Also by Lis Harris

HOLY DAYS: THE WORLD OF A HASIDIC FAMILY

LIS HARRIS

SIMON & SCHUSTER

NEW YORK LONDON TORONTO

SYDNEY TOKYO SINGAPORE

RULES OF ENGAGEMENT

FOUR COUPLES AND AMERICAN MARRIAGE TODAY

SIMON & SCHUSTER
ROCKEFELLER CENTER
1230 AVENUE OF THE AMERICAS
NEW YORK, NY 10020

DESIGNED BY KAROLINA HARRIS

MANUFACTURED IN THE UNITED STATES OF AMERICA

10   9   8   7   6   5   4   3   2   1

LIBRARY OF CONGRESS CATALOGING-IN-PUBLICATION DATA
HARRIS, LIS.
RULES OF ENGAGEMENT : FOUR COUPLES AND AMERICAN MARRIAGE
TODAY / LIS HARRIS
P.   CM.
1. MARRIAGE—UNITED STATES—CASE STUDIES. 2. MARRIED PEOPLE—
UNITED STATES—CASE STUDIES. I. TITLE.
HQ536.H35   1995
306.81'0973—DC20   95-457 CIP
ISBN 0-684-80826-9

FOR NICHOLAS AND DAVID

ACKNOWLEDGMENTS

I OWE AN ENORMOUS DEBT TO A NUMBER OF EDITORS with whom I was associated at various stages of this book's development. William Shawn encouraged me to write it and provided a milieu in which ambitious projects were cultivated, Sara Lippincott offered good advice about it, James Silberman and Ann Patty waited patiently for it, and Robert Bender's intelligence and enthusiasm for it sustained me in difficult times. I am particularly grateful for the good judgment and friendship of Robert Gottlieb, who offered helpful criticism and advice on the manuscript and without whose support at *The New Yorker* this book would probably not exist. My thanks go also to Ann Goldstein, to my agent, Georges Borchardt, to Eleanor Gould for more than two decades of brilliant editorial advice, to the librarians at Wesleyan University and The American Antiquarian Society, and to Anne Greene, Elizabeth Armour, John Bowers, Nora Sayre, James Chace, and James Lardner for their encouragement. It goes without saying that I am profoundly grateful to the eight people whose marriages are depicted in this book for agreeing to allow me into their lives and for giving so generously of their time and spirit. Last but not least, my thanks go to my sons Nick and David for their patience, good humor, and forbearance during this book's long gestation period.

CONTENTS

"Let me not to the marriage of true minds
Admit impediments."

SONNET 116, WILLIAM SHAKESPEARE

INTRODUCTION

LONG BEFORE MARRIAGE COUNSELORS, SEX THERAPISTS, quickie Vegas hitchings, *Ulysses,* mass nuptial ceremonies, Ingmar Bergman, personal columns, Freud, and *The Mating Game,* Americans were trying to improve themselves, singly and in pairs. The ink on the Declaration of Independence was barely dry before the colonists' ardor for overthrowing tyranny shifted into the private realm, and from that day to the present we have been virtually obsessed with the idea of making marriage, like the nation, "a more perfect union."

Hoping to explore the complexities of contemporary marriage in order to offer a kind of weather report on some of the factors that affect married people of different backgrounds, ambitions, and expectations, I spent several years visiting and talking with four couples: an upper-class couple, Sarah and Eaton McLane; a blue-collar couple, Claire and Michael Robbins; a middle-class African-American couple, Carlita and Samuel Jackson; and a resolutely egalitarian-minded couple, Vera and Neal Clark. (Their names and various identity-establishing details about their lives have been changed.) Their stories are not intended to represent a sampling, random or otherwise, of the scope of class, race, or social marital mores on the current American scene. Rather, they are the histories of four couples whose backgrounds were different enough to demonstrate widely varying ways of life and who were willing to permit me a privileged view of their lives. The couples shared various problems and passions, but the only view they held absolutely in common was that nothing in their premarital thoughts had in the least prepared them for the reality of wedded life.

In the early nineteenth century, men and women began to reveal a quickened interest in the yawning gulf between the idealized version of marriage described by their ministers or marital-advice books and the actual marriages they saw all around them. Then, as now, the highest expectations for friendship and romantic love were associated with the marriage vow. "I am . . . fully persuaded that the greatest share of happiness of which humanity is susceptible is derived from the conjugal connection," wrote Enoch Lincoln (who was himself not married and who later became the governor of Maine) on May 19, 1814, to the man who was about to marry his sister. But the wretchedness of so many husbands and wives also impressed social reformers during that period. The abolitionist Theodore Weld thought it strange that, as he wrote to his fiancée (and fellow abolitionist) Angelina Grimké, in all his wide acquaintance he knew no married couples who "embody in their example an illustration of what married life was designed to be." Nowadays, a steady flow of instructions and opinions concerning personal relations washes over us from every direction, and talk shows have popularized the idea that every domestic problem can—indeed must—be discussed freely and resolved, but there are essential mysteries in marriage that continue to elude us.

The huge nineteenth- and twentieth-century influx of immigrants into this country complicated American thinking about marriage. No generally agreed-upon model for husbands and wives exists; there are a thousand and one models. In our culture, as Margaret Mead has pointed out, not all men cross their legs with the same assured masculinity and not all women walk with little, mincing steps. Every American married couple develops a set of customs, a code of behavior, and a private language that are uniquely its own; as we approach the twenty-first century, marriage has come to seem the last institution on which we can leave an uncompromising personal stamp—the smallest social sphere in which we can test our assumptions about who we are or would like to be.

Dire predictions of the end of marriage as an institution have been common since the mid-nineteenth century. In 1927, the psychologist John Watson concluded from the general loosening of social and sexual mores that marriage would not last even fifty years longer. Yet, today, despite a soaring divorce rate, less than 10 percent of the population lives to age sixty-five without marrying, and that figure was pretty much the same in the eighteenth and nineteenth centuries. If the rate at which we marry has remained constant, though, little else about marriage has. In every class and every economic, ethnic and religious group, the face of marriage has undergone profound changes—psychological, sexual, and professional. Therapy or a therapeutic way of thinking has replaced duty as a guide for domestic imperatives; sex for fun and personal fulfillment has replaced the grin-and-bear-it Puritan notion of sex for procreation only; and the stepped-up pace of modern life, combined with the entrance of women into the workplace, has radically influenced the way husbands and wives regard each other. The dramas that devolve from those changes are the bone that novelists gnaw on most persistently, and the field of glory for whole armies of social scientists. Our preoccupation with emotions has been more than adequately recognized. According to the historian Lawrence Stone, the shift toward affectionate and voluntary family patterns was the most important social change to occur in modern times, and perhaps in the last thousand years of Western history.

• • •

SO much that is significant about marriage is hidden in the murky fastnesses of private life that trying to think about marriage as a whole is a bit like trying to think of the night sky as a whole. Before the dawn of the current age of expressiveness, most people didn't discuss their private lives much. Ethan Allen Greenwood, an early-nineteenth-century Massachusetts painter and lawyer, who owned an art gallery that eventually became the Boston Museum, kept a diary in which he recorded just about everything that happened to him—with one notable exception. On December 23, 1807, between entries that record a four-inch Christmas snowfall and his borrowing of a horse, he wrote, "Rode with the ladies to . . . Bedford. Where we dined and spent the afternoon. Returned and spent the evening agreeably—what I do not say here will not be forgotten."

In the last forty-odd years, however, scholars, undaunted by the erotically unknowable and the domestically unsaid, have plunged into the institutions of marriage and the family at an unprecedented rate, and what has struck them more than anything else is the increasing impact on people's lives of more freely expressed emotion and of the shifting status of women. In the 1980s alone, some nine hundred books about marriage were published, and that figure does not encompass the torrent of articles in newspapers and popular magazines, or the essays that fattened scholarly journals such as *The Journal of Marriage and the Family, The American Historical Review,* and *The Family Economics Review.* In general, all these works examine the deepest recesses of identity and personal behavior but leave the impression that most people—however able they may have become at vanquishing the demons of private life—still rarely talk about the really vital links between them.

Before the middle of this century, only a few intrepid souls ever attempted even quasi-scientific historical explorations of marriage; one was the Finnish anthropologist Edward Westermarck, whose *History of Human Marriage,* published in 1903 (the word "human" in the title is a tip-off to the kind of book it is), makes a brave, if heavy-handed, attempt to chart the origins and development of marriage everywhere. Writing without benefit of the municipal records, diaries, censuses, and letters that are a mainstay of modern research, Westermarck is clearly at sea much of the time, yet his struggling-in-dark-waters-but-plunging-on-anyway tone comes to seem rather endearing. For example, in a subsequent abridged edition of this book, he declares that "the institution . . . most probably developed out of a primeval habit"—that is, men and women having sexual relations with each other and having children. This habit was sanctioned by custom and law and in time became a social institution. Although he points out that similar habits are characteristic of other species of the animal kingdom, he is heartened by the fact that they are not to be found "among the very lowest"—invertebrates, for example. Noting that some form of marriage, whether monogamous, polygynous, or polyandrous, exists in all cultures, Westermarck traces its earliest sightings in antiquity. But after following that course for a while he concedes what virtually everyone inquiring into the history of marriage comes to realize, sooner or later, that many, if not most, early sources are inaccurate or unreliable.

Modern couples, and especially urban ones, often complain about their isolation from a larger community and their consequent obligation to fill roles—dear aunt, friendly cousin, helpful neighbor—that formerly were shouldered by a cast of dozens. But what were the great days for community—the Puritan era for instance—were hell for private life; the Puritan husband and wife were all but smothered by *communitas.* Colonial authorities were preoccupied with strengthening community ties, and marriage, like every other aspect of private life, was so closely scrutinized and regulated that neighborly snooping became a civic duty. In a sense, the colonists had no private life. Officials monitored their morals, set strict standards of behavior, were swift to punish transgressors—a happy era, surely, only for zealots, though a curious nostalgia for the tidiness of this cramped chapter of our history can be detected in the recent drumrolls for "family values." "Families are the nurseries of all societies," wrote Cotton Mather, voicing a sentiment that came to be invoked through the centuries by liberal reformers and conservative critics alike. "Well-Ordered Families naturally produce a Good Order in Other Societies." To preserve "Good Order," colonial courts not only investigated charges of fornication, promiscuity, and drunkenness but delved into the most personal aspects of married life, including the fulfillment of sexual roles. Colonists not only accepted the local authorities' intrusions into their marital affairs but regularly turned to them in times of domestic crisis.

Town fathers were called upon to counsel wayward husbands and wives and to compel men to marry their pregnant mistresses. Adultery was considered particularly dangerous, because it hinted at a fundamental breakdown of the society that permitted it, and in the Massachusetts Bay Colony, as every high school child who has read *The Scarlet Letter* knows, it was a serious crime.

Surprisingly, magistrates in the Plymouth Colony often recognized the sexual needs of both men and women in handing down court decisions, often found husbands and wives equally culpable in domestic disputes, often upbraided husbands and wives equally for what were alleged to be violent or quarrelsome ways, and often sentenced husbands and wives to be publicly whipped or subjected to some other punishment together. Nonetheless, because women's private interests were expected to be subordinate to family stability, women generally fared worse than men in the judicial process. Women only, for example, were faulted for marital "disobedience," and a wife's adultery was treated with far more severity than a husband's. In principle Puritan theology was firm in its endorsement of mutual affection in marriage, but in actuality marital stability was considered far more important than a couple's emotional responses, and in judging women the courts spoke far more often of deference and duty than of affection.

The basic inequality of husbands and wives derived its theological justification from the idea that a wife's duty to her husband was linked in a kind of unbroken chain that led back through monarchs to Adam and the Deity—a belief immortalized by a line from *Paradise Lost* that was regularly invoked by seventeenth-century ministers and town fathers: "He for God only, she for God in him."

In a treatise on the proper relations between spouses, entitled "Of Domesticall Duties," published in 1622, the arch-Puritan British divine William Gouge, who was widely read by his American counterparts, characterizes a husband as "a priest unto his wife" and a "king in his own house," and warns wives against addressing husbands with undue familiarity. Terms of endearment such as "brother," "cousin," "friend," "man," "sweet," "sweeting," "heart," "sweetheart," "love," "dear," "duck," "chick," or "pigsnie" were ill advised, he said, because they threatened a husband's dignity and put husband and wife on an equal footing. Gouge recommended that instead a wife add to her husband's surname the title "Master." The directives of a 370-year-old document may seem merely quaint, but in today's "total woman" marriage manuals there are echoes of the same message.

The affectionate terms in which colonial husbands spoke of their wives in letters and wills offer evidence of what common sense has already told us—that, despite the strains imposed by an unforgiving society, many men loved and honored their wives, and many women loved and honored their husbands, and that, as in every era, happy marriages flourished. What the great bulk of humanity, then or now, has made of the social constraints it lived with we cannot know, but one thing *is* certain: the Puritan ideal of mutual satisfaction in marriage was severely compromised by the stringent patriarchalism that governed domestic life and by the regularity with which colonial authorities put community needs before individual ones.

A disparity between publicly stated egalitarian marital rhetoric and conservative patriarchal practices of everyday life has been a constant throughout American history. In the eighteenth century, however, the community's grip on its citizens began to loosen. Even before the Revolution, pamphlets and magazine articles were vigorously questioning the relationship of parents and children, and of husbands and wives, and were using the same language they used to question the relationship between England and America. Tom Paine regularly published articles on marriage in *The Philadelphia Magazine,* which he edited in 1775; indeed, he even ran a sort of advice-to-the-lovelorn column. Though Paine himself was not a disinterested critic—he had been unhappily married and was permanently separated from his wife, who was English—his pleadings for divorce reform were echoed by many writers. After the Revolution, the first American novels— *The Power of Sympathy* (1789), by William Hill Brown; *The Memoirs of the Bloomgrove Family* (1790), by Enos Hitchcock; and *Parental Cruelty* (1797), by Mrs. Patterson—continued to explore themes of parental authority, individual moral obligation, and personal sentiment.

The Revolution had little impact on the civic lives of women, however. Despite much anti-patriarchal rhetoric, a more benign attitude toward children, and a newfound emphasis on familial expressions of tenderness, Abigail Adams could write in a letter to her husband, John, sometime after the colonies had secured their independence, "I cannot say that I think you are very generous to the ladies; for while you are proclaiming peace and good will to men, emancipating all nations, you insist upon retaining an absolute power over wives." Adams's customary epistolary salutation to his wife—"Dear Friend"—may have bespoken a notable change in eighteenth-century marital relations, and during the war he had noted with pride the competence of his wife in running the family farm, but his interest in the establishment of new ground rules at home was practically nil. In an earlier letter to her husband, dated March 31, 1776, Mrs. Adams made explicit her own revolutionary hopes: "In the new code of laws which I suppose it will be necessary for you to make, I desire you would remember the ladies, and be more generous and favorable to them than your ancestors. Do not push unlimited power into the hands of the Husbands. Remember all Men would be tyrants if they could. If particular care and attention is not paid to the ladies we are determined to foment a Rebellion, and we will not hold ourselves bound by any laws in which we have no voice, no representation."

Adams's reply eloquently attests to the fact that it would take a second American revolution to realize the social aims implicit in the first. "As to your extraordinary Code of Law," he wrote back on April 14, 1776 (less than three months before America declared its independence from England), "I cannot but laugh. We have been told that our struggle has loosened the bonds of Government everywhere. That children and Apprentices were disobedient—that schools and colleges were grown turbulent—that Indians slighted their guardians and Negroes grew insolent to their masters. But your letter was the first intimation that another tribe more numerous and powerful than all the rest were grown discontented. Depend upon it, we know better than to repeal our masculine system."

Over the last two hundred years, Adams's "masculine system" has in good part been repealed. But who would deny that elements of it still exist, or that most modern couples—especially those in the more privileged strata of society, who traditionally have the greatest stake in preserving the past—are burdened by its deadweight? And how can we calibrate the breadth of the changes wrought in people's domestic lives in this century by therapy, by feminism, and even by the nation's preoccupation with consumerism? The fact is that we cannot: we can only note that in the sweep of the life of a marriage, every couple writes its own elaborate epic, its own retranslation of history.

WE MAPPED IT OUT:

SARAH AND

EATON MCLANE

ON A COOL OCTOBER NIGHT IN 1958, AT A PARTY ON the Upper West Side, Sarah Blackwell was introduced to Eaton McLane, the only person in the room taller than she was. Sarah was twenty-four and had just returned from an exhilarating three-month trip to India. Eaton was twenty-nine. He had arrived at the party with a family friend, who was also a client of the brokerage firm where he worked, and he knew no one else present. Sarah knew nearly everyone; most of the guests were old school friends, and the rest were her relatives. It was an animated, tweedy crowd that radiated a kind of relaxed bookishness and old-shoe, Ivy League camaraderie—and a crowd in which Eaton, a slim, elegant figure in a neat three-piece pin-striped suit, looked a bit out of place.

Sarah had spent her time in India traveling with an exchange group called the Experiment in International Living. In the course of the trip, she had lived with several Indian families, had discovered a previously hidden talent for public speaking, and had enjoyed, for the first time in her life, a satisfying sense of her own competence. Large-boned, with penetrating blue eyes and clear, pale skin, Sarah stood slightly over six feet tall in her stocking feet. She was a kind, no-nonsense woman, with a deep laugh and a sharp wit. She wore no makeup except lipstick. Her friends and family adored her and considered her handsome, if awkward. Sarah had long thought of herself as a misfit. In her crowd, the belle idéal was dainty, cute, and blond. She had started out being all three, but in her pubescent years she had turned into a towering brunette with large hands and feet and a socially troublesome inability to dissemble. Like many other members of her family, she prided herself on her honesty and directness, and she could, and frequently did, intimidate the timorous. Sarah had had an interest in science since she was a small child, and this, too, had separated her from most of her friends in boarding school and college. She had graduated from Barnard in 1955; by 1958, most of her friends were married and some had begun to raise families. During those three years, Sarah had been teaching biology and chemistry, first at a private school, and later at a large public high school in upper Manhattan. There was no man in her life. She had had several love affairs, but they had not been the stuff of which marriages were made. Her parents had divorced when she was young, and she had recently begun to wonder if *she* was the stuff of which marriages were made—and, indeed, whether she really wanted to marry.

Sarah had never been close to her father's relatives, the Blackwells, who were mostly successful business people, but she was extremely fond of the Hardies, her mother's family. The Hardies were an old, prodigiously large, lively, and clannish tribe, and Sarah grew up warmed by their rituals and their affection. A few of the early Hardie settlers had been farmers, but most had become lawyers, teachers, painters, diplomats, or writers, and every generation took pride in its descent from its most illustrious forebear, a fiery eighteenth-century Scottish patriot who was hanged by the British. Through the centuries, the Hardie family had maintained a passionate interest in the machinations of government, and spirited political discussions were a regular component of family table talk. Sarah's childhood was spent among adults who clung to old-fashioned, patrician manners and mores and who enjoyed a high degree of cultural stability—a milieu made familiar to us by the novels of Edith Wharton. But the incursions of Freudian ideology, the depredations of the First World War, the sexual climate of the twenties, and the Depression had all chipped away at the foundations of that stability, and many of the joys and travails of Sarah's life could be traced to the ways in which she redefined what was possible for her within the changing constraints of her class.

Though Sarah's immediate family was richly endowed culturally and knew many well-connected people, they were poor compared with most of their friends and relatives. They had no trust funds to shelter them, no coupons to clip. Sarah's mother had not been able to afford college. She had begun working as a saleswoman in a New York clothing shop when she was eighteen, and both Sarah and her sister, Julia, who was three years older, had had to earn pocket money by taking odd jobs when they were still quite young. Sarah's father, a self-described "half-assed perfectionist of about fifteen different things," dropped out of Yale when an uncle who had been footing the bill for his education persisted in demanding more probity from him than he felt he could deliver, and afterward he worked at various jobs—bookseller, publicist, broker—with no great success.

Things had become particularly difficult after Sarah's parents' divorce in 1946. But straitened circumstances were hardly a novelty for someone whose family had lived through the Depression, and nobody Sarah knew felt disgraced by them. Before the divorce, Sarah's parents moved around a lot, fought a lot, and frequently left the two girls for long periods with their maternal grandmother, a warm, kindly woman who lived in Westchester County. When a rich relative arranged to send Sarah to boarding school, she went to her grandmother's house during school holidays. During the Second World War, her father joined the navy, and her mother took a job with the Office of Strategic Services (OSS) and moved with Sarah to Washington, D.C. (Julia was left with her grandmother, so that she could continue her schooling in Westchester.)

Sarah was lonely in Washington. She was left on her own a lot, and she did so much baby-sitting in those years that she had little cards made up saying BLACKWELL'S BABY-SITTING SERVICE. Her mother worked from seven in the morning to seven at night and was frequently exhausted, but she also had a full social life, and Sarah could not help but notice that she seemed to be in much better spirits than she had been when Sarah's father was around. She told Sarah that she liked her work and the independence of her life, and although Sarah's father rejoined them in Washington for a while after he was demobilized, he eventually left for New York, and he and Sarah's mother never got together again.

After the divorce, Sarah rarely saw her father. During the next few years, money became scarcer than ever, but her mother, now working for the Voice of America, seemed to manage well enough. The idea of supporting herself alone in the world held no terrors for Sarah. Though they were born into similar milieus, Sarah's outlook on love and money was markedly different from that of Lily Bart, the impecunious and unmarried heroine of Edith Wharton's 1905 novel *The House of Mirth*. (Lily would have been a contemporary of Sarah's grandmother.) For girls of Lily's class and era, as her bachelor friend Selden observes, marriage was still a vocation—the sole object, in fact, of their upbringing.

After college, Sarah lived briefly with her mother in a top-floor walk-up railroad apartment (one of a group of humble but much-sought-after apartments in the East Eighties owned by Vincent Astor, a family friend), but by 1958, when she met Eaton, she was living with three friends in the West Seventies, in a rent-controlled apartment that cost each of them forty dollars a month. She felt launched, but toward what she was unsure.

•   •   •

A casual observer, gazing at the rangy, confident-appearing figures of Sarah Blackwell and Eaton McLane that evening in 1958
might have been surprised to learn that they had grown up in
vastly different worlds. Sarah's family belonged to the liberal
wing of Waspdom that the sociologist E. Digby Baltzell admired
so much for its political consciousness, its inclusion of non-
Wasps in its circles, and its sense of social responsibility. The
Blackwells were politically engaged Democrats, and several members of Sarah's parents' generation had served as ambassadors
and advisers in the Roosevelt and Kennedy administrations.

Eaton McLane, on the other hand, had been reared in the rich,
conservative Republican enclave of Far Hills, New Jersey. Most of
the men of Far Hills spent their workdays on Wall Street and their
spare time hunting and fishing; the activities of the women,
which centered on preparing for, attending, or recovering from
charity functions, were closely monitored by the daily society
columns. Until about 1880, the pre–Civil War aristocratic class
that Sarah's family descended from and the post–Civil War plu-
tocracy that Eaton's ancestors belonged to had had little to do
with each other. But, as Baltzell has noted, the two groups began
to intermarry late in the nineteenth century, when the establishment of country clubs, cotillions, boarding schools, and men's
clubs, in which the two groups mingled, and the evolution of Ivy
League institutions from divinity schools to colleges for a secular
elite helped to weld the two groups into (in Baltzell's now famous
phrase) the Protestant establishment.

Like Sarah, Eaton had grown up with far less money than the
people around him, but, unlike Sarah, his family's money troubles had been a source of great anxiety to him. Money was what
counted at the city and country clubs that his mother and father,
an unsuccessful broker, belonged to—the Colony, the City Mid-
day, the Somerset Hills, the Seabright Lawn Tennis and Cricket,
and the Bedford Golf and Tennis—and the family's lack of it was
a constant subject of discussion. Eaton's mother was ignorant of
the details of the family's financial affairs for most of her married

life. Her husband would not discuss money matters with her, so she never knew exactly what their circumstances were, only that they were not good. Her father, the owner of a steel business, had at one time been quite rich, and Eaton and his sister, Elizabeth, who was three years younger, heard a lot of talk about the glory days of ten servants and two Pierce Arrows. But the children's maternal grandfather had lost everything in the stock-market crash—he died of a heart attack on Black Monday—and for the next two decades the family scrambled to get back on its feet. (Their paternal grandfather—a prosperous distiller and liquor wholesaler—had died before Eaton's birth, and the money from that branch of the family had evaporated.) By most standards, if not those of Far Hills, the family led a comfortable, even cushy, life. Until Eaton was eight years old, they had three servants; then they had two until the late forties, then one until his father died, in 1952. But, servants or not, there was always a feeling of panic about finances in the McLane household, a general sense of money running out.

After Eaton's father died, his mother was forced to sell their house, and the family moved to a second-floor apartment in a renovated barn on the estate of a friend in Far Hills. In Eaton's world, as in Sarah's, relatives and friends had a fairly accurate idea of the fortunes of the more impecunious members of their circle and felt obliged to provide a safety net. The McLane family was small, and though it, too, was venerable (family records of its Scottish, Dutch, and German ancestors went back to 1500), its members were not particularly clannish. Eaton's father paid for his son's education through the Far Hills Country Day School and St. Paul's; when Eaton moved on to college—Yale—the responsibility passed to a woman who was a close friend of the family. Although Eaton's mother doted on him, he had grown up in a state of cosseted isolation.

After college and a stint in the navy, Eaton worked as a clerk in a bookstore on Wall Street for a while—a job he rather liked, though it paid little. But an uncle on his father's side, whom he was fond of, told him that there was no financial future for him in the bookstore business and helped him get a job in one of the Street's more imposing brokerage firms. The size of the firm alarmed Eaton, but he was comforted to think that at last he had a career. When he met Sarah Blackwell he had been working at his new job for two weeks.

In college, Eaton had come close to marrying a girl he thought he'd gotten pregnant, but to his great relief, the pregnancy had turned out to be a false alarm. Still, he tended to agree with the Massachusetts politician Timothy Pickering, who wrote in 1799 that "marriage is a goal which every man, for his own happiness and honor and the good of society, cannot reach too soon." He was not actively searching for a wife, but somehow whenever he met a new woman the thought Wife? would blip across his consciousness.

Sarah and Eaton got into a long conversation at the party that night, and they enjoyed themselves so much that they decided to go on to a second party, to which he had been invited. Two weeks later, they traveled to Cambridge together to attend the Yale-Harvard game. She stayed with friends, and he stayed with friends. At the game, they sat in the Yale section, but Sarah cheered enthusiastically for Harvard, the alma mater of many of her uncles and cousins. Two and a half months later, they were married.

IN the spring of 1989, shortly after I was introduced to Sarah and Eaton McLane by friends of friends—who had explained to them that I was working on a project about marriage that involved interviewing couples of different social and economic backgrounds—I began visiting them more or less regularly to ask about their courtship and the evolution of their life together. By then, they had had four children—two girls and two boys. Eaton had become the president of a major brokerage firm, and Sarah had become a science-education consultant at a New York think tank. When, in a telephone conversation with Sarah, I first broached the possibility of interviewing them, she was interested but skeptical. A week later, we met in a Village coffeehouse to talk a little more about that possibility, and she said that, upon reflection, she had concluded that it might be "useful" to discuss the central issues of her marriage but that Eaton was appalled by the idea.

The first time I met Eaton—in a Chelsea restaurant a few weeks later—Sarah was there, too, and so were their two daughters, Mollie and Anne, aged twenty-eight and twenty-two, and their son James, who was twenty-one. (Thomas, who was a year older than James, was a filmmaker and lived in London.) Eaton seemed so dubious about participating in the project that I came away convinced that that was the last I'd see of them. As we were leaving the restaurant, he reminded me of an old society saw: Your name should appear in print only when you are born, when you marry, and when you die. Several weeks later, however, Sarah phoned to say that, after long deliberations and family consultations, they had decided to do it. (Eaton and Sarah were the only couple I spoke with who *wanted* their children to know from the beginning that they would be discussing their marriage with an outsider.)

ONE afternoon, about a week after that call, I paid my first visit to their home, a large, comfortable, sun-filled eight-room apartment on Central Park West. The McLane apartment exuded an almost preternatural coziness—the wood surfaces had a mellow burnish, and there were unphlegmatic ancestral portraits and old landscapes in the hallway, and original John Gould bird prints in the dining room—but it was not an establishment that proclaimed its occupants' wealth. Except for the antiquity and museum-worthiness of much of the furniture and the sumptuousness of some silver on a dining-room sideboard, it could have been the apartment of, say, the head of Columbia's History Department. There were several comfortable chintz sofas, a flowered needlepoint rug, and, neatly stacked on various end tables, numerous magazines—*Wilderness, Daedalus, Forbes, The Nature Conservancy, The Conservationist, The New Yorker, The Washington Report, Institutional Investor, The Sciences, The Nation, Harper's.* In every room were photographs of children, relatives, and friends, taken, for the most part, in country settings.

Sarah led me to a small, neat sitting room adjacent to the kitchen—an open kitchen, equally small—and offered me tea. Here, as everywhere, were photographs of the McLane children at all stages of development, and on one wall hung a picture of two pretty little girls—Sarah and her sister, Julia—outside a stable. It had been taken, Sarah said, when she was about eight and was "still cute. I wore size ten shoes and loomed over everybody by the time I was twelve," she said. "I was really ungainly. Everyone was better at sports, and by the time I got to boarding school I was shaped like a pencil and had straight, stringy hair—I was a disaster. I was fourteen and still hadn't had my period, and they put me in a dormitory room with three other ninth graders who all had bosoms, periods, and boyfriends. They wore stockings and pointy little flats. I clomped around in saddle shoes and ankle socks. It was a girls' school, but most of the students seemed to have boyfriends, who came from the boys' schools. Some of the girls had boyfriends they saw when they went home on vacation. Not me. I spent all my weekends, holidays, and summers at my grandmother's, and the social life of my grandmother's town revolved around the country club, which my family refused to join, because it was racist. Anyway, right through senior year there were *no* boys in my life. I did go to a few parties back home around then—my parents paid for me to go to the deb balls—but I hated them. I was greatly relieved when I was in an accident my senior year and my head was shaved and I had a terribly bruised face and I didn't have to attend any more of them. I was still too tall and too thin, and by then I was also wearing braces for my buck teeth. I thought, Well, I'm just one of those people. I had a lot of good times at family gatherings with my cousins, male and female—I mean, I have forty-one cousins—and my other relatives, but basically I had no social life."

I asked Sarah how big a role her parents played in getting her through this period.

"Zilch. My grandmother was the big nurturer of my childhood and the stable influence in my life. I spent more time with her than with either of my parents. But these were not matters I felt I could discuss with her. My mother is a great friend now—she's wonderfully intelligent and great company—but basically she wasn't all that interested in being a mother. I hardly saw my father after my parents divorced, in 1946, and when I did see him he was usually remote and quite sarcastic. I never told him anything. My mom sold bathing suits at Saks Fifth Avenue when I was young, and she kept on working at various jobs throughout my childhood. I think it was all really too much for her—the working and the mothering."

"And your sister?"

Sarah put a mug of hot tea on a small table for me and sipped iced tea from a mammoth dime-store plastic glass for a beat or two before she answered. Then she said, "Julia and I have become really close over the years, but it took a long time for that to happen. I'm a lot taller than she is now, but when I was young she was the enormous and strong one. She grew to her full height by the time she was nine, and she used to push me around a lot—I mean physically beat me up. She scared the hell out of me. I don't look back on my childhood with pleasure, as some people do. I was a miserable child."

Sarah told me that she signed up with the Experiment in International Living after she'd been teaching for a few years, because a friend had told her that it was a cheap way to travel. But what started out as a cut-rate tour became "a seminal experience," she said, adding "if I can use that corny word." On the trip out, the Experimenters, who were largely in their early twenties, landed in Beirut for a stopover and found the airport under siege. It was 1958, just after the United States invaded Lebanon. The Marines were occupying the airport, and Sarah and her fellow Experimenters, not entirely to their displeasure, had to crawl on their hands and knees to the waiting room and lie on the floor for ten hours while their plane was refueled and their safe passage negotiated; then, eyes popping out of their heads, they had to crawl back onto the runway to board the plane. In Bangalore, their group was trotted out before a crowd of some five thousand students squatting in the university courtyard and, to their collective horror, were asked to respond to political questions posed by the students. Alone among the Experimenters, Sarah Blackwell—who considered political debate mother's milk and had routinely spoken to forty people at a time in her classrooms—was unfazed. "I was totally at ease. I had no problem standing up in front of them. They would shout out questions, you know, and it was just like my family dining table. I loved every minute of it. They would say 'Why are the Marines in Lebanon?' and 'Why did you invade the Dominican Republic?' and I would talk about the government and how people I knew did not support these moves and how we disliked John Foster Dulles. It was exhilarating—it was unbelievable! And that was Day One. It went on for two weeks—not every day, but certainly five or six times. At one point the group leader left. She had been in India the year before, and she left to visit the Indian family she had stayed with. Amazingly, the group elected me to be its new leader. I had never been elected to anything in my whole life. I mean, I was a complete dud in high school and college. Now, all of a sudden, I was the responsible person—the person who made all the arrangements, the person who had to get off the train first and receive the flowers, or whatever. Every place had its own rituals, its own protocol, and you had to be sensitive and pretty flexible. One day you would be rooting around in some caves and spending the night in a hostel, and the next day you would be greeting the mayor of Benares."

While she was still in India, Sarah decided that her sense of independence and the exercise of her (apparently considerable) leadership abilities had both been thwarted in some way by her relationships with men. For several years she had been going out almost every night to parties or bars with men she hadn't been all that crazy about, though she had sometimes slept with them. She realized that for more than a year she had been bored and un-happy at these parties or bars and had merely been making a show of remaining in the marriage market. "I thought—you know—I don't want to go back to New York and start all over again, going out with these creeps. I don't want any part of that life. I'd always thought I probably wouldn't marry, and now I thought, Maybe I don't *want* to marry."

Back in New York that fall, Sarah threw herself into her teach-ing and successfully turned down all opportunities to return to the old stumbling-along-to-the-next-whiskey-bar-and-party rou-tine. Nonetheless, when she was introduced to Eaton she thought he looked "rather unusually nice."

FOUR days after my visit with Sarah, I met Eaton for lunch at a clubby-looking restaurant near his office in lower Manhattan. He gazed warily at me from beneath bushy brows, fidgeted with his fork, and reported that he had liked Sarah Blackwell from the start—her directness, her eyes, and, especially, her conversation. After they left the second party that night, he said, they kept on talking, over dinner at a small Upper East Side restaurant, and by the time they parted he felt "unusually good." Something he could no longer remember—maybe a business trip—kept him from inviting her out immediately. But he felt certain that he would see her again, and when he decided to invite her to the Yale-Harvard game he was confident that she would accept.

Eaton was born in New York City, he told me, and his parents moved to Far Hills when he was about a year old. "My mother worked for *Vogue* until we were born, and then she stopped working, except for a brief career selling real estate after my fa-ther died," he went on, "but even though she was usually around, my sister, Elizabeth, and I always had nannies, and the nannies did most of the child rearing. My father was rarely there. We never knew why. My mother's old nurse also lived with us until 1940, when she died. It may sound as though we were rich, but there was a great deal of anxiety about money in our house, and, though my mother was a staunch person, I think my father's frequent absences bothered her a lot."

When I asked Eaton if his father had played games or taken part in sports with him, he put down his fork, folded his arms, and said, "Never! Occasionally, he took me out hunting or shooting, and he did like to play games at birthday parties—he was very good at that. But ordinarily he just came home and sort of disappeared. Sometimes the two of them went out to dinner. They entertained a lot, too. Dinner parties. We had our own lives, Elizabeth and I and our friends. Most of my time was spent out-of-doors. All my interests were oriented toward nature. As far back as I can remember, I was always down in the grass looking at bugs and birds. I can still see the praying mantises on the lawn and the bat that lived in the toolhouse. I loved all that. I do to this day. I started collecting beetles when I was eight or nine, and I still collect them. When I was ten, I got interested in taxidermy. Mother's old nurse died about then, and they gave me her room. I filled it with aquariums and all kinds of bugs and butterflies and stuffed birds. That was my life. We rented a number of houses in Far Hills—I remember a big brown shingled house, and then a white house, where we lived from 1935 to 1941. Then a much bigger house, right across the road, which I really loved. There were miles of fields behind it, and I used to shoot crows and pheasants. My uncle Charles—my father's brother—had given me a shotgun, and I loved to go hunting. I didn't know anything about the environment then. I took it for granted. The neighborhood I lived in had lots of rambling, comfortable houses with a lot of land. There were literally thousands of acres to roam around in—miles and miles of fields, meadows, and woods."

As we talked about this part of his life, Eaton's expression softened, and he stopped eating. "When I got a little older, I got into a whole other thing—finding caterpillars," he said. "I had shooting friends, fishing friends, caterpillar-hunting friends. I was around twelve when I got the shotgun. I would go off, shooting rabbits or pheasants. Total freedom. I'd come home from school and just go off with the same group of four or five friends. I did everything with them. We'd go crow hunting, or rat hunting in the neighbors' henhouse. We'd wander for miles. A totally separate life. At home, they knew I had my own agenda, and I was left alone. I'd come home for dinner—they were formal dinners—but that was about it. When I went away to boarding school, in 1945, my life changed. I found it very painful. I missed my old friends and all the things we used to do together. I was hopelessly homesick. I dragged practically my full collection of bugs and beetles along with me, but there was no one who shared my interest in them. I'd never before been away from home for an extended period— I'd never even been to camp. I didn't want to grow up. The boarding-school world is quite tough, and I was just not prepared for it. I was not physically mature, either, and didn't like group sports. Eventually, I did get on the track team and even won a letter, and toward the end, when I'd made some friends, I liked it better. My family had moved again, too, from the big house to one that we owned, on a half acre. It wasn't little, this house, but there was no land to roam around on, and I hated it. My father's health started going downhill, too, when I was a teenager. He had heart problems. He was on the decline in terms not only of health but of money. He died when I was twenty-one. It turned out that there was *no* insurance—can you believe that? He hadn't taken out *any* life insurance, and all that was left of the family capital was twenty thousand dollars."

Eaton's father had stipulated in his will that any funds gained from the sale of the house were to be put in trust. The income from the trust—five hundred dollars a year—went to Eaton's mother, and the principal was to go to the next generation, after her death. Things would have been far worse after his father died if, once the house was sold, the three of them, thanks to the generosity of another family friend, had not been able to live rent free in the converted barn for the next six years. The barn-apartment was perched above long, lush fields. It was a place Eaton loved. Mrs. McLane's further real-estate endeavors did not meet with much success, however, and eventually their finances became really grim. Once again, a group of friends came to the rescue, giving his mother some money, which she invested well. With this fresh income and the agent's fees she collected from selling a house or two, the family was able to rent a guest cottage on another friend's estate. Eaton was still living in the cottage with his mother and sister when he met Sarah, but the boy naturalist who might well have settled down for life in some gentle outpost of the Nature Conservancy had developed by then into a man determined to make a lot of money and to follow in none of his father's footsteps.

Eaton could easily pinpoint the moment when the word "Wife?" ceased being an interrogative and coalesced around the person of Sarah Blackwell. It was occasioned by Sarah's need to use the bathroom at the Yale-Harvard game—an episode that Sarah had mentioned only in passing during her first long conversation with me. Before the game, she recalled, they had had a big lunch, with lots of beer. At halftime, when she set out for the bathroom, she kept bumping into friends, and by the time she reached it the line outside was so long that she gave up and returned to her seat. By the end of the game, she recalled, things were "really serious," but the field was jammed with people, and she and Eaton, who had gotten separated, kept on running into more acquaintances. Finally, in desperation, she relieved herself on the field, made her way to the bathroom, "finished the job," washed out her underpants, rolled them up in a ball, and put them in her pocketbook. When she found Eaton, she told him what had happened. She had no idea of the effect her confession would have on him.

"I told you I liked her instantly," Eaton said as we were finishing our meal, "and I'll tell you one of the reasons I liked her—her straight-as-an-arrow directness. She'd told me she had to pee, and afterward she just looked me in the eye and said 'I peed in my pants.' I'd never heard anything like that from a girl. She was direct. She was fun. Afterward, we went to a sort of cocktail party in Boston—we both had friends there—and that was the first time I kissed her. I remember looking at her at this friend's house—actually, it was my friend's mother's house—and she was wearing a dress with cuffed sleeves that were a little too short. But she stood there and smiled, and I thought, That's a woman I like—she's good looking, she's got a good personality, she's strong—and perhaps I could help her out if I could make a little money. I don't care that she doesn't have money, and she told me she doesn't mind my not having it, either—but I *really* like her."

According to Baltzell, upper-class men and women in the late fifties and even into the sixties, far more than Americans of other classes, still tended to marry people who could augment their power and status. In the world Eaton grew up in, inherited wealth and social position were crucial factors in choosing a wife. Love, looks, character, and achievement counted, too, but few sons of upper-class families—or, more to the point, few only sons of the decayed gentility—felt free to choose their wives solely on the basis of mere attraction. So, while Eaton would hardly have been anyone's idea of a heedless lover, his interest in Sarah Blackwell put him squarely on the modern side of the great divide between those who married for love and those who married (as until the late 1700s most people in the Western world had done for centuries) to increase their prosperity or advance their social position.

I asked Eaton why Sarah's directness appealed to him.

"I found it liberating," he said. "Her whole family was that way. Frankly, I'd never met people who were so blunt. Most of the group I grew up with were taught to maintain a neutral façade, to *never* hurt people's feelings, to be polite no matter what, and to say 'Yes, please,' and 'No, thank you,' and all that sort of thing, no matter how you felt in a situation. We were all brought up that way. Sarah and I had political fights right from the start, even though I wasn't very much interested in politics— I'm still not. But she cared, and cares, tremendously about these things, so she'd tear into me or anyone I knew whose politics she didn't agree with. Her mother, whom I came to love absolutely, has terrific manners, but she can cut you dead so fast. I mean, you'd say something silly, and the look that would come over her face would be just devastating. But there's an honesty there that is a tremendous relief. It is obviously a double-edged quality. When we had some people to dinner once, Sarah launched into a harsh critique of some private school, despite the fact that one of our guests was on the board. She just went on and on, until the man just exploded. 'I cannot believe you are a Hardie,' he said. 'You're just unbelievably rude.' Most of the time, though, I greatly admire her frankness. It wonderfully punctures pomposity and pretension."

After that first Boston embrace, Sarah returned to her friend's house "feeling very, very good," and in the bedroom, which she shared with her friend's baby, she reflected on the pleasure of the kiss. The baby mewed softly in his crib, and Sarah felt herself shifting into a heretofore unknown gear, or, as she described it, "I remember lying in bed, thinking, Hmm! Hmm!"

In November and December, Sarah and Eaton saw each other nearly every night. Most of the time, they slept together in her bedroom in the apartment she shared with her friends, and their relationship began to grow, as Sarah put it, "thicker and thicker." By Christmas, they had been seeing so much of each other that friends and family began to assume that they were a serious couple. Although there was some grumbling from Far Hills, nobody in Sarah's family thought it appropriate to question the sexual aspect of their courtship, and nobody Sarah knew would ever seriously have thought, much less recommended, that she should have waited for the wedding night to give up her virginity. In fact, the sexual freedom of her life had had its dismal side, including a difficult-to-obtain abortion—an experience she shared with a number of her friends. But she was not terrified of sex, as young couples of her grandmothers' and grandfathers' generation had been primed to be by such popular marriage manuals as George Naphey's *The Physical Life of Women,* published in 1871, which warned women that "more or less suffering" could be expected from the wedding night; or Sylvanus Stall's *What a Young Husband Should Know* (1907), which reminded men of the multitude of women who complained to their doctors that "the only rape that was ever committed on them was by their own husband the first day of married life." By Sarah's mother's generation, engagement, not marriage, signaled a relaxation of the barriers to sex, and, though there is some disagreement among historians and sociologists about the sexual norms of the 1950s, most maintain that the differences between male and female sexual standards were beginning to disappear and "permissiveness" was becoming the rule. Even so, neither Sarah nor Eaton considered the possibility of their living with each other for a prolonged period (as the next generation did) to see how well they would get along; an arrangement of that sort would have caused seismic tremors in the families of both of them. Instead, Sarah found her resistance to the idea of marriage lessening, and Eaton found his already primed predisposition to marry quickening. Once the idea took hold, they both proceeded toward the event with a remarkable degree of rationality.

IT had been raining while Eaton and I lunched, and afterward, as we walked along the shining, narrow, rain-spattered streets of the financial district toward his office, he described how he had arrived at his decision to marry. I remarked that theirs had been a short courtship and asked if he'd soon felt that he had fallen in love.

Eaton thought about the question before he answered, and then said, "No, no. I didn't think in those terms. I genuinely liked Sarah. I had fun with her. I thought she was intelligent. I could talk to her. I was attracted to her physically. I liked her family. I felt we could get on together. We had similar interests. Neither of us was religious. She's an atheist, I'm an agnostic. We both believed in abortion. She told me that she'd had one, and I thought she'd been brave and done the right thing. I'd told her that at one time I thought I'd got a girl pregnant, and that it proved to be a false alarm, but that I had certainly intended to help her get an abortion. Sarah was scientific-minded, and I was and still am fascinated by natural history, natural science. Neither of us had been part of the regular-guy, gung-ho, mainstream Ivy League life. We both felt like outsiders. I'm not sure I can describe my feelings. I love my wife in my own way. But I hate public kisses or holding hands. I always have. I'm rather a shy person. We've been married for thirty-two years. I don't think I would have had the passion of a Cyrano de Bergerac—let's put it in those terms—for an unobtainable woman. In fact, I made the decision to marry rather coolly. I said, 'This is a person I can live with. I think we will have fun in life. I think she's attractive and intelligent.' I remember making a toast at our bridal dinner, saying that it was good to find somebody I could love. That's what I felt. That wasn't passionate, schmaltzy stuff, but I knew that it would last. And I was right."

ABOUT a week later, I visited Sarah again, at the apartment on Central Park West. She was wearing jeans and a blue sweatshirt. Eaton, dressed in khaki pants and a torn-at-one-elbow old gray shetland sweater over a blue oxford shirt, was about to set off on a fishing trip. They had had a dinner party the night before, and, as Sarah and I were settling into the living room to talk, Eaton began removing the extra leaves from a large table in the dining room. The process was accompanied by quite a lot of rattling, and the noise bothered Sarah, so she asked him to take out the remaining leaves later. Eaton said that he wouldn't be long and kept on with what he was doing. After a few more moments of strained conversation, Sarah said "Jesus!" and stomped into the dining room and helped Eaton finish the job. Eaton thanked her, archly, and Sarah showily stomped back to the living room.

According to Sarah, when Eaton first broached the subject of marriage at a Christmas-week party, she felt quite ambivalent. "We started talking and the conversation went something like 'Where are we going with this?' and Eaton said he thought we should get married, and we sort of agreed that, well, maybe we *would* get married," she recalled. "But the truth was I really didn't know what to do. I was exhausted with the whole scene of going out with three or four people at a time, some of them wanting nothing but to get in your skirt and others wanting nothing whatsoever. The pressure was on, too. Not from my parents but from various relatives. One of my cousins had said, 'Well, are you going to get married, or what?' And an aunt pointedly remarked that I wasn't getting any younger. I really had fallen in love with Eaton in the conventional sense, I guess, but there was another part of me that said, 'Don't marry.' In India, I had discovered that I had certain qualities, and that I didn't really want to get married, because I was worried that marriage would compromise those qualities. I felt that marriage was obedience, subservience, so, even though I fell in love and all that, there was another part of me that was removed and stood outside and looked down at things. I've always done that. We fell in love, we got married, we're husband and wife, but at the same time we're two separate people who have really separate needs and interests. We have arguments all the time."

"Arguments or discussions?"

"Our friends call them arguments. We never feel constrained to shut up in front of people. They've often complained about it. Now most of them are divorced, and they're beginning to say, 'I wish I'd done that.' Eaton and I battle about everything."

Over tea—which I sipped out of an elegant old Spode teacup while Sarah drank iced out of her plastic glass—she described some of the more memorable battles. "In a way, you could say that all our fights—or most of them, anyway—have been about power. Both of us were brought up in a society where men had a lot of power. Eaton saw that men had the power, and exercised the power, and that those who were dependent did what they were told—jumped when they were told to jump—and I don't like that. I had an uncle—a tough cookie, a First World War army officer—who used to hit my cousin and me quite a lot. He frightened me. He's sitting right there." She pointed to a photograph of a heavily tweeded gentleman wearing a sportsman's cap and glaring at whoever was taking his picture. "He was married to my mother's sister, and had a daughter my age who's like my sister, because we grew up together. During the war, when my father was overseas and my mother was working so hard, I spent a lot of time at their farm, near my grandmother's house. They had horses, and he'd come out to the barn and find that, say, my cousin and I hadn't washed the bits but had just hung up the bridles; and he would get the horsewhip and come after us and hit us. We never spoke to anyone about it. We just sort of accepted it. But it made me *really* not like being pushed around—not even in more subtle ways, as I sometimes allowed myself to be as a young woman. By the time I met Eaton, I was tuned in to power issues, and we've struggled with them all along in our marriage.

"I'll give you one example. In the sixties, we went down to Washington to march against the Vietnam War. We went down with my friend Eva and stayed at the house of another friend, who was out of town. The morning after we arrived, Eva and I got up and started making breakfast, and then I went out and got the paper. "So I come back, put the paper on the dining-room table, and go on making breakfast. Eva and I are carrying our breakfasts into the dining room when Eaton comes downstairs. He sees the paper, picks it up, puts the whole thing under his arm, and goes into the kitchen to start getting his juice, or whatever. Meanwhile, Eva and I hit the table with our food, and I'm looking for the paper. I see from the kitchen doorway that he's holding it under his arm as he's preparing his breakfast. So Eva and I look at each other, and I say, 'We want to read the paper.' Well, he wouldn't give it up.

His response was 'I'll be right there, I'm just getting some break-fast.' So I went in and grabbed it, and we literally had a fight over the paper, and I remember that Eva was incredulous. I mean, she couldn't believe this. But I was furious. I had gone and gotten it, and he wasn't even ready to read it. It was just another case of 'I'm a man, and I want the paper, and I have a divine right to the front section first.'"

I asked Sarah if these encounters had changed in character over the years.

"Well, they go on, but I think I try to approach things a little more sensitively, and Eaton's become vaguely more aware of the power issue as an issue. But mostly he doesn't really think about these things, and that forces me into extreme positions. When we were first married, I thought wives were meant to get up in the morning and cook breakfast and do the dishes and all that, before work. I thought that that was what was expected of you. It didn't occur to me that you might share these responsibilities. Well, in the early days of our marriage, Eaton told me that he liked two fried eggs, two pieces of toast well done, and a cup of coffee every morning. This had never been an issue when we were staying in my apartment before we were married, by the way, because a bunch of people were always around, and there was usually a pot of coffee already made and somebody or other frying eggs. But af-ter we got married, my roommates left, and it became *our* apart-ment, and suddenly the whole climate changed. We were both working, of course, and there were quite a few times when I'd make the eggs and the toast, and Eaton would look at his watch and say 'I don't really have time to eat' and—*boom,* out he'd go. Gradually, it dawned on me that all was not well on the domestic front. We had a little talk about it, but it didn't seem to get us any-where, and things just went on the same way for a while, so I thought about it for some time, and then I just stopped cooking his breakfast. I never cooked it again.

"My mother and sister didn't handle things that way at all. They just sort of swallowed their resentments and pushed on, and, like them, I started out thinking, Well, I'm a woman and this is what we're supposed to do. I'd seen my mother go to work and do everything at home, too. And I know she resented it. Her way of dealing with these issues was to leave the marriage. When there was no husband around, she still had to do everything, but we did it with her. I don't think that my mother, or Julia, ever felt that they could negotiate these kinds of things. The feminist movement was wonderful for me that way. It hasn't solved my problems, but it's definitely given me a better perspective on them.

"Sometime after I had stopped cooking breakfast, we had another major fight, about frying pans. Eaton would make his scrambled eggs, or fried eggs, or whatever, and then he would leave the frying pan in the sink. He'd put his plate in the dishwasher—a major leap forward—but the frying pan would always be left in the sink, and I got tired of washing it. So one day I just left it in the sink to see what would happen. The next day, he used another frying pan, and the next day another, and so on, till he had used up all the frying pans in the house and they were all there, sitting in the sink. I just tried that as an experiment to see what would happen."

"And what did happen?"

"I can't remember. But the point is that Eaton just doesn't think about such things. He didn't do it to be mean or nasty. He didn't do it to say 'I am a man. I don't wash frying pans.' He just doesn't *think* about those sorts of things."

Sarah attributed Eaton's lack of consciousness about domestic details in large part to what she called "the tweeny mentality." "Tweeny" is a British word for a servant, which apparently used to have some currency among the Anglophile rich. "I wasn't brought up with servants," she said. "My grandmother sometimes had a farmer and his wife come over to help clean up, but they lived in a separate house, and you sort of worked *with* them. You didn't dump on them. You didn't treat them like— You know, the whole attitude that goes with having servants: when you drop things, the tweeny is going to pick them up. We went through a phase in which I went around a lot saying 'I'm not the tweeny!'"

Whatever the strains of the McLanes' lives, however, they were far outnumbered, as I was to learn, by the satisfactions of their marriage. They enjoyed good relations with their children: Mollie, the oldest, worked for an antinuclear organization in Boston; Thomas, the London-based filmmaker, kept in close telephone contact; James, their third child, was a law student at N.Y.U.; and Anne, the youngest, had recently dropped out of Sarah Lawrence and was temporarily living with some friends in Brooklyn and looking for a job. Mollie, James, and Anne were in and out of the house frequently, and at least once a year the whole family took an extended trip together. In recent years, they had traveled to Mexico, Bermuda, and Italy, and these trips, though they were expensive, tended to be highly restorative and beneficial to domestic harmony.

Both Sarah and Eaton liked their work. Sarah had a degree from Columbia in organic chemistry, and she had worked contentedly for the think tank for the past ten years. In the mid-seventies, Eaton had left his brokerage firm—where he had been made a partner—to become president of a distinguished but much smaller investment company. He was well thought of by his colleagues, and he made a lot of money—$600,000 a year. He sat on the boards of seven major New York cultural and educational institutions—a situation that served, in part, to confirm his place among the city's movers and shakers. Though he sometimes thought he might have enjoyed a career as a conservationist far more than managing people's investments, he still found time to spend many inspiring hours in woods, wetlands, and meadows.

During the week, except on evenings when one or both of them had to work late or Eaton had a board meeting, Sarah and Eaton ate dinner together and often went to concerts or lectures. They had a wide circle of close longtime friends and now and then had dinner with one or another of them or with one of Sarah's many relatives. They owned two country houses—one in Nantucket and one in a bucolic section of Westchester County, and they frequently visited a house owned by Sarah's mother, in Maine. They rarely spent weekends in the city. Sarah's mother had bought the Nantucket house in 1948 (for $5,000) as a place to take her city-bound daughters to, but she eventually found it a burden and sold it to Sarah (for a dollar). During the summer, Eaton and Sarah leased the house to pay the local taxes and for its general upkeep; they visited it themselves only in the late spring and the early fall. They bought the Westchester house in 1965, with a small inheritance Eaton received when his mother died. Westchester is where they go most weekends nowadays. The Maine house, which Sarah's mother bought in 1980, tends to be the gathering place for big family events and major holidays. During the course of an early conversation I had with him, Eaton frankly stated that he considers the wealth that in so many ways has softened the rough edges of his family's life central to his own happiness and well-being. He is fully aware of the fact that while most people of the middle and working classes have experienced dramatic downward mobility over the last decade, his fortunes have gone the other way, and he is grateful that he has succeeded where his father failed. In his marriage, too, Eaton feels lucky. He had been sorry for his mother and had vowed not to repeat his father's mistakes. It pleased him to look across the room and see Sarah reading a book, he said, or catch her eye in a crowded room. Drunken parties and marital promiscuity had been common in the well-appointed houses of his youth, and, though he was not a prig, he was determined that his own life would never resemble that of his parents' circle, and it has not.

THE McLanes' weekend house in northern Westchester is just a few steps from a well-stocked trout stream (one of the chief reasons, from Eaton's point of view, for their having acquired it). Built at the turn of the century and situated on a busy country road, the house is cheerful and spacious; they had it renovated recently, adding a good-sized kitchen wing and an entrance hall. It is white clapboard, has large windows with black shutters, and is surrounded by a wide expanse of lawn. On the left side of the house, a long sunporch provides a close view of a stand of graceful maples. The property includes thirteen acres of woods, and they adjoin other large wooded properties and a vast county parkland. At least one of the McLane children is usually around on weekends, and James and Anne, along with a schoolmate of hers, Robert Amis, were on hand when I arrived on a foggy Saturday in late winter. Robert, an aspiring furniture designer, had volunteered to cook supper for everybody, and when I got there, at about eleven in the morning, he and Anne were poking around in the cupboards and drawers of the sleek new kitchen and getting ready to prepare some parts of the menu. Robert, a serious cook, seemed to find the McLanes' stores and kitchen equipment sorely wanting. Half jokingly, he told Anne he couldn't believe that a family as obviously well heeled as hers had only the most humble supermarket vinegar for salad dressing.

"Well, forget it," said Anne, a tall, beautiful redhead with elfin eyes, who had recently begun working as an editorial assistant at a publishing house. "We're not a Fraser Morris family—we're an A&P family."

"But you like good food," Robert countered, as he whisked some of the offending vinegar into a bowl of plain-Jane olive oil.

"Yeah, well. But we just don't fuss over it. Any time Mom had to come home late from work when we were young, she'd write us notes telling us to heat up TV dinners."

"That's calumny," said Sarah, who had just returned with James from a nearby Caldor, where they had bought some knives and chopping boards for the kitchen and some odds and ends for James's new apartment in the city. "Maybe I did that once or twice, but there were a lot of things I cooked for you in advance. I froze things."

"Oh, yes, the famous chicken tetrazzini, staple of our childhood," said James, a dark-haired, intense-looking young man, smiling good-naturedly at his mother.

Anne began to make herself some toast. "Actually, that stuff was pretty good," she said to me. "But, really, we ate incredibly trashy food when we were kids. We were allowed to have any sweet kind of breakfast cereal—I mean Cocoa Puffs, Cap'n Crunch, Froot Loops, Frosted Whatever. We were the envy of our friends. Their mothers all had them on—you know—sprouts on toast, and sesame rice cakes."

Lunchtime that day was a catch-as-catch-can affair, in which everyone wandered off with a sandwich and a book or a newspaper to the wide sunporch or sat at the kitchen table, an old rickety affair with metal legs. Eaton, wearing a work shirt and chinos tucked into socks (he had been clearing paths through the woods and had tucked his pants into his socks to protect himself from deer ticks), made himself a ham sandwich and invited me to go antique hunting with him. Sarah would not be coming. "I hate tagging along with Eaton when he wanders around looking for things to buy," she said.

About ten minutes later, just before he and I headed out the door, Eaton said to anyone within listening range, "Well, wish me luck. I may come back with a new kitchen table. I'd rather like to find a big, round oak one and some old painted chairs to go with it."

Sarah, who was reading *Newsday* at the old kitchen table, with her back to a small TV set, looked up from the paper, gazed at Eaton, and said evenly, "But we never discussed what kind of table we'd get," she said. "You're just going to bring one home without my seeing it?"

James returned to the kitchen as this exchange took place, and he and Anne traded glances, like old foot soldiers at the dawn of another day of hostilities at Valley Forge. A pregnant pause filled the bright kitchen.

"Uh, no, no. Of course not. If we find something, you'll come back to have a look at it. Um . . . well, 'bye."

From conversations that Eaton had with antique dealers in various shops in the small towns we visited that afternoon, and from the practiced way he stuck his hand under various old tables and muttered "Fake, fake, fake!" and from ongoing comments in the vein of "Look at that! They didn't make anything after the early 1800s that looked *that* good," I gathered that he was considerably more knowledgeable about antiques than the average furniture buyer. In fact, he told me, almost all the furniture in their houses was inherited from his mother's or his father's family, and it was important to him that any additions be of the same quality. At an antiques show in one town and in the five or six shops we visited, we looked carefully at dozens of tables and chairs, but none appealed to him. Just before he started for home, though, we entered a small shop that had a number of seventeenth- and eighteenth-century pieces Eaton greatly admired. The owner "knew what he was doing," Eaton said, adding that in the past he had bought "a few good things" there. The shop smelled of costly must and old beeswax-polished wood—a smell that one observer of American upper-class life has pinpointed as an important "recognition signal" of all the grand rural redoubts of Old Money. The dealer, a fellow fishing enthusiast, exchanged brief rod-and-fly pleasantries with Eaton, then led him to an elegant Queen Anne dining table with a pale, glowing surface, saying that he knew that the piece would be to Eaton's taste. It was. But it was also too small to seat all the members of his family, and, though he did not appear slack jawed, as I am sure I did, when the price—$55,000—was mentioned, he shrugged and said that he had spent a lot on the renovation of his house recently.

On the way home, at my urging, we stopped at a yard sale on a road near the McLanes' house. Eaton does not like yard sales because the kind of furniture he admires rarely turns up at them, and this one did nothing to change his mind. Nonetheless, he approached an obviously picked-through assortment of lamps, chairs, and bibelots with polite attention and gave everything a cursory once-over. Eaton's dignified presence and boyish, toes-pointed out, clomping gait caught the eye of the woman who was holding the yard sale, and she seemed saddened when, before long, he strode away empty-handed.

Back at the house, Sarah and James were unwrapping some things they'd bought earlier in the day. Eaton, narrowing his eyes as he watched James set a new cutting board on a kitchen shelf, said, "Uh-oh, let's look at that. There's something wrong there." The board had three or four small, round holes in it. And as James handed it over, something minute fell to the floor.

"Those are beetle holes," Eaton said, looking quite pleased with himself as Sarah, James, and I peered at the board to see what he was talking about. "Let's look at the wrapper."

James extricated it from the garbage bin, and, sure enough, the plastic wrapper and a paper label had tiny holes exactly where the board had them.

"Where were you standing just now?" Eaton asked his son, and immediately both of them fell to their knees and pressed their faces to the linoleum floor. "I'm sure those holes came from a wood-eating beetle. They can do a lot of damage. I don't like the idea of one snacking its way through the floors and furniture, and God knows how many progeny it could engender!"

After a few moments, James said, "Aha!" and held up a small, purplish-black beetle. He presented it to his father, and Eaton dropped it in a jar for future delivery to the Caldor returns counter.

Eaton then took me on an antiquarian's tour of the house—a task that he found very satisfying, to judge from the little pats he gave a number of the pieces of furniture we passed. In the dining room, he pointed out an eighteenth-century Hepplewhite mahogany dining table, a Chippendale pine desk, and a mahogany demilune Sheraton card table (the only article of furniture in the room that he and Sarah had bought together). A 1905 painting of his mother, aged ten, with her hair blazing red over a white dress and a coral necklace, hung on one wall, and on the adjacent wall there was a small, gruesome print of a falcon eating a blue jay. The tour proceeded to the living room, where several bronze bird dogs and a bronze pheasant evoked pleasant memories of the uncle from whom Eaton had inherited them—"a great shot"—and of a group of Boston friends his uncle often hunted with. These and a bronze eagle with matted feathers embedded in the metal had long been a source of friction between Eaton and Sarah. To Sarah, they were symbols of the disgusting world of blood sport. To Eaton, they were cherished objects that brought back lyrical moments of his youth.

Passing by as Eaton was pointing them out to me, Sarah rolled her eyes and shook her head. "When *are* we going to get rid of those horrible things," she said. "Really, they give me the creeps."

"They're not horrible, they're French—and rather fine, as a matter of fact," Eaton said. "I love them."

Sarah shrugged and went on her way, apparently not attaching much significance to the matter.

That had not been the case with a Renaissance painting, originally the property of Eaton's grandfather, that had come to Eaton after his mother's death, in 1965. Sarah had mentioned it to me one day when she was recalling some of her more memorable battles with Eaton. The painting had inspired a kind of marital Armageddon. Immediately after Eaton acquired it, he hung it up in the living room of their Central Park West apartment. Eaton liked looking at it. The work of an unknown artist, it depicted a vacantly languorous, richly draped brunette Madonna, and he particularly admired the picture's elegantly carved, ornate gilt frame. Sarah, who loathed the painting on sight, was furious with Eaton for not asking her opinion before he hung it. But her strongest objections were antireligious. She did not want to look up at "a goddam Madonna" every time she sat down to read a book, she said. Eaton refused to take it down. They had a furious row about it. And another. But the painting stayed where it was. Eventually, Sarah announced that she would not enter the living room until the painting was removed. Eaton thought she was kidding, but, at a dinner party they gave a few days later, when everybody got up from the dining-room table after dinner and headed toward the living room for coffee, Sarah hung back and could not be coaxed into the room by anyone. More than a year passed before she crossed the living-room threshold.

Eaton recounted the episode to me as we ascended the stairs to look at some bedroom heirlooms. "My wife hated that painting, but it was like a Raphael," he said.

I mentioned Sarah's objection to its religiosity.

"But my grandfather was not religious. You mean even if we'd had a Raphael in there she wouldn't have liked it?"

I shrugged noncommittally. She probably wouldn't have.

"Well, it pissed me off. For more than a year! Finally, I sold it. I said, 'Life's too short. I didn't like it that much anyway.'"

Upstairs, Eaton showed me an 1830 tiger-maple cannonball bed, which was Sarah's, and a Sheraton tent four-poster, which was his. The beds were pushed together, but, though Sarah's had been made up, Eaton's was rumpled. As we passed by the beds to admire a Hepplewhite desk across the room, he glanced at the un-made bed and saw fit to remark, in a somewhat unconvincingly matter-of-fact tone, that, in their family, "we all make our own beds" and that in the city, where he and his wife shared one big bed, they usually made it together.

Dinner that night was a lengthy, chatty affair on the sunporch, enlivened by a great deal of reminiscing about the annual family trips. Sarah feels that it is important for all of them to get away to-gether, to touch base and have some fun, even if sibling rivalries sometimes make the trips less than the lovefest she has hoped for. She had a real gift for organizing interesting trips, James told me, adding that it was part of her "camp-girl persona." She planned them months in advance, and in recent years she had made up a big folder for each trip, filled with articles, maps, and various useful bits of information.

At one point in the conversation, Sarah made a passing refer-ence to her daughter Mollie's wedding. As far as I knew, none of the McLane children were married. And I had met Mollie several times without hearing any reference to a husband. I asked Sarah about this, and she answered matter-of-factly, "Oh, it's a *mariage blanc.* She never sees him. He's a Japanese student. They've been married for six years, but she only married him so that he could stay in the country."

Sarah went on to tell of the anxiety of Mollie and her husband when the immigration people had questioned them in separate rooms about each other's personal habits and histories; they had half expected to be found out, Sarah said, but they weren't. Since the day of their nuptials, at city hall, Mollie had hardly laid eyes on her husband, and, according to her mother, she rarely gave the relationship much thought. (A year later, Mollie would divorce the young man so that she could legalize a "real" marriage to a young man she fell in love with.)

There followed a curious discussion of marriage as a gesture of good will. Robert, who had cooked a delicious dinner featuring braised chicken breasts, thought that it wouldn't be a bad idea to seek out and marry a foreigner—some needy person in India, say, where he and Anne had traveled together a few years ago—so the woman could gain a foothold in this country. Anne agreed. Sarah and Eaton gave each other searching looks but said nothing. Except for Mollie and her *mariage blanc,* none of their children had so far evinced much interest in marriage.

After dinner, I asked James and Anne, who had stayed in the kitchen to watch a video, whether they thought that the high level of communication between the generations in their family was unusual.

"Extremely unusual," James said. "Perhaps we enjoy each other's company too much. We've all had to struggle for independence. Everybody but Mom has been to a shrink, you know. Well, let's see, I guess Thomas hasn't been to one. But, anyway, mine feels that maybe we all hang out too much with the family. I know what she means, but basically, we like each other more than anyone else we meet. And not just our immediate family. We're the same way with all our Hardie relatives. We'll be at some party, and the most interesting people there will turn out to be our cousins or aunts and uncles, or whatever, and we always end up standing around together in a big clump. People are always making fun of us because of it. But there are real problems connected with this kind of family. I'd say it's sad but undeniable that when we bring home our girlfriends or boyfriends, family acceptance is the crucial issue."

Anne agreed. "I don't know why," she said, "but the only people I've brought home who seem to meet with Dad's approval are rich, blond, Wasp fly fishermen—near copies of him, in other words. Everybody else gets criticized for something or other. But at least we can talk about these things with them. Particularly Mom. She was incredibly liberal with us. Practically as soon as Mollie and I hit puberty, she was saying 'Here's the money. Go to Planned Parenthood.' It was preemptive openness from the word go. My friends thought she was the coolest."

"But sometimes we worry that we have a model of a partnership that can't be duplicated," James said. "And God knows who will be able to fit into this family. I think it may be harder for us than it is for people who have less contact with their families. It makes us leery of bringing around people we're serious about. I don't bring anyone home for at least a year."

On Sunday morning, the McLanes rose at different times and wandered into the kitchen to make their own breakfasts. The music of Charpentier floated through the house. Sarah had tuned in to *Sunday Morning Baroque* on WFSU, a Connecticut station, and was sitting buried in the *Times* on the sunporch. Eaton was going through some barrels in the basement, getting rid of stuff that had been in storage since 1974, when they first leased the house. James was studying, and Anne was sleeping late. Robert had left in the small hours to return to his school—a small visual-arts school in Upstate New York. Periodically, Eaton surfaced with a beautiful old dish or glass vase and proudly displayed his find to whoever was around. Quite a few of these objects went immediately onto nearby shelves, inspiring snorts and wisecracks from Sarah. "I thought you were getting *rid* of these things," she said as she came out of the kitchen with a second cup of coffee.

Eaton was putting some Staffordshire figurines on a hall shelf. "I am, I am," he said. "I've found a lot of stuff that I'm going to sell. I'm just putting them here temporarily." "Uh-huh," Sarah said, and returned to the sunporch and the *Times.* About half an hour later, Eaton showed me a beautiful leather-bound edition of a book called *The Children's Hour*—a collection of fairy tales and stories I knew from my own childhood. His copy had been inscribed to his mother from her mother, on December 24, 1908.

"Mother was thirteen when she was given this book, and she treasured it," he said. "Her father lost his money three times—in 1914, the in the little depression of 1923, and in 1929, when he died. The first time, he made a recovery. The last time, of course, he didn't. After the first one, they had an auction and sold off many of the things my mother had grown up with, including the family's books. But a friend saw her crying when this book was being auctioned and bought it back for her. She was terribly grateful. I don't know how many times she mentioned the incident to me."

After lunch, Eaton went back to cutting paths through the woods, while Sarah stripped the beds, made them up with fresh sheets, and packed her clothes, occasionally flipping on the TV in the kitchen to monitor the progress of a football game. Sarah is a pro football enthusiast. "I don't know why, but it amuses me," she says. Eaton can't understand the appeal of any game played with a ball.

Helping Sarah make the beds, I asked her if it was true—as one of the children had told me the evening before—that she thought of herself as a socialist. She nodded and told me that she was a registered Democrat but strongly disapproved of the disparities in wealth that exist in this country. In the 1930s, she said as we tucked an old quilt under a pillow in a clean white case, her mother had been registered as a member of the Socialist Workers' Party, and, as a result—in the fifties, when McCarthyism was rampant—she'd lost her job at the Voice of America. "She has always been bitter about that, particularly because she never had any specific accuser," Sarah said. "And it changed our money situation drastically. I think I told you that I saw practically nothing of my father after the divorce, and that my mother was on her own economically. To tell you the truth, I didn't look forward to the times when I did see him. He criticized me constantly, and complained all the time, and he became more and more querulous, more and more alcoholic. As he got older, he began to make nasty remarks about blacks and Jews; in fact, he began to sound just like his mother, who was really something that way. One of the most embarrassing moments of my life was when Grammy Blackwell—as we called her—took me to Longchamps for lunch. I must have been around seven or eight. It was crowded, and we had to wait in line for a while, and at one point she just about bellowed, 'If there weren't so many Jews here, we'd have no trouble being seated!' God, I wanted to be swallowed up by the earth right there. What a horrible woman!"

A friend of Sarah's once described her to me as "your first pick for a lifeboat companion," because she had such a strong aura of competence. Self-reliance and unsentimental rationality were the cornerstones of her personality, and if recriminations and self-pity were not her style, neither was a capacity for prolonged anguishing over difficulties. James told me that all that any of the children had ever had to do was allude in passing to some emotional problem and their mother would whisk them—or, when they were older, tell them to whisk themselves—off to a psychiatrist. He thought it curious that her belief in therapy had never caused her to seek it for herself. Sarah's way of solving problems—particularly problems connected with her marriage—seemed to be to attack trouble head-on, and, if she got nowhere, to show by some act of defiance that she was not to be ignored. Anne and James both felt that, while their mother could not have been kinder or more sympathetic when something was troubling them, she always wanted their problems solved right away. She was notably uncomfortable talking about any still-unsolved problems of her own, and her children seemed to think she had none that she could not eventually solve.

Late on Sunday afternoon, a fog so thick that you could barely see the porch posts from the end of the driveway enveloped the house. Anne was painting some shelves on the porch, James was studying his law books, and Sarah began loading the car for the trip back to the city. Eaton came in from the woods, removed his socks, and began carefully examining them for deer ticks. Last week, he said, he'd found twelve on his pant cuffs and socks. This time, having found none, he looked up, asked if I was "comfortable and happy," and lit a cigar. He looked comfortable and happy himself. For a few minutes, Eaton and Sarah found themselves with nothing to do, and they just hung around the kitchen bantering and, mirabile dictu, flirting with each other. The fog lifted an hour later, and we all jammed ourselves into the car—an old Chevy Cavalier, which was loaded with food, law books, winter clothes that had been stored in the garage, and assorted treasures that Eaton had unearthed from the basement—and headed for the city.

ON a warm evening in early spring, not long after the Westchester weekend, I had dinner with Sarah and Eaton at their apartment. All three of us had arrived from our offices, and Sarah announced that she had work to do after dinner. While Eaton, who was wearing the same shredded shetland sweater and chino trousers I'd last seen him in, set the table and made us all drinks, Sarah, who had changed into jeans and a plaid shirt, cooked a meal of sautéed fish and steamed peas. Each listened attentively to the other's this-was-my-day-at-the office stories, and there were a few newsy exchanges about the children.

After dinner, Sarah excused herself and retired to a small combined study and guest room that had last been Anne's bedroom. Eaton then proposed that we look at some old family photograph albums, to give me a fuller idea of the world of his childhood. For the next hour or so, we scrutinized the fading records of a vanished world of long lawns, languid ladies in graceful brocade gowns standing near potted ferns, and prosperous bankers and merchants with bulging waistcoats. Included in the albums were society-page clippings that recorded the attendance of his mother and father at, for example, the Metropolitan Handicap at Belmont Park in the 1930s, and earlier clippings dealt with the social activities of his mother and her girlhood friends. For example, a 1919 clipping reported:

> Miss Anne Thomas, daughter of Mr. and Mrs. Thomas of this city, who is passing the autumn at Hot Springs, Virginia, is among the many well-known society girls who now carry walking sticks. This fad, which had its revival at Newport last summer, has now spread to the Southern resorts.

There were several pictures of Eaton's sister, Elizabeth, who died in a car crash in the early sixties. Photographs of Eaton's mother showed a pretty, reserved-looking woman with a pronounced cleft chin and a certain gritty determination in her face. These old pictures were either brown and white or black and white, and thus, Eaton felt constrained to tell me, I was missing the pleasure of seeing his mother's "rather amazing" red hair. His father was smashingly good looking, with an elegant handlebar mustache and a marked glint in his eyes. His expression was laconic, sensual, and challenging—the very image of the roué of silent movies. Many of the pictures were taken at various chic resorts in the years when Eaton's father was married to Eaton's mother; they show John McLane stretched out on a lawn or in a beach chair in the company of one or another beautiful woman. As Eaton peered at a few such photographs, his eyes narrowed slightly. "Well, these are records of some of the trips I told you about," he said. "Usually, my father went on these trips with a rich client of his—a sort of playboy, who had a house in Newport where he gave parties. Obviously, it bothered my mother—both personally and in terms of the money situation. She really resented these excursions. I don't know how often they took place, but there were too many. The marriage just was not good. I learned later on that they had had no love life at all during the thirties and forties. I'm not sure how I learned this. Maybe my mother told me. Maybe my mother told my sister, and she told me. But I gather that that's the way it was. I've always been sort of a women's libber, probably because of the way my mother's life turned out. I've always felt that women should have their own careers, their own lives. Once, while my father was away on one of his trips, one of the partners in his brokerage firm called my mother up and said, 'Can't you get him back? The market is good now. He's needed, and he's on these trips all the time.' She never forgot that. She told me that another time a good friend of hers who was in the brokerage business turned to her and said, 'John is heading for a fall, because he's not working hard enough.' I think she worried all the time that there would be some disaster. My mother told me these stories somewhere down the line, years and years ago, and I've never forgotten them."

I asked Eaton if he now had any major worries in his own life, and to my astonishment he shot back, "Money worries."

Incredulously, I asked him, "But surely you have plenty of money?"

"Now, yes, but if I got fired . . ."

"Who's going to fire you? You're the president of your company. Your colleagues think you're good at what you do."

"Well, you never know. There's actually a CEO who is in charge of the company. We know each other well and all, but . . . business can get bad. People get worried."

"You really worry about that?"

"I always have. My whole life has been lived with the idea of having a hedge against disaster. I have capital. I don't have debts. I will never repeat my father's mistakes. I want money for my old age, and to pass on to my children."

DESPITE Sarah's original misgivings about the idea of marriage, only a short time passed before she agreed to marry Eaton. The ceremony took place at the end of February 1959, in a small church in Westchester that was near her grandmother's house, and after a week's honeymoon in Puerto Rico, Eaton and Sarah returned to New York and their workaday lives. Though Sarah had initially been the more reluctant of the two, she soon settled comfortably into married life, and at the end of several months of living with Eaton she found, much to her astonishment, that it suited her quite well. Eaton, on the other hand, grew increasingly anxious, and even depressed, and often seemed distracted. During that period, not only had Sarah stopped frying his eggs but he had come to realize, with dismay, that his wife and his mother had a prickly relationship. ("She'd broken a valued object of my mother's, and she fought constantly with my mother's friends over politics," he told me.) And there was also a more serious problem. Eaton had made love to his wife every single night since their wedding—something he felt obliged by his marriage vows to do—and he had become utterly exhausted. Partly because of his upbringing, his sense of loyalty and duty had somehow become entangled with his idea of sexual performance. Except for Sarah, there was no one he felt he could discuss his situation with, and he was too embarrassed at first to broach the subject with her. So for a long time he said nothing.

Recalling that period of his life one evening several months after we had looked at the photographs, Eaton said, "I thought, Oh, God, I'm completely trapped. I can't do this. I'm tied to this person for life, and there's nothing I can do about it, and it's going to kill me. I was totally confused and depressed. Well, my wife finally brought it up, and I told her frankly what I had been thinking, and she was great about it. Great. But, you know, she was as much in the dark, really, about these matters as I was. So she suggested that I talk to some professional, and I did."

"You mean a psychiatrist?"

"Yes. And I ended up having analysis. I went to a doctor three or four times a week for a number of years. I found it extremely helpful, and the problems I had were resolved."

"Was psychoanalysis common in your world?"

"It was very uncommon at the time. It's an extremely conservative world, mine, and there was some stigma attached to the whole idea. I don't know if this is true today, but back then I never discussed my analysis with anybody, except that sometimes I would talk to Sarah about an unusual revelation. But we knew people, later on, who would come up to us at parties and say, 'I'm in analysis' and then start telling us about it. For some people, I think, analysis becomes the center of life. It helped me get on with my work and my marriage, and to lead a reasonably successful life, but it's been interwoven with a million other things. I've gone for help at more than one point in my life, as a matter of fact. But at the beginning of my marriage, when I was in actual analysis, it was very tiring. I was determined not to repeat my father's mistakes, but I needed to be able to think more clearly about the things that I was doing. You know, my mother took me to a psychiatrist when I was eleven, to learn about the facts of life. Despite her old-fashionedness, she could always face most things. In that respect she and Sarah are alike—but she could never talk about sex. Never. And all my father ever said to me about the subject was 'Don't masturbate.'"

"Was the psychiatrist your mother took you to a local person?"

"No. We made a special trip into Manhattan for the event, and—oh, God—it was a woman. I was absolutely mortified. I sat there with her, and she spoke very euphemistically about everything. She referred to my penis as my 'pipe.' She seemed incapable of saying the word 'penis.' She would say 'Your pipe does this, and your pipe does that.' Jesus! I knew I was blushing furiously, and I was veering between bursting into hysterical laughter and bursting into tears the whole time. I didn't tell my mother that an elementary-school friend had already tried to wise me up—though I didn't really understand much of what he had to say, either. He kept telling me 'Look, it's just like your frogs and toads.'"

One point on which Sarah and Eaton differed was their idea of their backgrounds. Sarah thought that she was "a regular, middle-class person." Eaton thought he would probably be considered an upper-class person, and he thought Sarah would be, too. Sarah thought that the differences in their upbringing were vast and significant; Eaton thought they were small and tended to downplay them. Though neither had known any of the other's friends or relatives before they met, Eaton felt rather strongly that they had been baked from more or less the same batter. One evening as we were looking at another photograph album, he pointed to a typed guest list for his parents' wedding. "Look at this," he said, smiling. The list included the name of Sarah's grandmother, also the names of her future stepfather and one of her cousins.

Several months after I'd begun meeting with the McLanes, Sarah's mother became ill and began a downward slide that was generally acknowledged to be irreversible. The McLane family took turns keeping her company in her apartment—especially on weekends, when no nurse was in attendance. Sarah was rarely anywhere else. She was so tired that she began feeling unwell herself, and, though she didn't begrudge her mother the time or effort, she did want to move her mother out of her apartment. Sarah suggested to Eaton that they sell their own apartment and buy one that would be big enough for all of them, or else perhaps find out if another apartment in their own building might soon become available. The McLanes were not in agreement on this question, and sometimes they fought about it. His mother-in-law's decline saddened Eaton greatly—he was truly fond of her—but he balked at the idea of selling their apartment, which had been his home for the last fourteen years.

My next meeting with Sarah took place while these discussions were going on. After we talked for a while about her mother's bravery, Sarah spoke of Eaton's close relationship with her mother and then of her own cool relationship with his. By the time they got engaged, she said, Eaton had already seen a lot of her mother, because they were always doing things with her family; she did not meet Eaton's mother until after she and Eaton had become engaged.

"She had, however, made her presence known," Sarah said. "Eaton told me that she was unhappy about our sleeping together during our courtship. We were spending our nights in my apartment, and his mother complained. She was of a different time. Most of her friends were much older, and she herself had had a governess hovering over her until she got married—at the age of thirty-five. And Eaton's father was forty-five when they married. He was tall and good looking, but his mother was Irish Catholic. That was considered beyond the pale and continued to be some sort of problem throughout their marriage. I know he worked hard at becoming socially acceptable—he knew all the right people, and he went to all the right places—but things did not go smoothly between them."

I asked Sarah if she and Eaton had discussed her future mother-in-law's complaints in any detail.

"We discussed everything. We still do. I think Eaton's openness—the way he was willing talk about anything—was what actually made me decide I could live with him. When we decided we would marry, we even picked the number of children we would have. My mother had lost two of her brothers during the war, and I said, 'Let's have a lot of children, in case—God forbid—we lose any.' And Eaton said, 'Well, two is too few, three would fight. Let's have four.' When Mrs. McLane and I finally met, I was on my best behavior, and I thought I was doing pretty well when I was introduced to her friends, though Eaton might disagree. But what surprised me a lot was that, really, he had no family. He had a mother and a sister, and he had an uncle he called Unk, whom I didn't meet until later on. That was it. Everybody else was gone. Another uncle had died some years before, and it was not many years later that Eaton's sister died in the car accident."

I asked Sarah if she saw any similarities between herself and Eaton's mother, as Eaton did.

We were sharing a Chinese take-out meal in her sitting room as we talked. She put down her chopsticks and permitted herself a sort of explosive, barking laugh. "No, no. We were quite dissimilar. She was very formal. She was very much interested in manners, something I was never famous for. She was very much into protocol. You know—'We've always done it this way, and that's the way we do it.' You sat down at a dinner party and in front of you was a menu. Not for a grand evening but for an evening where there were just twelve people at dinner. I mean, this was a very fancy world. She had strong feelings about possessions. I caused a scandal after I'd been at her house two or three times: I was washing the dishes and broke a wineglass. I said—perfectly innocently, I thought—'Oh, I'm sorry, I broke a wineglass,' and then I tossed it in the garbage and went on washing the dishes. Well, apparently I was supposed to cry and rant and beat my breast and fall on the floor, because it was one of four wineglasses that came from the king of Romania, or something. I was *heavily* criticized for not taking more care when I was washing it. But, you know, I just thought they were crazy. I mean, who gives a damn? So you break a wineglass—there are other wineglasses. I mean, it's nice to have nice wineglasses, but I just don't think that's what's important in life."

After lunch, Sarah settled herself on a small sofa and began sewing stuffing into some blue cushions for Mollie, who had just moved into a new apartment in Boston. As she sewed, she sipped iced tea from her favorite plastic glass. I smiled and said that it was certainly clear that crystal was not a high-priority item for her.

"No, it isn't. Someone did give us some Baccarat for a wedding present, but we've never been allowed to use it because Eaton's so afraid it would break." She looked at me wide-eyed, her eyebrows raised. "I'm serious. But I don't care, if that's the way he feels. It's a little weird, though. He inherited rings from his mother, and I'm never allowed to wear them. They're locked up in a box. To me, that's ridiculous. If I have a great ring, I'm going to wear it. If I lose it, so I lose it."

I asked Sarah what else had struck her about the world that Eaton grew up in.

"The people I met in Far Hills were absolutely different from the people I knew. They seemed to be very rich but not very well educated—certainly not thinking reeds, as they say—and they drank a *lot*. I don't want to characterize them unfairly, but after we were married we spent time down there, and Eaton allowed as how he hated them and never wanted to see them again. And, of course, I got into political arguments with people. I would be with someone who would make a remark about some ethnic group, or they would express admiration for Eisenhower . . . Well, I cared a lot about politics. Eaton's family was Republican and violently anti-Roosevelt, and the younger people out there were certainly very anti-Kennedy. They thought Nixon was swell. My family had been so caught up in the McCarthy era that Nixon was like the end, the enemy! And my family had been very much involved with the Roosevelts. When Julia skipped the fourth grade, she was allowed to stay at the White House for the weekend. I mean, how else do you reward someone for skipping a grade? But what surprised me most about Eaton's family and the people in their circle was that they were not really politically aware. They were not leaders in public life. They were just not tuned in to the life I was accustomed to. They played music and talked about it, but they didn't go to concerts, or anything. Mrs. McLane had gone to the opera in the glorious twenties, but that was all gone. She played bridge, and she read the Reader's Digest Condensed Books, and after dinner they watched television."

What qualities of Eaton's, I asked, had compensated for the differences in their backgrounds?

"Well, I just liked him. He was fun to do things with, and he liked doing many of the things I liked to do. He liked being outdoors, he liked skiing, and I would go to the theater and he would come along and he seemed to like it. He has taken on more of the coloration of my family and my existence, I would say. He's turned away from the Somerset Hills Club and the backgammon and the plaid-pants stuff. You know what I mean. I don't know—it just seemed to me that we did have things in common. We both had gaps, and we have discussed them many times. He can listen to a recording of someone singing an aria, and after a few seconds he'll tell you, 'Oh that's Licia Albanese, in 1959, and the conductor is So-and-So.' Which I can't do at all. And he's much more knowledgeable about art than I am. Actually, I'm color blind—not for primary colors, just shades. We've learned from each other. He never cared about travel much, and I adore traveling, so he's become a traveler with me. And God knows I've spent far more time in the woods with him than I would have if I hadn't married him."

IF there was one area in which you might expect a certain dimming of the bright light of rationality that Sarah and Eaton prided themselves on beaming into every cranny of their lives, it was the realm of sex. But to a remarkable degree, this seems not to have been the case. Each spoke obliquely but appreciatively of the other as a sexual partner, and both said, separately, that they had arrived at a state of erotic felicity via a path of frank discussion. These discussions rested on a bedrock of affection, Sarah said, without which they probably wouldn't have dared to talk so frankly with each other. Affectionless sex, a growth industry in an increasingly body-centered, secular society, had in fact been a feature of both their amatory histories, and they looked back on those interludes with little joy. Like many of their friends who had come of age at the dawn of the go-go years of sexual liberty, when "Why not?" was probably the most often repeated sexual question, they had affected a sexual sophistication that was based on little actual knowledge or experience—a modern strategy that seems to have replaced the Puritan need to assert one's bona fides as a virgin. Before they married, however, they had settled the matter of sexual fidelity—a subject about which they were of one mind.

Eaton: "Where I grew up, there was an awful lot of wife swapping among my friends. And they were constantly getting divorced and remarried. By the time I got married, I had come to the conclusion that the open-marriage idea—this business of screwing around with other women—was not going to work. I felt that if Sarah was going to go off and do it I would say 'You shouldn't,' and I also felt an obligation to say that I wasn't going to do it."

Sarah: "Having affairs has not been an issue, because we agreed not to have them, and we haven't. As far as I know. That was not the way we wanted to live our lives—particularly because of the circumstances of both our homes. In the short time that we spent visiting Far Hills, we saw all these other couples, and they did a lot of screwing around. It wasn't quite 'Throw the car keys on the floor,' but almost. These things were going on, and we just didn't want to be a part of it."

For a brief period in the early days of their marriage, Eaton was still taking home a relatively small paycheck; Sarah, who continued to teach school, was earning more. The hotel in Puerto Rico where they spent their honeymoon was modest, and they didn't have much in the way of spending money while they were there. Nonetheless, they had a wonderful time. Sarah learned in situ about her husband's passion for beetle collecting—something she'd only heard him talk about previously. They spent hours crawling through fields chasing Staphylinidae, or rove beetles.

Within a very short time of their becoming lovers, Sarah and Eaton had rather bluntly confessed to each other that there was a lot about sex they did not know, despite the considerable number of hours they had each logged in various beds. Both reluctantly admitted that their experiences had not been entirely satisfying. For Eaton, the obscurities of the pipe lecture, his loss of virginity at a Cuban whorehouse during his freshman year at Yale, and subsequent collegiate excursions to another whorehouse in Palm Beach, his depression after he broke up with the girl he thought he had impregnated, and his frustration with the many "nice" girls who were impossible to bed had all left him feeling vaguely confused and desirous of fathoming the deeper mysteries of love-making. Sarah had had similar feelings. Neither of her parents had ever discussed sex openly, and her own adventures had erred, she felt, on the side of tentativeness.

"We basically knew nothing about sex," she said one afternoon when the subject came up. "And as far as I could tell, there were few ways of learning about it. After my freshman year at Barnard, I was baby-sitting for a family on the North Shore of Massachusetts, and behind some books in the library I came upon Van de Velde, the world's most terrible sex-advice book. I read it from cover to cover, of course, and found it completely imponderable, and that was the extent of my technical knowledge."

The book that Sarah referred to is *Ideal Marriage: Its Physiology and Technique,* by the Dutch gynecologist Th. H. Van de Velde—a popular guide for the sexually perplexed during the 1940s and 1950s, though it was originally published in 1926. Written in the relentlessly hearty, hortatory style of the doctor-savant (the title page quotes Balzac: "Marriage is a science"), *Ideal Marriage* is a mélange of textbook physiology, Christian moralizing, literary aphorisms, and advice on sexual techniques which is phrased in flowery language. In the preface the author mentions that he is working on a second volume, to be entitled *The Prevention of Conjugal Aversion,* and is planning a third about marital fertility and sterility. Van de Velde writes with an air of goodwill and boundless optimism: "I show you here the way to Ideal Marriage. You know the honeymoon of rapture. It is all too short and soon you decline into that morass of disillusion and depression, which is all you know of marriage. But the Bridal honeymoon should blossom into the perfect flower of Ideal Marriage; may this book help you attain such happiness.") But his old-fashioned paternalism must have offended many of his female readers: "The wife can do much to avert that fatal marital ennui by independent interests, which she persuades him to share. For instance, an interesting book, or journey, or lecture, or concert, experienced, enjoyed and described by her, with sympathy and humour, may often be a talisman to divert his mind from work and worry, and all the irritations arising therefrom. But of course he, on his side, must be able to appreciate her appreciation and her conversation." And virtually every Van de Velde reader, male or female, who came to his book hoping for a quick fix for some problem must have gotten hopelessly bogged down in his digressions. The following example, about genital odors, is illustrative:

> The seminal odour of Orientals is stronger and more acrid than that of the "Caucasian" West. The semen of the healthy youths of Western European races has a fresh, exhilarating smell; in the more mature men it is more penetrating. In type and degree this very characteristic seminal odour is remarkably like that of the flowers of the Spanish Chestnut (marron), which also vary according to the conditions of the trees and the atmosphere and are sometimes quite freshly floral and, then again, extremely pungent and quite disagreeable.

According to both McLanes, it took time—years—and some patience to figure out where they wanted to go in this department. Sarah put it this way: "I knew people who seemed to know about sex instinctively. I have a friend who looks like a total prude, but she had intercourse when she was fourteen, and she knew all about masturbation and orgasm from birth, practically. I don't know how she found all this out, but she did, she tells me now. So there were people even in that era who knew about these things. But Eaton and I were not among them. Despite our previous experience, we didn't know what we were doing, and so we learned. We had to talk a lot. We studied movies and books. There was a book that came out in the late sixties called *Everything You Always Wanted to Know About Sex but Were Afraid to Ask,* and I read it, and it told me things I hadn't known about homosexuality, for example, and other things as well. Certainly when we were first married we didn't know what we were doing. But there has been a natural progression. I never set a specific standard, because I didn't know what was good."

● ● ●

THE better I got to know the McLanes, the more I came to marvel at how high a value they placed on rationality, and how, in its steadiness, the flow of their life called to mind the genteel, solidly placed country gentry of the novels of Jane Austen—hardly a practical model for most modern lives. This is not to say that the irrational hasn't had its part in the McLanes' lives, nor that there weren't issues in their marriage that continued to trouble them. Almost always, these issues had to do with egalitarianism or money, and the resulting discussions and anger were of a kind that could have arisen in no era but our own.

In the forties and fifties, when Sarah was coming of age, antifeminist ideologues were far more visible and audible than their feminist counterparts. In books and magazine articles, academicians and pop writers alike castigated intellectually lively or independent-minded women as "masculine" and suggested that all professionally or academically ambitious women were neurotic man-haters. Margaret Mead, in a discussion of the options open to women in the generation in which she grew up (well before Sarah's), wrote that the societal pressure made her feel that one could either be "a woman and therefore less an achieving individual, or an achieving individual and therefore less a woman." Those who chose the achievement path, she said, often gave up the chance to be "a loved object, the kind of girl whom men would woo and boast of, toast and marry." This was hardly less true in Sarah's day. The sixties and seventies brought radical changes to the professional and private lives of women, but how much have their domestic lives really changed even now? If the sociologist Arlie Hochschild is correct, not much. In her 1987 book, *The Second Shift*, Hochschild recounts interviews with a wide range of couples in which she questioned them closely about how they arranged their lives. She found that the great professional leap forward of the women she interviewed had rarely been accompanied by more than meager progress in the sharing of household and child-rearing tasks. Worse, many of the women were performing an elaborate psychological high-wire act by trying to convince themselves and their friends that their husbands helped out more than they did, in order to put a more modern face on their unions. The McLanes, although they may come across to casual acquaintances as a traditional couple, have, on the whole, a remarkably egalitarian marriage. Nonetheless, their differing views about money and the division of labor have been a continuing source of rancor.

At first, they had a joint checking account, but that did not last long. "Eaton was writing checks for lots of things I didn't want— fishing rods that cost a hundred dollars," Sarah said. "Our rent by then was two hundred and fifty dollars a month, so a hundred dollars was a lot of money. Neither of us was earning a hell of a lot—I was still teaching, and his salary at the brokerage firm was fairly modest—but he had no sense of budget, and no sense of constraint. Sometimes he would overdraw our account. His atti- tude was 'You want something, you get it.' And I would say, 'But we can't afford it,' and he thought I was out of my mind. When I met him, as you know, he was living with his mother. He'd lived briefly with some friends in the city, but mainly he'd lived at home, where someone else took care of things, and so the whole concept of, say, Con Ed, and turning off the lights—whatever— never occurred to him, and still doesn't. If we walked back to the bathroom right now, or any place he's been, you'd find all the lights on. He finishes shaving, he walks out of the bathroom. I don't mean to make a major issue of it, and obviously we can af- ford it now, but when we started out, we couldn't. He just seemed to feel that there were certain things he could not do—like shop at sales or stand in a line. He's *never* gone to the post office. Never bought a stamp. His secretary gets stamps for him."

In the late sixties, Eaton bought a painting for two hundred dol- lars at an auction held by the children's nursery school. Although Sarah was at the auction, too, Eaton never asked her whether she liked the painting or wanted to buy it. "He bought the painting because it looked good for him to participate in the auction and buy a painting," Sarah told me. "He never asked me if I wanted it.

I had nothing to do with it. He just bought it. It was the final straw. I was so mad that I took my money out of the joint checking account, and I've never put it in an account with him since, ever. We had a huge fight. And from then on, if he overdrew his account, it was his problem."

In 1970, a few years after the incident at the auction, Eaton's brokerage firm made him a partner, requesting, as was its custom, that he invest some capital in the firm as part of the deal. At that point, Eaton had no savings to draw on but knew that he would lose face if he wasn't an investor, so he asked Sarah whether he could mortgage her house on Nantucket. She willingly agreed, and that investment became, she says, "the foundation of his capital." In the ensuing years, Eaton's salary got larger and larger, while Sarah's earnings as a teacher and, later, as a science curriculum consultant, remained modest. But Sarah felt that she had come to Eaton's rescue at a crucial time, and every time they fought about money she became furious when he advanced the theory that since he was earning far more than she was it was all right for him to make unilateral purchasing decisions and spend his money as he saw fit.

By the time the McLanes' children were toddlers, Eaton was making enough money, he thought, to hire an English au pair to help with the children. There were other au pairs over the years. They made a big difference, but they didn't clean the house, or do dishes, or accompany the family to the country on weekends. Despite the privileged life she led, Sarah, like the great majority of working wives and mothers, would still rush home from work, shop, cook dinner, clean up afterward, and see to the children's needs in the evenings. One weekend in Westchester, she cracked.

"Eaton would sleep late on Saturday morning, and I would get up and get the kids' breakfast and play with them, and so on, and I was getting exhausted. I realized that I was doing all the shopping, all the cooking, all the cleaning, and putting out the garbage in snow and rain. It was also clear to me that we were spending much more money than we were taking in. I confronted Eaton one evening with some of these things, and he said, 'OK. I'll take out the garbage.' That lasted about three weeks. Then we began to have big fights about other domestic chores, and one day in 1974 there was a knock-down-drag-out fight about money that culminated in our sitting down and looking at the books and the fact that the children went to private school—Eaton wouldn't consider sending them to public school—and he saw that we were really headed for disaster. So we decided to give up the Westchester house, even though we loved it. We were going to sell it, but we were lucky enough to find people to rent it right away. We didn't know how long it would be before we could get back to it, but it turned out to be thirteen years. That same year—1974—we gave up the au pair. We just felt we couldn't afford it. The children remember vividly the evening their father told them that he was having financial troubles and they would have to give up the house, because they were all sitting around the table, and he broke down and wept.

"That next period of my life was horrendous. The children were still little, and they would come home to an empty house. I worked out intricate schedules for them to go here, there, and everywhere. The summers were a particular nightmare. Because of the four tuitions, we were living very close to the bone, so we never traveled, we never did anything. But leaving the house was the culmination of years of living above our income. After that, it wasn't ever again so bad, because Eaton became more able to acknowledge these things."

At about the same time, Eaton was having serious misgivings about his job. His firm was being transformed, in Sarah's words, "from sleepy old preppie to twenty-first-century yuppie." Everything was getting computerized. The already large staff was growing larger, most of Eaton's mentors had died, and he did not feel comfortable in the new milieu. When a friend in another highly respected but smaller brokerage company offered him a job as its president, he felt instinctively that accepting it was the right thing to do. Sarah agreed.

Succeeding in the business world was especially hard on Eaton, according to Sarah, because "he didn't give a damn" about business when he started out—or not the sort of damn he would have given if he'd become a conservationist or an entomologist. Whatever Eaton's feelings about his job and its rigors, the large sums of money it eventually generated justified for him his withdrawal from the general day-to-day upbringing of his children and from most of the domestic chores. If in other aspects of his life he struggled to be a "modern" man, in these areas more traditional thinking prevailed, and when he talked about his role as family provider the words he used were rather uncharacteristically bureaucratic and impersonal. Because he began now to make substantially more money than Sarah did, he felt he had an impeccable argument for contributing less on the domestic front. That belief remains firm to this day, though the issue has inspired the biggest fights of Eaton and Sarah's fight-filled marriage. Sarah is not the only member of the family who has found fault with Eaton's hands-off-the-children-and-the-feather-duster position. On a visit from London, Thomas, a strikingly handsome young man (he looks like a kinder, gentler version of Eaton's father), mentioned to me that his father did not seem really interested in him or his brother and sisters until they emerged from early childhood. "It was hard sometimes to understand some things about him," Thomas said. "I mean, we knew he loved us, but, for instance, you couldn't ever just jump in his lap—he'd get annoyed, and he obviously didn't like it. Sometimes his distance was a little scary."

"I didn't spend a lot of time taking care of the children," Eaton said late one evening, about a year after I'd first met him. "I didn't change diapers. I didn't play with them a lot. I had the idea that dealing with the children was essentially the woman's responsibility, and the male responsibility was to support the family structure. I have used the analogy of the tree—I'm sure if my wife heard me use it now she'd throw up—but anyway I have the feeling that, somewhat similar to a tree, I have to keep the structure supported by my earnings. I knew that we were going to have four children and that it was going to be expensive. I wanted them to go to private schools, and also to college, and to have the same opportunities that I had as a child. I knew that Sarah had neither the money nor the capacity to make the money that would enable them to have all that. So that really was the main obligation that I had as a participant in this family unit."

I asked Eaton if he thought that Sarah had ever accepted his view of his role in their marriage?

"No, she hasn't," he said. "You know, there are things I may not like about her, but when things are going well, I forget about them. In that sense, our marriage is like an accordion. When things are going well, the accordion is closed, and I just don't think about her faults. But when things aren't going well the accordion's open, and everything about her bothers me. I think my attitude toward our roles has always been a source of friction. But I simply cannot do everything she would like me to do. I have to single out certain things that I feel responsible for and comfortable with. We've had terrible fights about these issues. I remember one fight when Sarah turned to me and said, 'I'm not coming back here anymore unless you do more work in the house—vacuuming, sweeping, cleaning things.' So we worked out a deal whereby, at the end of the weekend, I would do certain rooms and she would do the other rooms. And that worked for quite a while. We mapped it out. And now it's gotten to the point where, if she cooks, I'll do the dishes. If I cook, and I do sometimes, she'll do the dishes. We still fight about these things all the time, but she ought to understand how much sweat I go through to do what I do."

Eaton's *apologia pro vita sua* had been stoutly articulated one night in 1971, in the form of a manifesto he wrote after everyone had gone to sleep, for delivery to Sarah the next day. At the time, he was still at the first brokerage firm, and the family had been keeping some horses at a stable near the house in Westchester. The manifesto was entitled "I Want a Husband," and it read:

I want a husband who cuts wood; brings up wood; lays fires; builds bookcases for all my books, and cabinets for the records; fixes fuses and shorts in the electrical system; drills the walls and paints the cracks that develop from leaks; clears out the gutters; varnishes the porch wicker; buys, carries, and loads the salt into the water softener; picks up the garbage when the raccoon dumps it; gets out the rat traps and poison; examines the house for termites and carpenter ants; repaints the screens; points up the fireplace; puts up the storm doors and windows; resets the flagstones when they crack and heave; saws up the dead elms and trees blown down on the lawn; knows the cycles of fertilizer, weed killer, planting, so that the lawn is at least more than 50 percent grass; gets the pool replastered and painted so that it doesn't leak; copes with the complexities of the pool system and water pump, tank, toilets, furnace, radiators; digs in the asparagus; moves the hydrangea; cuts back the wisteria; mows the meadow with a sickle bar; digs out the poison ivy; cuts briars; transplants the peonies; primes the apple trees; puts the fencing around the pool, the garden, and the pasture for the horses; lugs in 100-pound bags of sweet feed and oats; builds the lean-to; puts up the saddle racks; rat proofs the feed bin; changes the tires when flat; tries to lift 70-pound suitcases onto the roof rack; drives unquestioningly 100 miles when I am tired from working all day; unloads the car.

And, most of all, I want a husband who makes enough money for me to send my kids to school. Enough so that I can go to the opera and ballet and theatre when I want to. Enough so that I can spend my time working on the town's advisory conservation council, involve myself in town planning, work on the boards of those institutions. Enough so that I can take a week in Dominica or St. Croix in the winter or go salmon fishing in Norway or go to the Cape or England in the summer. Enough so that I can hire a nurse for the children and a gardener for the country. Enough so that I don't have to run the old car into the ground. Enough so that I don't have to put up with the politics in my office or be polite to customers I can't bear and deal with the treadmill of up at 7:30—subway at 8:30.

Eaton's conviction that he regularly shoulders a good many un-
noticed or underappreciated responsibilities is probably shared
by hundreds of thousands of husbands of strung-out working
wives. But, long as his list of tedious chores was, a comparable
list of Sarah's at the time, had she thought to compile one, would
probably have filled a small notebook, and, whereas many of the
items on Eaton's list happened only occasionally, those on
Sarah's would in all likelihood have represented tasks she did day
in and day out. In the last forty years, because of the demographic
reality of the two-job family, the domestic and child-rearing help
that men give women has shifted from being a kindly supplemen-
tary gesture to crucial support. In 1950, fewer than 30 percent of
the country's married women with children worked; by 1986, according to the United States Bureau of Labor, 68 percent did. In
1950, 23 percent of the married women with children under six
worked; by 1986, 54 percent of such mothers had become part of
the labor force. Until recently, it was actually so rare for women
with children under the age of one to work that no records were
kept of the phenomenon. Today, 50 percent of such women work,
and, all told, two-thirds of the nation's mothers do. Only 20 percent of the men in Hochschild's study shared the housework
equally with their wives, and, even when men shared some
household tasks, women still seemed to do a full two-thirds of the
routine domestic chores. Since 46 percent of all women who
work earn less than $10,000 a year and a fifth of all full-time
working women earn less than $7,000 a year, few can afford
household help or child care—unless their husbands pull down
substantial salaries. In the absence of a comprehensive national
policy on child care, most women must see to their children's
needs as best they can, and the lower they are on the economic
scale, the less adequate is the care they find for their children.

Sarah's own cri de coeur on the subject of domestic labors appeared one day in 1982, in the family message book—a thick spiral notebook in which everyone puts telephone and other
messages, and which Sarah saves as a kind of quotidian record of

family life. She has amassed quite a collection of these notebooks, which are filled with grocery lists, lists of chores needing to be done, requests from the children for cash, requests to the children to stop leaving piles of dirty dishes in the sink, scoldings, angry responses to scoldings, fond little notes from the children to Sarah and Eaton and vice versa, angry exchanges between children, guest lists for birthday parties, birthday-gift wish lists, doctors' appointments, doodles, requests to borrow the car, and bus schedules. In the 1982 book—among many notes about someone's staying over at a friend's house, irritable exchanges about messy rooms, and a copy of "Heloise's Boric Acid Roach Exterminating Formula" with an arrow pointing to it and a note from Sarah saying "This is what I want for my birthday!"—is the following clipping, from the *New York Times* of Tuesday, March 16, under the headline DOMESTIC STRIKE ENDS:

Fed up with having to serve as what she described as "mother, cook, driver, laundress, go-fer, and money-changer," Mary Ellen Shaver went on strike against her children last month. She said she was through with being their servant, until further notice.

Mrs. Shaver, of San Ramon, California, said yesterday that her strike, which began February 8, had worked and that she had called it off over the weekend because her three children had "shaped up" and abandoned, at least for now, their "slovenly ways."

Although her husband, John Shaver, was not a target of her strike, he has joined the children in accepting equal shares of the household tasks, Mrs. Shaver said.

"We wrote an agreement and everyone has a copy," she said. "The children will have to keep their own rooms clean, observe a curfew, and try to be more courteous to one another."

In the first days of the strike, the children—Beth, 18 years old, Meg, 15, and John, Jr., 11—ate a lot of peanut butter sandwiches and one of them learned how to make macaroni and cheese, said Mrs. Shaver.

It was when they tired of that fare that serious negotiations began to end her strike.

Neither frank discussion nor fighting nor good-natured cajoling was ever successful in changing Eaton's mind about the proper apportionment of responsiblities for rearing the children. He feels no particular regrets about the way things worked out. In this respect, he says, theirs was merely another "traditional" marriage, and if he had the chance he would not do things any differently.

Sarah, on the other hand, still considers the period, now long past, when her husband failed to accept what she believed to be his obligations as a spouse, a father, and a "decent person," one of the bitterest in her life. "Sometimes his hands-off attitude created *serious* problems," she said one evening. "I mean, the usual thing was he would say, 'I can't get up in the night because I have to go to work tomorrow'—even though I was also going to work. But the idea was, you know, that his job was more important, because he earned more money. I could never get through to him about how unfair that was. But there was one Saturday when I was finishing my M.A. at Columbia when I had to go to the library, so I left the kids with Eaton. I think it was the winter of 1965. We already had Mollie and Thomas. Mollie was four, and she got into a desk drawer in another room. He was sitting in the living room reading. She found a pocketknife, and she opened it, and she cut her face with it. Of course, he was horrified. But then he took her to the emergency room and didn't pay any attention to what they were doing, and they sewed her up as if it were her leg. When I came home from the library, he and Mollie were back from the ER, and I found out later that the sutures were very inappropriately done. She had this *huge* scar on her face, and she has it to this day. Eventually, I took her to a plastic surgeon who made the scar less noticeable, but it was terribly upsetting and traumatic. I blamed myself for leaving her with him, if you can believe that, but I also blamed him, because he was totally in his own world—and I don't really impinge on that, and the children don't. Nothing does.

"So I learned that I couldn't trust him. In effect, I never left him in that situation again. I know it sounds awful, but it's the truth. I just sort of accepted the reality of it. I mean, when they were babies he just had no interest in them except as sort of scientific experiments—he'd ring a bell on one side of the room to see if they'd turn their heads. That's how he had fun with them. He'd shine a light on them and see if they'd jump. He loved that. He cuddled them a bit, I mean he wasn't an ogre, or anything, and he did exercise male authority later on when it was needed, as I gather some fathers seem unable to do, but, basically, he just wasn't interested in babies."

I asked Sarah if she had ever said to herself, "Well, he doesn't have enough regard for me, we're not compatible"?

"We are extremely compatible, *and* he has no regard for me in those ways," she answered. "I think there are certain things you have to accept about people. It's made me furious. We scream. We throw things. We've had terrible periods of not speaking, and terrible periods of lots of things. The basic root of the problem is that he doesn't know how to think—in the sense of putting himself in their shoes—of other people. The idea of anticipating things, for instance. If someone's going to be here for lunch, he doesn't think, Well, now someone has to set the table. He'll pick up the serving platters and come into the dining room and say, 'The table isn't set'—like 'Where's the tweeny?' And it's not because he's trying to shirk his job. It just hasn't crossed his mind. Oh, he's made some revisions. He has. He will now clear the table when we have people for dinner. But that took, easily, twenty years. And it only happened because I said that I wasn't going to have people to dinner anymore. Our fights are pretty all out. Once, in the middle of one, he told me to leave. 'Get out if you don't like it,' he said. So I went across the street and rented an apartment."

"You did?"

"I didn't actually sign the paper, but I told him I had. I came back and said, 'I found an apartment. I'm going.' Then he thought that maybe it wasn't such a hot idea after all. But, you know, in

some ways, I've never thought of marriage as an absolutely permanent situation. Probably because I never planned for marriage
or expected to be loved all my life. When I told Eaton about the
apartment, I figured he'd probably change his mind, but I wanted
to demonstrate that there *was* an apartment right in the neighborhood that I *could* rent that day."

I asked Sarah if she could remember what that fight had been
about. She couldn't, but she was sure that the essence of it was
his failure to acknowledge the reality of some basic grievance
she had.

"You know, he's never known where I've worked, what I've
done. I've been working as a science-curriculum consultant at my
present spot for more than ten years, but I've heard people say,
'Where does your wife work?' and he'd say 'Ah . . . what's it
called again?' You know—that kind of thing. It depresses me. But,
basically, he's a very nice man, and I'm glad I'm with him, and
he's never hit me."

I laugh, but she doesn't.

"No, seriously, I'm quite terrified of that."

SARAH and Eaton laugh a lot when they're together, and, except when they're fighting, their friends like to be around them;
not only are they good company but the longevity of their marriage and the confidence of their bearing seem to convey to people around them a welcome sense of stability. Eaton appears as
solid as a Roman senator, but in truth the pressures of his interior
life have occasionally disturbed its smooth surface violently and
rudely.

About ten years ago, when his work had been particularly demanding and there was a lot of tension at home with his teenage
children—Eaton apparently had a hard time handling the parent-
child wars of the period—he rushed home on the subway in the
middle of the afternoon to get a book of Japanese prints. Eaton
loves and collects Japanese prints, and, through his firm, he had

learned that a famous collector had just died. His firm was the man's executor. The book he was racing home for had plates of many of the prints in the deceased's collection, and Eaton hoped to be able to purchase a couple of the originals. But while he was still on the subway, he began to breathe so fast that he thought he might be about to faint or have a heart attack. A doctor he consulted that same afternoon told him that he had been hyperventilating, gave him various tests, and had him walk around with a heart monitor for twenty-four hours. It emerged from these measures that nothing was wrong with his heart; he had simply had a panic attack. Over the next few weeks, every time he slid through the subway doors he expected to have another one. The surface calm of his life had in some way been pierced, and he recalled that he'd had "absolutely no idea of what was going on."

Several months later, while he was giving a speech at an out-of-town business meeting, it happened again. "In the middle of the goddam speech," he said. "I had to stop talking. It was so absolutely mortifying. I thought, Jesus, that's the end. My life is falling to pieces. So I got the name of a shrink who my doctor said knew about these things, and I went to him and said, 'Listen, you've got to get me out of this, I don't know what it is, but something is happening, and it started on the subway, and now it's extended to my speech making, and I *have* to make speeches and appear in front of people.' Well, we did it through chemicals. If I have to make a speech now, I take a Valium. Or, if it's a major speech, there's a drug called Inderal I can use—actors use it—and that has completely solved the problem. I don't like the Inderal, because I feel a little droopy when I take it. But it doesn't affect my performance or my manner of speaking. So if I have to make a speech in front of thirty people, or something like that, I just take one and don't have to worry."

I asked Eaton if he had ever discovered the underlying cause of the attack.

"Well, I went to the therapist for a couple of years to figure it out, and we trolled out whatever demons there were. It didn't seem to be one precise thing. We would talk through these things—my relationship with Sarah, and my children, and everything you deal with when you go to a shrink. I like the guy. He's a very nice man. A decent guy. I still like him."

One afternoon in May, over a lunch of canned tomato soup and pâté in the kitchen, Eaton got onto the subject of how he had fallen into the kind of work he did. "To be honest with you," he said, smearing some pâté on a slice of French bread, "I never liked business very much. I didn't know what I wanted to do when I got out of college, but I really didn't want to go into business. These businesspeople would come to Yale, and you would go to see the people from Lever Bros. and Procter & Gamble, and the advertising agencies, and I would think, Oh God, this is boring, boring! I wanted to try to go into conservation, I wanted to be a pianist, I wanted to be a doctor—I didn't know what the hell to do. I finally decided the only thing to do was to go into business—to make enough money so I could do all the things I like to do. And my whole family had been in the investment business. So I sort of backed into business, but it turned out to have been the right move to make. I still get to spend a lot of time in the woods. I fish. I collect my beetles. But I never *imagined* that I'd get this far."

I asked Eaton if he had any idea then of the kind of life he'd like to lead, and the answer came back as swift as an arrow: "The life I'm leading now. Sarah and I have often talked about this. If we inherited, say, a hundred million dollars, we would continue to live right here. We'd still travel the subway. I might buy a few more antiques, because I like them. But I honestly don't think I'd change my lifestyle. I would not get a chauffeur. We don't need trappings."

The path to Eaton's eventual good fortune was smoothed considerably, of course, by the fact that at the time he was looking for a job the CEO of the firm he initially joined was a friend of his mother's—a man of the old school, whom Eaton came to admire tremendously, and who felt, as Eaton did, that successful businessmen ought to help their communities. But his mother's friend retired in the mid-seventies and was replaced by a younger man, with an entirely different outlook. In a general discussion among the partners about the direction the firm should be taking in the next decade, Eaton mentioned that he was a trustee and fund-raiser for several organizations that helped provide housing and educational and legal services for inner-city groups that had been abandoned by the government, and he suggested that the firm get more deeply involved in such projects. His new boss didn't feel that outreach work was appropriate, because it took too much energy and time away from business. Eaton thought his response was "cheap" but "typical of today's businessman."

Like most of his colleagues, Eaton is a Republican, but he often finds himself voting for Democrats, and did so in 1992 for Bill Clinton. He is also vehemently pro-choice. Mollie and Thomas both remembered that as children they helped their parents distribute Planned Parenthood leaflets at a local fair in Westchester. The position that the Bush administration took on the abortion issue consistently infuriated Eaton, and so did its general two-faced approach to the environment. Unlike Sarah, however, Eaton does not enjoy political arguments. Also unlike her, he will sometimes let an offensive statement—a colleague's anti-black or anti-Semitic remark—slide. Sarah thinks that his lack of self-confidence and fear of alienating people are what silence him. Eaton says, "Such talk is more common than people think; you cannot squabble about it all the time. There are always a lot of anti-Semitic comments and racial slurs against minorities in business. A kind of quiet whispering. It's never done publicly. I hate it. But I hear it all the time."

One day, Eaton remarked to me, "Sometimes I don't know if I'm a Republican or a Democrat, or really what I am, because in many ways, as I've told you, I'm rather apolitical. I do feel very, very strongly about the environment and overdevelopment. Those are things that put me on the side of the Democrats. I really loathe the Republican Party's positions in these particular areas, and I certainly don't share the feeling of a lot of my colleagues on

Wall Street about blacks and poverty and welfare. I think we've got to have some kind of better support system for people in need. But I'm very conservative about financial issues. Something that's always bothered me about the Democratic Party is its tendency to throw money at things. But, of course, the irony is that Reagan was one of the biggest spenders that we've ever had, and the whole savings-and-loan mess is just revolting. Now, Sarah will tell you she's a socialist. And this is where we really do differ, and we've fought about these issues ever since we got married. She knocks business all the time. But I know that there are an awful lot of people in business who have a lot of integrity and are basically honest. One of the running arguments Sarah and I had when we were newlyweds was about the railroads. She would always point out how badly run they were and say that they ought to be nationalized, because the people who ran them were out for themselves, and not for the people who took the trains. My position was—and is—that it's a lot harder than you think to do these things, and that many big public institutions are not all that well run in this country. By and large, businesses do try to do the best they can. I'm in business, and I know that you get knocked and criticized for decisions—you get second-guessed constantly—but you have to make the decisions. I'm on Wall Street, which is a hotbed of greed today, and this may sound ridiculous, but most of the people I've dealt with are honest people. I mean that. Anyway, Sarah can be awfully rude when she disagrees with someone's politics. I'm sometimes nervous about taking her to functions where some of my more conservative friends are. And sometimes even the children have objected to her high-handedness when she thinks she's right. She's *extremely* opinionated. She is invariably friendly and considerate with the people she comes in contact with who are sort of on the bottom rungs of society; sometimes I just wish she would extend the same courtesy and politesse to members of her own class."

• • •

IN the late spring, Sarah drove up (and ferried over) to Nantucket, as she does every year, to spend a weekend opening up the house for the season and readying it for the summer tenant. A few days before she left, she invited me to join her for part of the weekend, but warned me that it might not be much fun because there was a lot of work to do. And there was. Apart from brief interludes for lunch, tea, and dinner, Sarah worked without cease for two days. The Nantucket house is the very model of a modest, comfortable old seaside summer retreat. Built at the end of the last century, it is bright and airy, and it is about a five-minute walk from the ocean. Most of Sarah's neighbors there are year-round, working-class people. The house has three small, sunlit bedrooms, each painted a bright pastel color; a smallish living room, filled with comfortable furniture; and a pocket-sized kitchen. Some time ago, Sarah had painted the kitchen walls a deep green and decorated them with white silhouettes of all the big bass and bluefish that Eaton had caught over the years, and inside each fish silhouette she or Eaton had carefully noted the date and place of the catch. The furniture and bric-a-brac were humbler than anything in their Westchester place, but, like all their houses, this one had a careless air of expensive, aesthetically pleasing coziness.

With some help from me, Sarah scrubbed and painted the trim of the porch screens; aired the bedrooms and made up the beds with crisp embroidered linens she'd bought at an auction in Maine; cleaned the kitchen; painted some porch furniture; and scrutinized the house's deepest recesses, both upstairs and down, to see if the winter cold and damp had caused any damage that needed repairing. Stripes abounded, throughout the house, giving one the general impression of being inside a Matisse painting. There was a green-and-white striped chair and sofa in the living room, blue-and-white striped mugs in the kitchen, and a blue-and-white striped cloth on the dining-room table. The walnut stairwell was covered with a weathered rag rug, and near the front door a profusion of venerable fishing rods and tennis racquets filled an equally venerable umbrella stand. Sarah had arrived on Friday, and I joined her the next day. In a telephone call the night before, she'd told me that the major task she was setting herself for the weekend was pruning the hedges and bushes in the backyard. Sounding quite pleased with herself, she boasted that she had been pruning since early that morning and had kept going until she couldn't tell the honeysuckle from the lilac.

She returned to that task on Saturday, and, except for a short break to pick me up at the ferry, she worked hard at it all day. Recently, she had discovered the charms of a light, easily manipulated electric chain saw. It was an efficient tool, and she tremendously enjoyed wielding it. Until seven o'clock Saturday night, she tugged and sawed away, freeing lilac bushes from the encroachments of the honeysuckle, and a beautiful old pear tree from the encroachments of the lilac bushes. When it got too dark to see outdoors, we began working on the inside of the house.

Sometimes Eaton or one of the children helped Sarah at the beginning of the season, but she was also accustomed to doing house-opening tasks alone, and she went about them with the practiced rhythm of someone who knows exactly what is required. For instance, even though I was present, she left the radio on all day, because, she said, she liked to hear a voice when she came in from outdoors, so that she "didn't feel lonely." It was, I realized, the only time I'd ever heard her use that word. I helped out mainly by dragging the fallen vines and branches into a nearby wooded area (it held the final resting place of the family setter), and after about four hours of steady labor time began to fall away. My skin itched and my lips became parched, but the greenness all around and the salt air were bracing. I glanced over at Sarah, tall and determined, hacking away at the gnarled vines, and looking for all the world like some pioneer homesteader. There was sweat on her brow, and her hair was plastered to her face, but she was clearly in her element. By the time two piles of branches had grown to about twice my height, it was 3:30 in the afternoon, and I needed a break. Not Sarah: she seemed to be welded to the electric saw and to have become Diana, Destroyer of Vines. She barely noticed when I staggered to a nearby pond on the pretext of checking the bird population. Afterward, I took a slow walk along the seashore. When I returned to the backyard, Sarah was still sawing away, standing waist-deep in a pile of branches and vines and humming to herself.

Eaton had more than once spoken to me with awe of Sarah's "amazing" energy, but only now did I realize its mythic proportions. In a way, her furious energy was a reproach and a challenge to the genteel traditions of her class. Edith Wharton, in her memoir *A Backward Glance,* complains that she knew "less than nothing" about the women of previous generations of her family, "with pearls in their looped hair, or cambric ruffs around their slim necks," because most of them left no record of their lives and were not very well known even to their husbands. For the men, like Walter Scott, who wrote about them, the "gentlewomen were 'a toast' and little else," Wharton went on. "Child-bearing was their task, fine needlework their recreation, being respected their privilege." No one could say that the McLanes had not made themselves known to each other; and their deep mutual understanding probably could not have come without the fury of their battles.

When night fell, Sarah reluctantly put the saw away and came into the house, and we finished the remaining chores. The sun had made her face rosy, and her jeans and purple sweatshirt were covered with grass stains, but she didn't look tired. Mollie telephoned from Boston and Thomas called from London, and she told them both in an offhand way what she'd been doing for the last two days. We ate supper and drank some wine, and she said that Eaton was off fishing somewhere and wouldn't be able to call until the next day, but she knew he was having a good time, because he was with an old school friend he liked a lot. Eaton probably knew that Sarah was having a pretty good time herself.

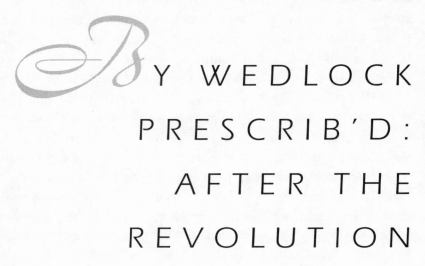

BY WEDLOCK PRESCRIB'D: AFTER THE REVOLUTION

WHEN THE REVOLUTIONARY WAR ENDED, WOMEN WHO had run the family farm, tavern, or business in their husbands' absence returned to their old chores and duties, and in the clear light of the Republic a noteworthy asymmetry in the dignity and status of husband and wife suddenly became more visible. In September 1794, *The Massachusetts Magazine* published some "Lines Written by a Lady who was Questioned Respecting her Inclination to Marry":

> With a heart light as cork, and a mind free as air,
> Unshackled I'll live and die, I declare,
> No ties shall perplex me: no fetters shall bind,
> That innocent freedom that dwells in my mind.
> At liberty's spring such draughts I've imbib'd,
> That I hate all the doctrines by wedlock prescrib'd.

Few early champions of women's rights attacked marriage per se; rather, they advocated a kind of domestic feminism aimed at educating women to become better wives and mothers and in general at improving their lot within the context of marriage. Indeed, it was almost impossible to imagine women's lives in any other context. Bachelors might establish satisfying lives in the greater world, but the unmarried woman—equipped with few skills that were useful outside the home—was like a baker without an oven.

Both in Europe and in the American colonies, the illegitimacy rate shot up during the middle and late eighteenth century—a development that has generally been interpreted as a sign of a growing sense of individual choice and independence among young women, and perhaps it was. The incidence of premarital pregnancies in America in that period—30 percent of the female population experienced them—was not equaled again until the 1960s. But the rising illegitimacy rate could just as well be accounted for by the fact that, as society became more mobile and the community less controlling (and less willing to intervene on behalf of "wronged" women), men found it easier to abandon the women they had made pregnant.

The English essayist Mary Wollstonecraft called in her writing for a radical restructuring of society that would enable women, married or single, to enjoy the same legal and social status as men. Wollstonecraft, whose *Vindication of the Rights of Women* (1792) became the cornerstone of the American women's movement, theoretically disapproved of marriage, but she married the political philosopher William Godwin (he was also officially opposed to marriage) in 1797, after learning that she was pregnant with his child. Historians have exaggerated Wollstonecraft's antimatrimonial beliefs, making her seem hypocritical for marrying Godwin, but what she disapproved of was the mores associated with marriage, not the institution itself. In fact, as she wrote in *Vindication of the Rights of Women,* she considered marriage "the foundation of almost every social virtue."

None of the sentimental novels so widely read throughout the nineteenth century advocated the single life, nor did they shrink from describing in excruciating detail the horrors that fallen women were prey to. Most of those novels, indeed, might well been entitled *Marriage*. The genre's modernity, such as it was, consisted largely of the way its authors applauded young women like Constantia Dudley, the heroine of the American novelist Charles Brockdon Brown's *Ormond* (1799), for refusing, usually at considerable economic cost, to enter into loveless marriages. After Constantia's father loses all his wealth to an embezzler, she sells her books and jewelry, supports her family with needlework, reconciles herself to a diet of cornmeal mush thrice daily, and steadfastly rejects offers of marriage from men she does not love, though marriage appears to be the sole means by which she could improve her material existence.

One of the regular contributors to *The Massachusetts Magazine* in the 1790s was Judith Sargent Murray, who shared many of Wollstonecraft's views but wrote about them in a more practical vein. In *The Gleaner,* a collection of her essays published in 1798, Murray drew on the arguments of Locke not only to plead for immediate changes in women's education but to chide parents for making marriage the only goal of their daughters' lives.

It was an abiding fear of early civic leaders and social theorists alike that female independence would pose a danger to marriage as an institution, and the term "Wollstonecraftism" was long understood to denote a kind of unleashed mad-dog feminism. The linking of Wollstonecraft's name with loose morals and unwholesome predilections was caused by Godwin's decision to publish his wife's memoirs in 1797, after she died in childbirth (of puerperal fever, like thousands of her contemporaries). The memoirs made it clear that many of her published theoretical views—including her endorsement of free love—were based on actual experiences of her own. Wollstonecraft revealed not only that she and Godwin had had premarital sex but that she had had several lovers before him and had borne an illegitimate child. The memoirs transformed Wollstonecraft, in the world's eyes, from an interesting, harmless, literary novelty into a pariah. American advocates of better education for women now felt compelled to dissociate themselves from Wollstonecraftism, and the general tone of the social agenda formulated by the husbands of the Republic for their wives remained essentially what it had been as spelled out in the loftily sentimental and flatly conservative 1795 Columbia College commencement oration, whose subject was "Female Influence." In it the speaker called up a tableau of "the accomplished woman surrounded by a sprightly band, from the babe that imbibes the nutritive fluid, to the generous youth just ripening into manhood, and the lovely virgin," and exhorted her to "contemplate the rising glory of confederated America," to "consider that your exertions can best secure, increase, and perpetuate it," and to remember that "the solidity and stability of the liberties of your country rest with you."

THE much discussed separation of workplace from living space that occurred in the 1820s when men began to leave home in significant numbers for factories and offices brought about a further—and perhaps more far-reaching—split between the worlds of husbands and wives: moving work away from home caused men and women to feel an artificial remoteness from each other. Though the gradual entrance of women into the working world over the next hundred years would eventually restore a sense of mutuality of interests and horizons, the fact remains that for most of the nineteenth century the daily lives of husbands and wives had little in common. Even women who did work tended to work at home. In the 1870 United States Census —the first in which employed women were counted—four-fifths of the working women tallied were employed either on farms or in domestic service. The only type of work that bucked the trend was teaching. At the beginning of the nineteenth century, most teachers were men, but by 1870 two-thirds of the teachers in public and private schools were women. The shift seemed inevitable to the educator and lecturer Catharine Beecher, who wrote in an 1841 *Treatise on Domestic Economy* that women and children were a natural combination, and declared it "chimerical" to hope that men could overcome their characteristic "aversion to the sedentary, confining and toilsome duties of teaching and governing

young children" when they had available to them the "excitement
and profits of commerce, manufacture, agriculture and the arts."
Of course, this "excitement," however inspiriting, was understood to be extremely taxing, and even brutal. So, as capitalistic
society became more complex, the modern wife was expected by
her husband not only to be a paragon of virtue and a moral educator but to offer him healing solace and respite from the harsh
demands of the masculine world. Occasional whimpers of dissatisfaction were also heard from the Provider. The absolute separation of men's and women's spheres struck the Unitarian
clergyman and social reformer Samuel May as equally horrible
for men and women. "The terms in which the two sexes are generally spoken of," he wrote, "seem to imply that men must go
forth, take part in the collisions of political party, pecuniary interest, or local concernment; get themselves careworn, perplexed,
initiated, soured, angry; while women are to stay at home, and
prepare themselves with all the blandishments of maternal, sis-
terly, conjugal or filial affection to soothe our initiated tempers,
mollify the bruises we have received in our contacts with other
men; and so prepare us to strive with renewed resolution, and
bruise or get bruised again."

Oblique criticism of marriage from the male point of view pep-
pered nineteenth-century fiction. Writers as diverse as James Fen-
imore Cooper, Herman Melville, and Mark Twain all created male
characters whose mobility and freedom could exist only away
from the inhibiting constraints of married life. Natty Bumppo, the
solitary hunter of Cooper's "Leatherstocking Tales," roams as he
pleases because he has virtually nothing to do with women. Although Cooper himself was happily married and apparently lived
a life of domestic serenity, D. H. Lawrence concluded that Natty
was a kind of "wish fulfillment" figure for Cooper, who, happy or
not, felt tightly bound by his marital obligations. Natty, on the
other hand, "had no business marrying," Lawrence went on. "His
mission was elsewhere . . . he does not give much for the temp-
tations of sex. Probably he dies a virgin." Lawrence believed that
the nineteenth-century unmarried wandering male character rep-

resented a new kind of womanless, childless being—"hard, iso-
late, stoic and a killer."

Far more often, however, that character assumed a more benign form: the bachelor. Like the poor, long-suffering virtuous
woman, the besieged bachelor was a staple of nineteenth-century
American literature. One of the bestselling novels of 1850 was
Reveries of a Bachelor, by Ik Marvel, the pen name of the writer
Donald Grant Mitchell. Mitchell's book—reprinted thirty-nine
times before 1859—contrasts the quiet freedom of a bachelor's life
with the prospect of a tumultuous and duty-bound life with
women. The central character evades a potentially entrapping at-
tachment and winds up strolling down a country lane with his
gun pouch and dog—a scene that, with a horse substituted for the
dog, came to be replayed in a thousand and one Western movies.
It seems odd that the pioneer couple never played the same
larger-than-life role in the popular imagination that the solitary
wandering male did, but it is not difficult to see why. In the vastly
expanding nineteenth-century American world, the geographical
and economic possibilities held out to men must have appeared
endless, and the homebound, narrow world of women stultify-
ingly small.

In the 1840s, when the American women's movement began to
take shape along with other social reform movements—child welfare, prison improvement, and the abolition of slavery—the utter
dependence of wives on their husbands became a recurrent subject of public discourse. Refused seats at the 1840 World Anti-
Slavery Convention in London because of their sex, Lucretia Mott
and Elizabeth Cady Stanton, who are generally considered the
founders of American feminism, began to campaign zealously for
women's rights, and in 1848, in Seneca Falls, New York, they
helped organize the first feminist convention, which issued a
"Declaration of Sentiments." Based on the Declaration of Independence, it began with the words "All men and women were
created equal," and those words inspired many women to begin
working in earnest for the right to vote.

It was not easy for most early feminists to find the time or energy to work for their cause, and they faced vigorous opposition from their husbands and fathers. Moreover, they were so unused to assuming roles of political power that not one of them felt capable of chairing the Seneca Falls Convention, and in the end the job had to be given to Lucretia Mott's husband. Sustaining a public life while meeting the crushing demands of the home was a constant difficulty for the early women's-rights crusaders. Usually, they helped each other out. Susan B. Anthony, the only early feminist who actually remained single, frequently came to Stanton's rescue, and Stanton often expressed her gratitude. But in all her letters there is not even an oblique suggestion that Stanton ever considered the possibility of asking her husband to share her domestic duties.

THROUGHOUT our early history, American wives enjoyed greater legal rights than their British counterparts. Married women's property rights broadened somewhat in the first years of the Republic, and inheritance rights improved for women with the abolition of the rules of primogeniture and of oldest sons' double shares and with the granting of equal status in inheritance statutes to daughters and sons. In the states that had chancery courts—New York, Virginia, and South Carolina—women obtained far more legal independence and exercised their right to own property without much difficulty. By the middle or late nineteenth century, even in those jurisdictions without chancery courts women were granted the right to own property and clearer rights to their shares in the estates of their deceased husbands.

But if the old patriarchal order of the colonial era was dead by the nineteenth century, there was yet to be established an accepted modus vivendi for husbands and wives living in the industrial age (as, in a sense, there is yet to be established one for the postindustrial age). Diaries and memoirs bear eloquent testimony to the existence of rich erotic lives and harmonious marriages in the nineteenth century, but the new leisure made possible by the machine created problems of its own. Middle- and upper-class women, freed from the daily round of grinding but essential work at home as their husbands went off to work else- where and servants took care of the heavy chores, now became unhappy in their idleness, depressed by their newly exalted posi- tion of priestess of the home, and frustrated by the uneasy knowl- edge that their reproductive roles had come to be their most tangible asset in the household economy. Individually, they con- fessed in their diaries to feelings of boredom and isolation that collectively created a virtual epidemic of invalidism among the women of the middle and upper classes. The redoubtable Catharine Beecher, traveling around the country in 1871, discov- ered "a terrible decay of female health all over the land," which appeared to be "increasing in a most alarming ratio." Private jour- nals of the time, both the women's and their husbands', record an almost universal inability to account for what was going on.

The newly established gynecological profession attributed the deteriorating health of American women to sexual ailments stem- ming from the very nature of womanhood, and from the early 1870s on, doctors were treating women surgically for psychologi- cal disorders that went by diagnostic names as varied as "nervous prostration," "neurasthenia," "hysteria," "dyspepsia," "depres- sion," "hyperesthesia," and "cardiac inadequacy."

Until well into the twentieth century, women were being sub- jected to what a number of researchers have characterized as a kind of undeclared war on the female genitalia. The tone of the era is well captured by Dr. Horatio Storer, an enthusiastic early advocate of surgical treatment for women's mental disorders: he wrote in 1871 that woman "was what she is in health, in charac- ter, in her charms, alike of body, mind and soul because of her womb alone." Actually, there was a difference of opinion among doctors as to which part of a woman's sexual anatomy was most responsible for her woes. Although clitoridectomies were never a really popular surgical procedure in America, they had become a way of checking female masturbation and curing mental problems as early as the 1860s and were still being performed as late as 1904 (with one isolated case reported in 1948). Oophorectomies, or so-called normal ovariotomies—removal of the ovaries to cure insanity—were first performed in 1872 and came to be far more widely practiced. All told, 150,000 women in the United States probably underwent the procedure.

The supposed dominance of the reproductive organs over a woman's whole being theoretically made her uniquely vulnerable to mental peril. "With women, it is but one step from extreme nervous susceptibility to downright hysteria, and from that to overt insanity," one doctor wrote. In a climate created by such views, the expansion of women's horizons was thought by the majority of the American public to be, at best, misguided and, at worst, threatening race suicide. The notion that husbands and wives might actually flourish in a friendly, and not rigidly separated, domestic arrangement was rarely mentioned (except in a few utopian communities—real or literary—and even they generally followed patriarchal lines). The supposed dominance of women's reproductive system over their brains implied that if women were changing they could do so only by becoming more masculine. The Woman Question was thus portrayed as a shoot-out between the brain and the uterus for dominion over the female persona.

The most extreme interpretation of this battle was offered by a doctor named Edward C. Clarke, whose book *Sex in Education, or a Fair Chance for the Girls* was published in 1873 and was reprinted seventeen times in the next decade. After reviewing contemporary medical theories, Dr. Clarke became convinced that higher education for women would cause atrophication of the uterus.

Marital-advice books were rarely addressed to men. Warnings against masturbation and exhortations to practice self-control surfaced intermittently, but, all in all, remarkably few words were addressed to the private stresses and strains experienced by husbands. Men married to the unhappy, nervous, and occasionally suicidal women of that epoch were, for the most part, unable to understand what was happening. They frequently accompanied their wives to doctors' offices or went alone to seek advice. In addition to surgery, rest cures and respites from the anxieties of daily life were generally prescribed for the wives—more idleness for those already awash in a sea of ennui.

AT the beginning of this century, marital-advice books—among them *Plain Talk on Avoided Subjects,* by Henry Guernsey; *Quiet Talks on Home Ideals,* by S. D. and Mary Kilgore Gordon; and *The Relations of the Sexes,* by Mrs. E. B. Duffy—railed against cheap romantic novels with matches based on physical attraction and approvingly described the ideal marriage as a union of two supremely sober, undersexed people, who would live quietly until death sent them to their well-deserved reward. The crucial role that a wife played in laying the foundation of her country's social values continued to be a theme in those works. The character of her progeny and the success of her husband—the fate of the nation!—still depended, the advice books suggested, on the wife alone. Men were encouraged to look for thriftiness, chastity, good domestic skills, and tenderness in a wife; and women, because of their supposedly feebler sex drive, were expected to be less swayed by passion and subsequently more rational in deciding on a suitable husband. Nonetheless, despite a growing flexibility and openness in courtship around the beginning of the century, men still initiated courtships and decided when and whom they wanted to marry.

The first Americans to call for radical change in marriage itself were a group of social critics which included the writers Edward Bellamy, Thorstein Veblen, Lester Frank Ward, Charlotte Perkins Gilman, and Theodore Dreiser. The economic injustices of the institution were a particular target of these turn-of-the-century writers. Bellamy objected to the relentless pressure put on men by the need to support wives and families; Veblen disapproved of the acquisitive nature of the patriarchal marriage and the idle lives it imposed on women; Ward and Gilman criticized courtship patterns that reduced women to marketable goods, and the artificiality of living in a world so rigidly divided into masculine and feminine spheres; and Dreiser wrote dark, lyric meditations about marriage, sex, and work. In *The Man-Made World; or Our Androcentric Culture,* published in 1911, Gilman compares wives to sheep, and their husbands to unwitting shepherds. "In some grazing regions," she writes, "the sheep is an object of terror, destroying grass, bush and forest by omnipresent nibbling; on the great Plains, sheep keeping frequently results in insanity, owing to the loneliness of the shepherd and the monotonous appearance and behavior of the sheep." Gilman shared with the feminist Olive Schreiner (who once described the marital relationship as "female parasitism") the belief that the "sexio-economic" relationship of men and women was a form of legalized prostitution.

In the late 1880s, Gilman herself was unhappily married to a young painter she did not love, and suffered from extreme lethargy and depression. To find a cure for her illness she visited a well-respected Philadelphia specialist in female ailments, Dr. S. Weir Mitchell. Mitchell refused to look at a letter that she had sent him describing her symptoms (mere "self-conceit," he told her), assured her that her problem was not "dementia" but "hysteria," and advised her to keep her baby with her at all times, to take extra naps, and never to touch a pencil, pen, or brush as long as she lived. Gilman followed his advice for a number of months and nearly went mad. In her autobiography she describes how she found herself crawling into closets and under beds to hide from her own distress: "The mental agony grew so unbearable that I would sit blankly moving my head from side to side." Not long afterward, her marriage broke up, and she moved, with her baby daughter, to Pasadena. There she recovered and even thrived, writing thirty-three articles, twenty-three poems, and ten children's verses. Eventually, she moved back East, continued writing and married again, happily.

Gilman's writing draws on evolutionary theory to reverse neatly the arguments of the medical "experts" and contemporary conservative social critics. If the separate-sphere arrangement was allowed to continue, she said, it would threaten women's capacity to survive. If the doctors thought too much education would cause women's uteruses to atrophy, Gilman worried that disuse of the brain would have the same effect on the rest of the organism.

Doctors, utopians, and feminists were unanimous in their belief that the sequestered life of the "civilized" wife had made her sickly; they just disagreed about the causes and the cures of the sickness. Among the not so "civilized"—that is, poor American women, many of them immigrant workers—the need to work for a living brought them more contact with men, even though in the mills and the factories the sexes tended to be kept separate.

Poor women, of course, did not enter the labor market for feminist reasons but because they needed to. If upper- and middle-class feminists were wont to idealize and glorify the world of work, poor women, like poor men, knew full well the darker side of wage labor: their problem was not ennui but dank factories, unhealthy sweatshops, harsh living conditions and the ever-present threat of disease, especially tuberculosis. Noting that, despite all the misery of working-class life, the women of the lower classes did not suffer from the same nervous maladies that afflicted upper- and middle-class women, one doctor suggested that the cause of these maladies was surely overeducation: "Education which has resulted in developing and strengthening the physical nature of man has been perverted through folly and fashion to render woman weaker and weaker." The poor woman was also spared the surgical knife because she was seldom considered a suitable subject for surgery, that is, she could rarely afford to take the long rest cure usually prescribed to follow the surgery. Plainly, the Victorian cliché of limp womanhood owed a lot to what one writer of the time described as "the monstrous assumption" that women possessed "but one set of organs—and that these are diseased."

If the majority of the activities that were carried out until the mid-nineteenth century in the home—making clothes, manufacturing soap, weaving cloth, baking bread, and so on—had been removed to other places by the industrial revolution, leaving middle- and upper-class wives stranded and bored, it did not take long for a virtual avalanche of time-consuming tasks to be granted them, thanks largely to the efforts of an ingenious early-twentieth-century chemist, Ellen Richards—the mother of what was at first called orkology, then euthenics, then domestic science, and, in more recent times, home economics. Because it was observed that Americans were continually packing up, and moving on to new homes and jobs, magazine articles and books fretted about our national restlessness and bemoaned the erosion of the idea of the home as sanctuary and castle. Into the breach stepped Richards, who, instead of welcoming the changes brought about by industrialization as a way of freeing women from domestic drudgery and enabling them to find more challenging labors in the outside world (as feminists were doing by then), hoped to lure the housewife back into the cottage and give new purpose to the woman's sphere by portraying wives as scientists, economists, and medical technicians on the front lines of disease prevention. The recently popularized germ theory of disease, with its emphasis on the dangers of disease lurking in ordinary places and the beneficent results of good sanitary conditions, gave the new model of housewifery its biggest boost. Culling through popular magazines of the years 1900 to 1904, the feminist writers Barbara Ehrenreich and Deirdre English found evidence of extraordinary anxiety about contagion; even the titles of the magazine articles of that era, such as "Books Spread Contagion," "Contagion by Telephone," "Infection and Postage Stamps," "Disease from Public Laundries," and "Menace of the Barber Shops," attest to a widespread preoccupation with the menace of germs.

While feminists, with their focus on suffrage, tended to neglect the subjects of courtship, marriage, and sex, contemporary writers did not. The old sentimental novels of an earlier era, which, as William Dean Howells put it, "romanticized . . . painful devotion and bullied adoration with auroral gleams of religious sentimentality," no longer seemed relevant to modern men and women moving in a less cloistered world. In his last novel, *The Vacation at the Kelwyn's,* which was published in 1920, Howells satirized the treacly romances of the 1860s and 1870s that he had grown up with, and the heroines who measured their suitors' worthiness by their readiness to risk their lives for them or their tendency to contract some terrible, life-threatening disease. Howells found it mystifying that even educated people seemed to have read those novels voraciously and to have found their melodramatic version of life appealing. But what may have seemed like melodrama in Howells's time (and ours) probably seemed like social realism to an earlier generation, when "fallen" women were ostracized for life, life-threatening diseases were rampant, poverty led to the poorhouse, and redemption through marriage was a commonly held article of faith.

AT the beginning of the nineteenth century, the Blackstonian idea of a wife's interests merging with her husband's prevailed in the laws governing domestic relations, but by the middle of the century the new notion of equality and dignity for wives had created a new model of the husband and father as a benign, sympathetic judge rather than a severe, watchful patriarch. A patriarchal bias remained central in domestic law, but its main source was the home, not communal customs. Some legal reforms actually took women one step forward and two steps back. By the middle of the nineteenth century, however, judges had begun to grant women the right to claim damages for seduction or breach of promise. While this was good news in terms of giving women an active legal identity, it was, on the whole, bad as a social litmus test, because, as the legal historian Michael Grossberg points out, in *Governing the Hearth,* it "was one aspect of the Victorian redefinition of sexuality." He explains, "In their attempt to control sexuality, many Victorians stressed the passionlessness of normal women; some tract writers even denied women's sexual feelings. Judges not only accepted the new advice, they made the law conform to it. Men were penalized for being ruled by their passions, women were understood to be passive victims of their seducers."

Then, in the early twentieth century, the legal and social climate shifted once again. The legal community criticized breach-of-promise suits as unfair to men (because the all-male juries tended to favor women)—indeed, a form of "sanctioned blackmail"—and they gradually disappeared into legal purgatory.

Other changes in domestic law and domestic relations that originated in the nineteenth century included the nudging to the sidelines of religious authorities as arbiters of marital mores by reformers, expert social scientists, and lawyers; a growing judicial support for and then a tempering of that support for common-law marriages; and, in 1862, the passage of the Morrill Act, which made polygamy illegal in American territories and eventually led to the prosecution of more than thirteen hundred Mormons. There was a legal shoring-up of the states' and territories' bans on interracial marriages but, after the Civil War the infamous prohibitions against slave marriages became defunct. Though there was increasingly strident public opposition to limiting the size of families there was a far more enthusiastic widespread private commitment to family planning. Most forms of contraception available today—except, of course, the pill and progesterone injections—were known in the nineteenth century, though some were known by different names, such as "womb veils," and until 1873, when the Comstock Law declared the public dissemination of information about contraception illegal, newspapers and magazines were filled with ads for birth-control devices and services. A declining fertility rate reflected, in part, the desire of women to control their own bodies, but, according to the demographer Robert Wells, "The one fact that stands out above all else is that both men and women decided to limit childbearing because they thought it would improve their lives as well as those of their children." Already, the legal battle was joined over abortion rights, and the battle shows no signs of drawing to a peaceful conclusion a full century later. There was a decline in the let's-keep-the-family-going-at-all-costs-because-the-Republic-depends-on-it way of thinking and a strengthening of the idea of the family as a collection of separate individuals with separate legal rights; and, in general, there was the ongoing evolution of family law as, to quote Michael Grossberg, "a mix of common-law rules, statutory commands, and private practices and prejudices."

The nineteenth century also witnessed the gradual liberalization of divorce laws, along with a marked increase in the number of divorces across the country. In 1867, there were 10,000 recorded divorces in the United States; in 1906, there were 72,000—a sevenfold increase that far outstripped the rate of population growth. Needless to say, the perpetual national worry that the republic's mainstay, the family, would not withstand such an assault reached epic proportions. As president, Teddy Roosevelt worriedly observed that "there is a widespread conviction that the divorce laws are dangerously lax and indifferently administered in some of the states resulting in a diminishing regard for the sanctity of the marriage relation." Then, between 1900 and 1920, the divorce rate doubled. The number of single women also rose, and criticism of marriage became, in certain circles, almost fashionable. Without much success, churches throughout the country mounted a strong campaign to preserve the traditional family by making the divorce laws stricter again. But in the new century a new generation of reform-minded social scientists, more understanding of human fallibility than their clerical brethren, refused to see the rising divorce statistics as reflecting either a moral or a legal breakdown. "Law does not create divorce," Carroll Wright, the first U. S. Commissioner of Labor, had said as early as 1888. "Divorce occurs when the husband and wife are estranged. Law steps in and defines the status of the divorced parties." The divorce rate continued to climb (three million divorces were legalized between 1926 and 1940), stabilized briefly in the 1950s, accelerated sharply in the 1960s, and reached a peak in the 1970s. It declined again slightly in the early 1980s. Nowadays, one out of two marriages in the United States ends in divorce and it would probably take a supertanker to contain all the ink that has been spilled by psychologists, historians, and sociologists in their attempts to account for the staggering fact of mass divorce.

Conservative social critics often claim that the gradual social acceptance of divorce over the last decades has made our commitment to marriage less binding; liberal ones point to the well-documented share of human misery that divorce spares the unhappily yoked. A number of explanations have been advanced for the undeniably sharp rise in the rate of divorce in our century, many of them manifestly ludicrous. The most intelligent ones have emphasized the rising expectations that people bring to marriage (and the need for husbands and wives to assume roles that were once played by extended families, clergy, and less preoccupied friends); the radically changing roles of women; the passing from view of the traditional male-headed family economy and the decline of vital communities. The fact is, however, that no one really understands why so many marriages break down. Yet, alarming as the divorce rate might be, it has in a sense merely taken up the slack left by the radical shift in the mortality rate. In 1850, only 2 percent of the American population lived past age sixty-five; today, 75 percent of the population does. So, though there are obviously crucial differences in the ramifications of the two events, divorce now does what death used to do: it wrenchingly separates people from each other, sometimes paving the way for remarriage. In fact, three out of every four divorced women eventually remarry, and the remarriage figure for men is five out of six. In colonial times, the average marriage lasted about twenty years, but, because people died at such an early age, marriages of ten years or less were not uncommon. Today, marriages that do not end in divorce last an average of forty years, and stresses and strains develop over a time span that had no parallel in the short-lived unions of earlier periods.

THREE

*G*ETTING SOMEWHERE:

MICHAEL AND

CLAIRE ROBBINS

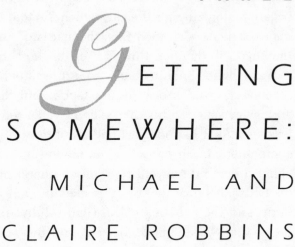

WHEN I FIRST MET MICHAEL ROBBINS, BRIEFLY, IN 1987, he was suffering from what a friend and fellow worker of his in the Freehold, New Jersey, Local of the Oil, Chemical, and Atomic Workers International Union called "a quadruple economic by-pass." Four different plants Robbins had worked for had closed—in 1968, 1973, 1986, and 1987. He had recently been hired as a chemical worker at a nearby factory for what turned out to be a short-term job, and he and his wife, Claire, were living in a small rented apartment in Laurence Harbor, New Jersey. By the time I really got to know him, in 1989, he had bought a house in nearby Matawan and had found a better job with a local chemical company. Claire, who had previously been a waitress and exercise instructor, was also working nearby, dispensing needles and medicine at a local hospital.

The small Jersey-shore community where Mike and Claire lived was about an hour's train ride from Manhattan. In a brief telephone conversation, Robbins had agreed to pick me up at the station, and he arrived a bit late and conspicuously, with a billowing black cloud of smoke wafting out of the back of his car, a rusted 1974 Oldsmobile. As soon as we had greeted each other, he began apologizing for the car, which, he told me, was the bane of his existence. "Call me Mike," he said, and then embellished his theme. "The damned thing's been in the shop all week, but it's still not right." Robbins had a round, weathered face, wary, intelligent gray eyes, a droopy mustache, and thinning brown hair, and, even seated in his car, he conveyed a sense of profound restlessness. As it happened, I had a not dissimilar vehicle, so I was sympathetic to his car woes and made some little dismissive joke about them, but he went right on enumerating the many faults of his Olds. "It's overdue for an inspection, but it's got a hole in the floor, and the exhaust leaks." Claire didn't like the smell of the fumes that wafted inside, he said, and she wouldn't ride in it; she drove a small Honda that was only about six years old and was in far better shape.

As we drove the short distance from the station to his house, Mike alternately sipped diet Pepsi and dragged on a cigarette. In the long period I was to spend getting to know him—several years—there was probably not a single moment when he didn't have a soda can, a cup of coffee, or a cigarette in his hand. That day, he was dressed in an old pair of jeans that rode low on his hips and a Bruce Springsteen T-shirt, and a large tattoo of a peacock decorated his right arm. (Springsteen, I learned later, was a hero of his for supporting the community's efforts to help keep the 3M plant open while Mike was working there.)

Mike looked incredibly tired but ready to grapple with anything life might drop on his doorstep—a look I associated with seasoned country-and-western singers.There were deep creases under his eyes. The plant where he worked ran twenty-four hours a day, and he worked a swing shift, so his sleep hours were always changing. The routine was hard on the body and the nerves, but it was shared by his fellow workers, and he considered it nothing out of the ordinary. The way things turned out, Claire was usually leaving for work when he arrived home or vice versa.

The neighborhood that Mike and Claire live in is about a ten-minute drive from Raritan Bay, but nothing about it suggests proximity to a beach or water. It is a respectable working-class neighborhood with no signs of grinding poverty yet with none of the marks of middle-class prosperity. Most of the cars in the driveways resemble Mike's, a good number of the houses are in poor repair, and the yards are strewn with plastic gewgaws and broken toys. Two large German shepherds and a Malamute inside the front door began barking furiously as we pulled up the driveway of a small bungalow-style house. After he unlocked the door, Mike immediately let them out a back door onto the deck of a rather forlorn-looking but spacious yard. Inside, the house was immaculately clean and jammed with innumerable bouquets of pale pink-and-blue paper flowers, china figurines, doilies, crocheted pillows, and mood messages, such as a wistful-looking plastic Snoopy hanging on the back door which bore the balloon caption "I need a Hug." A plastic sign near the kitchen light switch read "All stressed out and no place to go." A white ceramic pig hugged the dishwashing-liquid bottle by the sink; a huge bouquet of paper flowers dominated the wooden kitchen table, where Mike and I sat down to talk; and on almost every shelf and wall, and every cross beam, Garfield-the-cat stuffed toys, plastic stickers, and ceramic miniatures peered out. The kitchen, like the rest of the house, was spotless.

Mike grew up and lived the early part of his adult life in Plainfield, only about an hour's drive from where he lived now. But he felt as if he had actually had two lives, he said, because he was a recovering alcoholic, and all the years before he stopped drinking—eight years had passed since he had his last drink—seemed to have been lived in a kind of dream. He met Claire in 1969, several years after he split up with his first wife, and they'd been together ever since—except for a six-month period in 1980, when they were estranged. Mike couldn't remember the specific occasion of their meeting. He recalled only that it was in the spring and that they'd started living together a few weeks later. He was twenty-nine at the time and was drinking heavily, though not as heavily as a few years later. It seemed to him that Claire had just shown up one evening at the Smithfield Tavern, a now defunct establishment in North Plainfield. Everyone he knew headed for the Smithfield after work. It was, he said, "a second home."

His real home had not been a happy one. Until his parents got divorced in 1959, when he was nineteen, "they fought like cats and dogs—they hated each other," he said. "They still do now, after thirty years, even though they've been divorced all those years. These were two clashing personalities. My father worked for Western Electric—his whole life. He started as a line worker and retired as a supervisor. He saw the same people at work every day—they knew each other well. It's been totally different for me and the guys I work with. In my dad's generation, you put in your time and you reaped your rewards. That just doesn't happen anymore. I had a *bad* relationship with him but an OK one with my mother. They were strict disciplinarians—especially my dad. He was a tyrant. I was never close to him. I still can't get close, though I sometimes try. Mostly I don't see him. He meant well, but he was . . . a prick."

Without interrupting himself, Mike tossed his empty Pepsi can into the garbage and reached into the refrigerator for another. "He scared the hell out of me. He'd get angry about just about anything and hit me—with a strap when I was little, with his hand when I got older. He was *always* anxious. He'd say, 'Don't go near the brook, you might drown,' 'Don't go out and play football, you might get hurt.' Anything my father would tell me not to do when I was a kid, I'd do it. I rebelled. I'm still a little like that. You can't ever tell me I can't do something. My mom more or less stuck up for me, but my dad—never. I think he was mad at me because I was the reason for their marrying. I have a younger brother, Paul—he's a pipefitter, and he lives in California, no wife, and he moves around a lot. My dad was always saying 'Why can't you be like Paul?' And don't forget, I grew up in the fifties, when you were considered a *criminal* for doing things that are considered normal today. For instance, when I was in the eighth grade my friend Charlie and me—he's a cop now—were thrown out of school for telling a dirty joke to a girl. Not loudly or anything. Quietly, like I'm talking to you. We were sent to the principal, and he said it was the worst thing he'd ever heard of in all his years of teaching and he said, "Go home and tell your father that you're expelled for good." Well, I could never talk to my father, and I'd be damned if I was going to tell my mother what happened. Charlie had the same problem. So we decided to run away from home. We bought a bag of jelly doughnuts and hid in the woods all night. Really, it was the fear of our fathers that made us do it. It was wintertime, though, and at about three or four in the morning I got cold and went home, scared to death. And, you know, he didn't do a thing. He just looked at me. Anyway, my parents went to talk to the school, and I went back a week later. My dad made my life hell for that week though. He was a strange guy.

"I lived in a normal neighborhood, but our house was always a mess—not dirty but filled with junk. He would always start something, but never finish it. He would start an addition upstairs and leave it half done. He always had a lot of projects going; and, between all of those different projects and fighting with my mother, nothing ever got done. The house wasn't that old, but it always looked more run-down and shabby than the other houses in the neighborhood. Anyway, I *hated* being at home. But I had no interest in school. I was thrown out of high school—for real this time—in my senior year, basically for being a pain in the ass."

I asked Mike if he knew what he wanted to do when he left school.

"I wanted to work. I wanted to leave home. I didn't see any future in school. I'll be honest with you—even if I had stayed, it wouldn't have made any difference. I went right to work for the United Printing Company, as a flyman—a printer's helper—taking magazines off the press and stacking them on pallets. That was the beginning of my voyage into overtime. I averaged ten hours a day. There were fourteen hundred people at that plant. I was there for nine years. I expected to become a journeyman printer eventually. There was nothing in the English language, as far as I was concerned, called 'plant shutdown.' And then it started happening everywhere. These were places that everybody's parents had worked at. They had worked there all their lives, like my dad. I worked with people who had been with United for nineteen, twenty-eight years. It took twenty years to go from flyman to journeyman—promotions went strictly according to seniority, but it didn't seem like such a long time to me. I was making pretty good money. I had my own apartment."

During that same period, Mike had married a local girl, and they had had two children—a girl in 1964 and a boy in 1966. "Gail was seventeen when we married, I was twenty-three," he said. "But we didn't know what we were doing. It only lasted a few years. She left me in 1966 and took the children fifty miles away. That was a bad, bad time. My whole world caved in. She left me for one of my best friends, a guy I had worked with. So she's left me, and after a while the plant shuts down, and then both my grandparents died, and so did an uncle I had really liked. I guess you could say that I went square to hell for a while. That's when I *really* started drinking. Ever since I'd left high school, I'd been sort of a weekend drinker. I used to play pool and drink. But after I broke up with Gail and she took the kids away I gave a lot of wild parties, and before the plant closed I even drank on the job—though I never missed a day's work. You had three-quarters of an hour for lunch, and I'd have a sandwich and a couple of beers. After I clocked out, I headed straight down to the Smithfield. Most of the guys who went to that bar, we all knew each other from school, and we had close friendships. It was a dump, but I felt safe there. Hell, my grandfather had gone to the same damn bar. After my marriage broke up, I just about lived in there."

Many of Mike's contemporaries at the Smithfield eventually got drafted and sent to Vietnam, and several died in the war, but Mike escaped because he was married and had two children. He was, in a sense, at war with himself, though, and headed into a downward spiral he felt helpless to arrest. Nearly eleven and a half million Americans lost their jobs over the next decade because of plant closings. A large proportion of them failed to find new jobs, and almost a third of those who did were paid at least 20 percent less than they had been. The Oil, Chemical, and Atomic Workers Union, in a 1986 report arguing for the creation of a national superfund for displaced workers, pointed out that the side effects of prolonged unemployment among its members included rising alcoholism, crime—especially child and spouse abuse—suicide, and sickness.

In the next few years, Mike's car, a '66 Plymouth convertible, was taken away because he couldn't meet his payments, but he somehow acquired an old jalopy—a 1948 Ford—and he drove it without a license, because his had lapsed; he lived briefly with a runaway from Chicago; he was thrown out of his apartment for not paying the rent; he was introduced to marijuana by a friend he'd moved in with, and once introduced, he renewed his acquaintance with it almost daily; and, though he saw his children from time to time, his relationship with them grew more distant every year.

In 1969, he went to work for Universal Steel, a mill that made stainless-steel tubing and pipes. Initially, he worked as a draw-bench operator, pulling pipes away from the heavy machines that made them, then he operated an overhead crane, and later on he worked in the plant's pickle shed, where the carbon was stripped from the pipes in troughs of hydrochloric and nitric acid. It was dangerous and unhealthy work, but Mike didn't mind it. He has had quite a number of jobs that were both physically taxing and boring, and several that involved working with toxic chemicals, but he claims that he's never had a job that he absolutely hated.

He was still drinking heavily when he met Claire. She, too, had recently ended an early marriage and had two children—a boy, Bob, who was six months old, and a girl, Melissa, who was two. Mike was then living in the apartment of a friend who had recently moved to Florida, and Claire and her children moved in with him in the late spring of 1969. "It just seemed like a good idea at the time," Mike recalls. Neither of them envisaged any kind of long-term arrangement. Even after several months of living together, he hadn't any strong feelings of commitment. But on December 2nd of that year, while Claire was out for the evening with a girlfriend, she was in a bad car accident—her friend hit a tree head-on—and everything changed.

"She almost died," Mike said, taking a long drag on a cigarette, "and, though we'd been together for a while, I never realized until that day how much she'd come to mean to me. She was in the hospital for three months, and when she came home I had to nurse her around the clock. She was in a body cast from her neck to her toes. Then she was in a wheelchair for another three months. She had to learn to walk all over again. I didn't worry about anything but taking care of her. Her mother took Bob, and for a while her sister took care of Melissa. In some ways, I was growing up, but also I had been drinking so much that my thinking was stalled. I was twenty-nine, but I might have been nineteen, mentally. I mean, I wanted to have a farm, I wanted to be famous, but I never made any plans. There'd been a layoff at the mill, which in this case was good, because it gave me the chance to be with Claire. I don't know what we would have done if that hadn't happened. On the other hand, it became hard to pay the rent, and we got evicted."

He and Claire moved into the apartment of the friend who had been driving the car the night of the accident. She had sustained only minor injuries, and eventually, when Mike was rehired at the steel mill, she helped take care of Claire. Despite Mike's heavy drinking and pot smoking, he was considered a good employee and was well liked by his co-workers. When Claire was able to get around by herself, they found an apartment in North Plainfield. But then the mill shut down in 1973, and they decided that they might do better in another part of the country—perhaps Pennsylvania, where Mike had heard there were jobs. So he borrowed five hundred dollars and, with high hopes, "set off west." Claire's mother thought Bob should stay with her a while longer, but they took Melissa along. Somehow, they succeeded in driving only twenty-five miles, checked into a motel that rented small cottages, and spent all their money on a weeklong binge. Feeling embarrassed, but still determined to leave town, they drove back to North Plainfield, borrowed a few hundred dollars more, and took a cheap apartment above a mattress factory in a small, prosperous, prim New Jersey town that they both came to hate.

Mike soon found a job in a textile mill, but he was extremely uncomfortable with his middle-class neighbors, who, he says, were snobbish, straitlaced, and unfriendly. ("If you didn't go to work in a shirt and tie, they acted like you were some kind of bug.") During this period, he started taking amphetamines, and at one point had to be hospitalized because he had developed amphetamine psychosis: he believed the townspeople were trying to kill him. In a sense, his paranoia was based on a germ of social reality. Mike *was* a blot on the town's squeaky-clean horizon: he was rambunctious, he got behind on his rent, and apparently the town fathers decided that on the whole they did not want him around. Shortly after he got out of the hospital, he came home from work one day to find the door to his apartment boarded up. When he tried to take the boards down, he was arrested at his own front door for "breaking and entering" and thrown in jail for a week. Claire was jailed, too—basically for creating a ruckus when she found out that they had arrested Mike. A neighbor who was their one friend in town, a black man, phoned Claire's sister, and she came and fetched Melissa.

All plans to shift their venue having been effectively scotched, Mike and Claire returned to North Plainfield. They camped out for a while in a friend's cellar before moving to a cheap apartment above Mike's old haunt, the Smithfield Tavern. Melissa was back with them by then, but Bob was still staying with his grandmother. Though Claire was not alcoholic, she, too, had begun to drink heavily, and her mother refused to return Bob to her. In fact, what had started out as a temporary arrangement became permanent. Bob lived with his grandmother for the remainder of his childhood.

Mike and Claire moved into the apartment over the bar in 1974 and stayed there about a year, scrimping by on Mike's unemployment. Then a drunken bar patron staggered upstairs one night, and threatened them with a gun. No one was hurt, but Claire's mother and stepfather had been worrying about her for some time, and the incident convinced them that she was not in safe hands. The next day, Claire's stepfather invited her to bring Melissa and live, gratis, in a garden-apartment complex that he owned. The invitation explicitly excluded "that bum." But Claire pressed her stepfather to allow Mike to join her, and eventually he relented, and even hired Mike to work at the complex, painting apartments and grooming the grounds. (Claire too, worked for her stepfather briefly, as a rental agent.) Mike made intermittent attempts to stop drinking and taking drugs but somehow never fully grasped the effect they were having on his life.

After that, he worked for a while on a production line at a glass-manufacturing plant—a place he would characterize only as "a sweatshop." He considered himself fortunate when, in 1983, he landed a job in the videotape production department of 3M, a company known for its benevolent paternalism and excellent worker benefits. Mike enjoyed the job and liked his co-workers more than he had at any previous place of employment, but his drinking, he said, had gotten "out of control." He began to get the shakes, and suddenly he realized he had a bona fide problem. Between 1976, when he began working for Claire's stepfather, and 1981, when he started at the glass factory, he had been in and out of hospitals and detoxification and rehabilitation centers, for long and short periods, an astounding seventy-five times. Counselors and therapists tried but failed to help him. In the midst of all this, Claire left him, saying she was tired of the terrible fights they had been having for years and his nearly perpetual state of drunkenness. Not long afterward, 3M fired him for drinking on the job.

"Well, like they say, I'd hit bottom," Mike told me, taking a long pull on his soda. "This time when I went to a rehab place it dawned on me that they were talking about something real. I couldn't blame Claire for leaving. I was nasty when I was drunk, and the big-time fights we were having weren't good for Melissa. So I started paying attention. Before that, I'd been given the tools to sober up—the meetings, the people to talk to, the sponsors—but I never used them. For the first time, I began to take the whole business seriously."

While Mike was talking, Claire, a tall, leggy strawberry blonde with a long face, deep blue eyes, and pale skin, got home from work. Her eyes did not at the moment have much expression in them, and she, too, I observed, had a tattoo—a delicate rose that curled around the top of her right wrist. It was about 4:30 in the afternoon, and she looked tense and tired. She greeted me with a weak smile but looked past Mike. She had an earache, she said, and was going to lie down for a while. A few minutes later, Melissa, a small, poker-faced, tousled blonde, came in, carrying her six-month-old baby, Willie. Melissa was nineteen. She switched on the TV, but soon got into a heated argument with her mother, which terminated only when Claire announced loudly, "She's driving me crazy," and fled to her bedroom, slamming the door.

Melissa also slammed the door to her bedroom—a tiny room that was about a foot or so away from her mother's. The baby was playing in his playpen, with the light of the TV flickering across his feet. Earlier, Mike had mentioned that Melissa couldn't read. She had always been a poor student, he said, but no one had really understood why until she turned eighteen, when Mike, whose last name she has legally made her own, had her tested, and learned that she was dyslexic. Mike found a special school for her, but she dropped out when she became pregnant. Mike argued for an abortion; the baby's father was not someone Melissa wanted to live with, and Mike wanted her to go back to school. Without being able to read, she could neither pass a driving test—though she knew how to drive—nor hold a job, and she depended on Mike and Claire in a thousand ways that she resented and they often did, too. Mike thought it crucial that she learn to "stand on her own two feet." He had, in fact, not been so much *against* her having the baby as in favor of her gaining a degree of independence, but his view had not prevailed.

The baby began to cry. Claire came out of her room to pick him up and quiet him, and she and I talked for a while in the kitchen while she rocked him back to sleep. Looking out the kitchen window, she asked, lightly, if Mike had told me that they'd had a baby together in 1972, but it had died.

I said he hadn't. Mike stared at his well-worn work boots.

Claire put the baby in his crib, lit a cigarette, and said that both she and Mike had wanted a girl, and they got a girl. "Mike named her Joanne. He had already left the hospital and was handing out cigars. Our friend Matt was going to be the godfather. They told me she died of pneumonia. God only knows what really happened. She was healthy when she was born. My gynecologist asked me afterward 'What happened?' and I said 'I don't know. You tell me. You're the doctor.' They delivered a healthy baby, and in eight hours the baby was dead. I was lying there, you know, and they weren't bringing me the baby, and I knew the procedure—they take the baby away for a while and then they're supposed to bring it to you. So this doctor comes in with the nurse, and the nurse had a needle in her hand. And I knew that you were not supposed to get a shot after you've just had a baby. They said, 'Your baby is very sick. We're having trouble suctioning her . . . the mucus . . .' I said, 'Let me see her,' but the doctor said, 'I don't think you want to see her now.' I said, 'I do. Of course I do. I want to see her now.' But they wouldn't let me. I think I was crying. I know I was shouting. Then the nurse literally threw me over and shot me up. I guess it was a tranquilizer. She said 'Calm down!' and the girl in the next bed started to freak. So the nurse said, 'We're moving you out of this room.' There were babies all around me. But I just kept saying, 'Where's my baby? I'm not moving anywhere. Where is she?' I was young."

"She was twenty-four," Mike said. "I was a little older—thirty-two—but, you know, we just sort of accepted what they told us."

"I was young and stupid," Claire went on. "I'm listening to them like an idiot. Drugged. Nodding my head. Then I panicked. My phone hadn't been turned on yet, but the nurse said, 'The switchboard is going to put through any call you want to make. It's free of charge.' Later, I realized what must have been going on. But right then it didn't click. I tried to call Mike, but he wasn't home, so I called a neighbor of ours, and the neighbor saw Mike coming up our driveway and said he'd get him. When Mike got to the phone, the doctor came in again, and I'm trying to tell Mike something's wrong with the baby, and the doctor grabs the phone and he's talking to Mike, and I could hear the doctor go, 'Yeah, ummmm, uh-huh,' I didn't know that Mike was asking the doctor if the baby was going to live and the doctor was saying No. So Mike knew before I did, and he said he was leaving right away. Twenty minutes later, they came in and said the baby had died. Then they told me that if I wanted to I could go down and see her. Really, to this day I don't know why she died."

A little later, Claire said she needed some things from the store, and invited me to go along for the ride. Like the kitchen, her white Honda had Garfield knickknacks dangling from or clinging to every surface. On the back window, a sticker proclaimed "Anyone who has a clean car is sick." Since it was late afternoon, I asked Claire if she was shopping for the evening meal. She wasn't. She needed some supplies from the drugstore, she said, and she added that she and Mike almost never ate together. He shopped for his own food, and when Melissa was hungry she usually grabbed something from the refrigerator or shared a take-out meal with Claire. Meals in general tended to be solo affairs, except for Thanksgiving. Claire herself was a vegetarian and didn't eat very much anyway. She had cooked at an earlier stage of her life, she said, but these were modern times, and she didn't see why she should work *and* cook. "A lot of the time, we're just not here together. I'm up at 5:30 and out of the house by 6:30. I punch in at

7:00. We're usually on completely different schedules. Sometimes Mike's here during the day, but with all the overtime he works, he's usually asleep. We don't really see each other that much. I eat my main meal at lunchtime in the hospital cafeteria."

As she drove, Claire chain-smoked and, at my request, talked about her early life. It was a subject she usually avoided, she said, and her voice became flat and sing-songy—as if the events and the people she described were of no great interest to her. I learned that she was born in Brooklyn but her family moved to Westbury, Long Island, when she was four, and lived there until she was thirteen. That was 1961, the year her father died. Most of his life, he'd worked in a factory mixing cement, she said, and though she did not then relate her father's death to any environmental hazard, he always complained about stomach problems and wound up dying of stomach cancer, and she'd since wondered if something at his work had caused his cancer. "He was an incredibly hard worker—he meant everything to me." Her mother had never worked before her father died, but afterward she worked part-time as a server in a high-school cafeteria. By then, they'd moved to Hillsboro, New Jersey, where a cousin had found them a cheap apartment. But her mother hadn't had to work for long; she quit her job on remarrying, in 1965. Claire's father had actually been her mother's second husband (the first had died), and Claire had had three half sisters from the previous marriage. One had died six years before, one was living in Florida, and the other on Long Island. The sister who died had lived nearby, and Claire had often visited her, but she'd rarely seen the others. Contact with her mother, who was widowed again in 1980, was almost exclusively by phone. Claire, for reasons she did not really comprehend, hated long trips. Her mother was basically healthy, though she never seemed to marry healthy men. Claire herself was as pale as parchment and, all in all, looked far from robust. Her medical history included a hysterectomy in 1985 and a benign tumor removed from her breast a few months ago.

Claire said that when her father died, "I went a little wild on my mother for a while." As she grew older and joined the work world the idea of finding a profession or some sort of temperamentally satisfying work never crossed her mind. Sometimes, she said, she regretted her lack of ambition "to be something." She said she wasn't a reader, but the visions of wider horizons presented by movies and television tantalized her and sometimes vexed her. "We were raised to be housewives—to, you know, just grow up and get married. What did my mother do? She cooked and cleaned and crocheted and baked. When I was sixteen, she met this man who became my stepfather. She met him in a funeral home—he was an undertaker, and he also had a finger in a lot of pies, especially real estate. In 1965, she started having dinner with him, and within a year they married and she moved to his house, in North Plainfield. I hated him."

The drugstore that Claire had driven to was in a shopping mall. As we cruised the aisles, I asked Claire if she had ever become reconciled to her stepfather.

"I came to love the man, but it took a long time. He used to yell and carry on a lot, but we were close. My own father never yelled. Dad's family was Catholic, but nobody in our family was religious. My mother's family was Methodist, and that was how we were raised, but religion wasn't a big deal for us. My mother didn't keep up with Dad's side of the family. My dad had seven brothers—I have *seven* uncles somewhere, but I've lost contact with all of them. I've tried to find my grandmother on my father's side—she found me once and we wrote to each other, but I've lost her address. She's probably dead by now."

Claire's shopping basket became filled with shampoo, cosmetics, and various beauty aids. "I went to Sunday school," she went on. "My mother made me. I made my Communion. I did all the legal stuff. I believe in God, but I don't go to church. I don't have time. My father didn't care about religion, but when he was dying a priest came in and told him that he wasn't really married to my mother, according to the Catholic Church, because she wasn't Catholic. My father threw him out. He was buried a Protestant."

The year Claire's mother remarried, Claire herself married a man she'd met at her half sister's house on Long Island. She was spending a lot of time there to get away from her stepfather, whom she had not yet learned to like, and she married, she says, basically for the same reason, and "to play house." Her new husband, a line worker in a chemical-manufacturing plant in New Jersey, was twelve years older than she was. By the age of nineteen, she had two children, Bob and Melissa. They were born a year and a half apart. The children gave her joy, but her marriage quickly went sour. Her husband turned out to have a violent temper and he beat her. She stayed with him for three years anyway, until late 1968, then she moved, with the children, to an apartment her stepfather (who had opposed the marriage from the start) found for her.

In the next months, Claire would sometimes hire a baby-sitter and spend the evening with friends. Often they would end up at the Smithfield Tavern, which Claire described in terms similar to Mike's—a place where "everybody knew everybody." Like Mike, she could not recall the occasion of their meeting. At some point "we just sort of got together," she said. From the start, she realized that Mike was a heavy drinker, but ten years passed before the word "alcoholic" found a fixed place in her mind. Of their moving in with each other she recalls only, "We got together. I don't remember how it went. But it was cheaper for us to live together, and he had a place, and I just moved in with the kids. My stepfather and my mother couldn't stand Mike, because he drank so much. But he was a lot nicer to me than my husband." At that point, Claire was still more than a little afraid of her husband, but Mike told him to stay away from Claire, or else. "He left town," Claire said. "And that was it. The kids never saw him again, and he hasn't been around since. Nobody really knows where he is."

On December 1, 1969, Claire's mother came to the apartment to pick up Bob, who was going to spend the weekend with her. Her husband's real estate investments had begun to pay off, and they had moved to a large and comfortable house on the Jersey shore.

Claire remembers the date vividly because it was the day before her accident. The next evening, she decided to go out with a girl-friend of hers. They planned to visit Mike's mother and go on to the Smithfield Tavern for drinks. Originally, she'd thought she might take Melissa along, but Mike, who was aware that they would be drinking, persuaded her to leave the girl at home. In fact, they drank far too much, and on the way home her friend drove head-on into a tree. Lying in traction in the hospital, Claire was told that she was lucky to be alive, and she realized that Melissa probably would have died if she had come along. While Claire recuperated, her daughter stayed with Claire's youngest half sister. By then, as far as Melissa was concerned, Mike was her father. She calls him Dad, he considers her his daughter, and throughout her life he has tried to be as helpful as possible to her. At the time of the accident, though, he didn't feel he could care for her properly. Bob remained at his grandmother's. After a year, when Claire had learned to walk again, Melissa came home, but Claire's mother held on to Bob. "She conned me out of my son," Claire said, over coffee in a local diner, her voice registering the enormity of the event only by a small, sharp intake of breath. "My sisters supported her, too. They kept saying, 'Let her raise him for a while. He's better off.' My stepfather was becoming richer all the time. Bob got anything he wanted. I explained all this to him re-cently. He never really understood what happened. When Mike started really drinking hard they threatened to take me to court, to take Bob away from me legally. I didn't fight them. The acci-dent just sort of took all the fight out of me for a long time. But it definitely brought Mike and me closer together. Before that, we didn't really know we cared for each other."

The head of Mike's old union had described Mike to me as a man who had had a lot of problems. Without being specific, he'd said that many of the people Mike worked with, shared those problems, but that he was a "real go-getter." Over several years, I took the train ride through the bleak New Jersey flatlands to Matawan to visit the Robbinses whenever their schedules permitted—usually every few weeks. Mike is a talker and is clearly somewhat lonely. Because of his history, he was grateful simply to be alive and functioning, and had the redeemed person's vivid curiosity about the outside world. But it was hard to get together with him, because he seemed to be always working, even when he wasn't scheduled to work; he frequently had to change his plans at the last minute after being asked to work overtime.

When Mike and Claire were around each other (which wasn't very often), they usually acted testy. Claire seemed either annoyed with Mike or ready to be annoyed with him. Mike's "official" view of his marriage when I first got to know him was that he and Claire had gone through some terrible times together, but that things weren't so bad now that he was sane and sober, and they would probably get a lot better if he could just get a grip on his bills. With his drinking days behind him, he had set himself the goal of getting a car and a house and he had acquired both—though the car was decrepit, and the house was small and overpriced at $96,000. On the whole, he would say, in the manner of a man trying to convince himself of something, he wasn't doing so badly. The horrendous battles he'd always had with Claire had settled down to small, mean skirmishes. He couldn't complain.

Claire was less sanguine about their marriage. She often looked depressed, and on the few occasions when they happened to be in the house at the same time, she tended not to linger in Mike's proximity for long. Neither Mike nor Claire ever offered the other any food or drink in my presence, and though I spent hundreds of hours over several years sitting around in their kitchen, neither of them ever offered me any food or drink beyond a cup of coffee—once. It was not rudeness; they were always welcoming and generous about sharing their meager spare time with me. It was just not their custom to indulge in small pleasures or to create warm interludes of communality by the usual means, or to think in terms of social occasion. Both visited their relatives from time to time, but their family ties did not seem to be a vital part of their daily lives and the same could be said of their friendships. Neither Mike nor Claire belonged to any community, church, or civic organization. They never had people to dinner. Mike read the Newark *Star-Ledger* every day but considered most of the events described in it irrelevant to his own life. Claire never read the paper. Like Claire, Mike read few books, and they rarely went to the movies but instead often brought them home to play on their VCR. They didn't know their neighbors, and for them their neighborhood was for the most part an aggregate of separate lives beheld from a distance.

When I met Mike, his base pay was $28,000, Claire's was $12,000, so they were way above the poverty line, and, with the megaovertime that Mike invariably put in, he could make more than $45,000 in a good year. Even so, the Robbinses seemed poor. Though their income may have been sufficient, it somehow did not give them a decent independent life or fill them with confidence that the wolf was not breathing hotly at their door. Mike believes that he is better off emotionally than his parents, because they hated each other. "I love Claire and Claire loves me," he says often, but without much emphasis. Mainly, he is grateful for the comparative lack of Sturm und Drang at home. But economically and socially, he says, he is surely worse off than the preceding generation was.

The sense of permanence that was central to his father's generation came in large part from having one or, at most, two jobs for life, which offered possibilities for self-advancement, secure pensions, and upward mobility for the next generation. For people like Mike that idea has vanished. He recognized with dismay the fact that the intimate neighborhood connections of his childhood had no counterpart in the place where he now lived, which, even physically, had a kind of tentative look, as if a government bulldozer might arrive at any minute to clear it away for a highway bypass. Although he is earning more money than he had ever dreamed he would, the house cost so much and his mortgage payments are so high that he struggles every month just to meet his current bills—and it still bothers him that the house doesn't have a basement, which he was brought up to believe should be a part of every decent house. The trend of downward mobility that began in the early seventies has, of course, cut across every class, but the loss of benefits and a secure footing for blue collar workers has been the most dramatic, because their tie to middle-class life was secured so recently, and the skills and qualities that conferred it—craft expertise, loyalty, thrift—became so sharply devalued.

Lest the picture of a declining standard of living be overdrawn, however, one might well remember some of the less attractive attributes of working-class life a mere hundred years ago. The slum the British sociologist Robert Roberts grew up in, in Salford, England, and wrote about at the end of the last century, for example, though deeply rooted in human connectedness, was, like its counterpart in American cities, a place of filth, disease, and soul-destroying tedium. "In summer," he wrote, "houseflies and bluebottles swarmed, every kitchen alive: sticky, foul-smelling paper traps dangled about, dark with writhing bodies. And the bed bugs! With the warm days they spread in battalions first in the hovels, then in the better-class houses, where people waged campaigns against their sweet-odoured, sickening presence. The lime-washed bedrooms. . . . Through summer days one saw the 'fever' van carrying off some child, who only too often would be seen no more."

If from a middle-class perspective Mike Robbins's life seems almost terrifyingly devoid of social glue, he is nonetheless far freer to venture forth from the confines of his house than was his turn-of-the-century counterpart and is much more aware, through television and movies, of the world beyond his doorstep. In the bad old days "leisure for men without the few coppers to go into a tavern meant long empty hours lounging between kitchen chair and threshold," Roberts pointed out. "How familiar one grew in childhood to these silent figures leaning against door jambs, staring into vacancy waiting for bedtime." And if Claire's economic dependence on her husband and general frustration about her

life seem to reflect some kind of ongoing working-class chattel-
dom, how much worse was the plight of her turn-of-the-century
counterpart, who lived, as Roberts put it, "in a kind of purdah" after marriage. Survivors among his generation's old working class
remember "the many women broken and aged with childbearing
well before their youth was done," he wrote. "They remember the
spoiled complexions, the mouths full of rotten teeth, the varicose
veins, the ignorance of simple hygiene, the intelligence stifled
and the endless battle to keep clean." On the other hand, whatever the degradation of the turn-of-the-century working-class milieu, it is noteworthy that in popular songs at least the home was
forever being sentimentalized and exalted. And, in Roberts's
words, "songs about its beauties were forever on people's lips."

WHEN her son, Willie, was about a year old, Melissa, Claire's
daughter, moved out with him and established a household in a
nearby garden apartment with Daryl Picket, a young man she had
met not long before. Daryl was a construction worker who spe-
cialized in building gas stations. Mike disapproved of the move at
first—neither he nor Claire had warmed to Daryl, who was a
rather close-mouthed young man—but his qualifications as a
good provider and a willing father for Willie soon outweighed his
lack of congeniality. Moreover, Claire and Melissa, with some distance between them, began to get along better; Claire adored her
grandson and baby-sat as often as she could. It was Willie she
looked forward to seeing when she came home from work, she
said, and even when she was tired, she would often pick him up
on her way home and keep him overnight.

Meanwhile, Mike was working harder and harder and accepting so much overtime that for two years he never had a full
weekend off. Claire, too, was working hard. In the fall of 1990,
she decided to take an intensive three-month emergency medical
technician's course. She wanted to earn more money, and the
course was a first step toward getting an E.M.T. license. Classes

were held Monday and Wednesday nights in a building about a mile away from the Robbinses' home. On Mondays, there were lectures, and on Wednesdays the students practiced emergency medical help techniques. They were also required to be on call to assist the local rescue squad on its middle-of-the-night excursions, and Claire, in the first few weeks of her training, was summoned to help someone whose nose was broken in a bar fight, a number of people with severe abdominal pains, and several victims of car accidents. A device called a Plektron, which emitted an ear-shattering screech, was installed in the Robbins house when Claire signed up for the course, and it went off whenever there was a car accident or any other kind of emergency within the local area. Usually, this would happen when Mike had just got home from work and was beginning to drift off to sleep. There were many Plektron-inspired arguments. Claire dropped out of the course after a while but began taking it again the following fall, and then thought about dropping out again. She wasn't sure she was ever going to make it through, she said, because her day job was extremely tiring, and she found it nearly impossible to have her sleep interrupted by a middle-of-the-night emergency call and then get up at 5:30 to go to work. The year 1990 was a difficult year for the Robbinses in several respects. Early in the year, Melissa had had a miscarriage, become pregnant again almost immediately, and become so sick that she had to have an abortion.

"It was a bad pregnancy," Claire said one afternoon when I was sitting at the kitchen table with her. "She looked scary. She was down to eighty pounds. I really thought for a while that she was going to die. She was awfully sick, but she wanted the baby so bad— Well, when she told me that she'd better have an abortion I knew how sick she was." According to Claire, Daryl had not behaved well when Melissa was in the hospital. He had visited her but had refused to take charge of Willie after work or try to make arrangements to have him looked after during the day; the diapering aspect of the job alone, he said, was more than he could handle. Mike, of course, had felt similarly incapable of caring for Melissa when Claire was hospitalized twenty years earlier, but Daryl was a lot soberer than Mike had been back then, and the temper of the times had changed sufficiently so that Daryl's reaction seemed churlish. Since somebody had to take care of Willie, Claire took three weeks off from work without pay to do it. She had considered putting him in a day-care center, but her boss, a woman, suggested that she take the time off without pay and look after the baby herself. In the hospital, Melissa said she didn't want to live with Daryl anymore, because he'd been so unsupportive, but Daryl talked her into coming back.

A few weeks later, she returned to the school that Mike had found for her, which had been helping her with her reading problem. She was slowly learning to read, but she still needed to be driven to the supermarket and the laundromat, because she felt that she couldn't yet read well enough to pass a driver's test. Once, while I was in the kitchen talking to Claire, Melissa called to ask Claire to help her figure out whether a package she'd brought home from the supermarket contained chicken breasts or fish, and she spelled out the letters on the label.

EARLY one gray fall Sunday morning in 1991, I arrived in Matawan during a period when Mike and Claire had not been getting along very well, and a heated argument took place. Melissa needed to be driven to the laundromat. Mike's car was again overdue for an inspection, but he didn't have the money to fix the things that were wrong with it, so he and Claire were both driving Claire's car that week—except when Mike drove his stickerless car to work, hoping he wouldn't get caught. On most weekends, Melissa loaded laundry into Daryl's car, and he took it to the laundromat, usually on Sunday, but Mike—forgetting that he didn't have a car—had offered to take her that Sunday. Claire wanted Mike to pick Melissa up right away. She had chores to do and needed the car. Mike wanted to wait awhile. He was tired. He had worked a twelve-hour shift the night before and had just gotten out of bed. During the week, the Plektron had sounded while he was out in the car, picking up a carton of cigarettes, and Claire had had to run all the way to the E.M.T. building—a distance of about a mile and a half—in the middle of the night. Claire was telling me about the incident when Melissa called, and she and her mother got into a fight about the laundromat trip. After a great deal of shouting, Claire slammed the phone down and accused Mike of reneging on his promises. More shouting. I retreated to the bathroom, the only space that was more or less out of the line of fire, and, when I returned, Mike was handing Claire the car keys and telling her that he was going back to sleep and that he would help Melissa after Claire finished her chores. "Come on," Claire said, turning to me. "Let's get out of here before I go nuts."

In the driveway next to the house, there were two other old cars next to Mike's ailing Oldsmobile and Claire's Honda—a rusty blue Plymouth and an ancient tan Chevrolet. I asked Claire why they were there and (half knowing the answer) whether they were operable. It turned out that the Plymouth belonged to Mike's brother, who drove it whenever he came East, and the Chevrolet was just an old heap that Mike used to drive. Neither car was registered.

After a brief stop at the drugstore for some aspirin, Claire began a long search for a Halloween costume, which I at first assumed was for Willie, but which turned out to be for herself. Claire liked Halloween. The hospital where she worked threw a big Halloween party for the staff every year, and she prided herself on showing up in something nice. A certain amount of competitiveness was involved, she admitted: she'd worn the same witch costume for several years and didn't want to show up in it again. She bought ready-made costumes, she said, because she had no gift for sewing, but most of the ready-made things were flimsy, and she was worried about not having enough money to buy a good one. A friend of hers had rented a costume somewhere in Red Bank for sixty dollars. She was hoping to spend fifteen or twenty, but all the costumes we saw, even the bad ones, cost at least thirty dollars. In the course of a subsequent discussion about the inadequacy of her $12,000 yearly salary, it emerged that most of the family bills—mortgage, taxes, gas and electricity, house and car repairs, insurance, general household expenses—were paid by Mike. She was responsible for the phone bill and paid for her own food and gas, but often ran into trouble. She confessed to being a poor money manager—she was an impulse shopper and found it nearly impossible to budget her money. "The phone's going to be shut off tomorrow because I forgot that I was supposed to pay them a hundred dollars on Friday. So I have to leave work tomorrow, and pay it, and hope they haven't shut it off yet."

I asked Claire if she carried credit cards. "I *wish* I did," she said with considerable heat as we pulled into a local mall. "My girlfriend has a Sears card; if *she* wanted a costume she'd just charge it. She lent it to me a few times and I paid her back when I got my paycheck. The truth is, I can't really afford this costume, but I *have* to get it, so this will leave me short on food and gas money this week."

After several hours of unsuccessful searching at four different warehouselike department stores, we finally arrived at costume nirvana—the adult-Halloween-supplies section of the local Sears outlet. There Claire found a slinky outfit that she looked good in and liked. It consisted mainly of a black cape, a short black skirt, and (for a bit extra) a red wig; the general effect was to transform her into a sexy mod elf. It cost twenty dollars more than Claire was planning to spend, but she looked so stricken when she peered at the price tag that I offered to put it on my credit card. She accepted, promising to pay me back as soon as she could.

Over lunch in a nearby diner afterward, Claire said she had been pretty depressed in recent months. She and Mike weren't getting along, and, as always, they didn't seem to have any way of resolving their problems. "He's so jumpy. And everything is money, money, money. Sure, money's a problem. But when you work where I work, and see people dying, you see that it's not the main thing in life, believe me. You've got to live while you can."

After Mike sobered up eight years ago, Claire said, he changed in ways she had yet to adjust to. For one thing, he seemed to lose sexual interest in her. Some years ago, he'd had a brief affair with a young woman, and they'd fought about it and talked a lot about what had led up to it. They had both agreed that there had been a general lack of communication between them. Things got better, she said, but eventually they drifted back to the old pattern of fighting, holding grudges, and avoiding each other. Claire had ordered a salad for lunch and smoked as she ate her meal, occasionally propping up her forehead with long, red-tipped fingers. When she needed to talk to someone about things that were on her mind, she said, she called up an old friend of hers named Bob Mills, or talked to one or two women friends at work. Mike had some friends he confided in, too—particularly a woman friend whom he used to work with at 3M.

"I have my friends and he has his, and that's the way it goes. Once in a while I go out, but not with Mike. He just doesn't go out. I used to think he was in love with his friend from 3M, Molly Peters, but I don't anymore. Mike's just not romantic. My girl-friend—a woman I work with—if she so much as sneezes, her husband sends her roses, and she talks about how he rubs her feet when she's tired. It gets on my nerves. I was sick for three weeks recently. I was going in to work, though I felt like hell. Mike never asked me how I felt. He would *never* send me flowers at work. He doesn't do any of that stuff."

On the rare occasions when they manage to talk about what is troubling them, "it ends up being a big fight," Claire said. "I know he tells Molly a lot of personal stuff. She knew about his affair before I did."

One of the revelations of a famous study of working-class couples published in the early sixties was that the growing psychological awareness of the college-educated middle class was rarely reflected in the lives of blue-collar couples. Most of the couples interviewed for the study tended to be fatalistic not only about their marriages but about their lives in general, and viewed the major forces affecting them as beyond their control. Until recently, reserve, not self-disclosure, was the emotional skill that working-class men and women drew upon in times of stress and, if that ancient strategy did not solve problems, it did help preserve some of the fictions that kept marriages rolling along. Nowadays, working-class couples are still less likely than their middle-class counterparts to seek the aid of therapists or psychologists to help them with their problems, but the therapeutic way of looking at the world has nonetheless drifted their way—through social workers; drug- and alcohol-abuse counselors; ministers, who are apt to have studied psychology along with the Gospels; and, above all, through movies and television and popular magazines.

Mike Robbins had had many conversations about his emotional life with professional people, mostly with counselors at the detoxification centers he visited on his long journey to sobriety, and somewhere along the way he had absorbed the idea that intimacy was a central human value and that open communication lines were the path to it. Claire saw a therapist briefly during Mike's initial serious sobering-up period, but she seemed less conscious than Mike of the emotional fault lines of their marriage, and less willing to broach them as a subject of discussion. Even so, her assessment of their marriage was more open-eyed than his. Through television and magazines, she, too, had absorbed some of the shibboleths of feminism and pop psychology, but they were overwhelmingly undercut by a far stronger traditional set of values which stressed rigid male and female roles. Sometimes modern egalitarian notions and her old-fashioned ideas clashed head-on. She had "gone off the beam," she said, when she learned that Mike was having an affair a few years back (the young woman he was involved with told her about it), but when they tried to sort out what had gone wrong and Mike complained that she hadn't been paying any attention to him, mentioning that she never made meals for him—not even breakfast—she told him that she shouldn't even be working, or that she should be working only part-time, "for her own needs," as many women in her mother's generation had done. Claire feels that because she works so hard outside the home she should not be expected to cook. Mike does not find fault with her logic but wishes she could share his feeling that it is really the pleasure of eating together that they are missing. He usually sounds wistful rather than angry when the subject comes up, but he says he has never really considered the possibility of taking part in general meal-preparation—though he often cooks a chop or a steak for himself. On the other hand, Claire is far less demanding of her husband's cooperation around the house than many middle-class women are. Mike prides himself on his tidiness—he never drops his dirty socks on the furniture, or leaves wet towels on the floor—but it would never occur to him to help with the housecleaning chores. "She takes care of all that," he explains, in the manner of one describing a phenomenon as natural as the rising of the sun. Claire, too, takes it for granted that cleaning up and child care are her lookout. Though far fewer working-class women are at home all day now, as they were in the previous generation, the household help that they get from their husbands is still considered a favor, not an obligation, because traditional roles—though they are changing—are still accepted uncritically in the essentially conservative American blue-collar world.

Claire's solution to feeling overworked and undervalued—her refusal to cook—actually mirrors a national trend. In the 1970s and early 1980s, researchers found that the so-called leisure gap had increased substantially for working wives: they seemed to have far less free time than their husbands. But more recent studies have shown that the leisure gap has decreased—and, in some cases, even disappeared. In *The Second Shift,* Hochschild noted that "men weren't doing *more* housework and child care, women were doing less, and putting in four to five hours less on the job as well." Instead of trying to persuade their husbands to take on more domestic chores, working wives were cutting back both at home and at work.

MIKE lost all his union seniority when he left 3M in 1981 to dry out. The company reluctantly hired him back again after he sobered up (Claire and the company nurse, who had gotten him into the successful detox program, begged them to let him return), but put him in at the lowest grade-level union job—in the tape-rewinding department. All the other workers in the department were women, and the assignment was apparently understood to be a kind of insult. But Mike took great pleasure in the job. A quota had to be met every day, and he always managed to surpass it. He liked the women he worked with, and one of them, Molly Peters—who lived in a nearby town with her boyfriend— became a close friend. Mike says that in truth he loves Molly and has more than once entertained the idea of enlarging the terms of their friendship, but had always decided against it, because he suspects that "it would ruin things if sex were involved. "He values the friendship the way it is, and though he theoretically yearns for friendship and intimacy to be conjoined he is doubtful about the chances of its actually happening. His life-rescuing encounter with Alcoholics Anonymous and the therapeutic world seems to have stimulated a kind of hunger for a richer daily emotional life but left him utterly bewildered about how to acquire it.

Claire occasionally talks to her women friends—mostly work friends—about personal problems, and, as she'd told me, she has one close male confidant, Bob Mills, a boiler-room operator and avid motorcyclist who used to work at her hospital. Mike calls him "Biker Bob." Claire also knows and likes Molly. Once, Claire remarked to me that she wished she and Mike could speak as openly to each other as they could to their friends, and she thought it might be useful to visit a marriage counselor—but she quickly added that it was unlikely that a marriage counselor could get them anywhere. She attributes most of their marital problems to flaws in Mike's character ("He always thinks he's right") or to their different approaches to life ("We have nothing in common"). On the other hand, Claire says that Mike is basically a kind person—good about giving her money when she needs things and bailing her out when she gets into trouble with the telephone bill—and that she doesn't mind having to ask him for money all the time. The idea that they might pool their money, as Mike has often suggested, so that they might work out a budget and have a common fund available for everyday expenses seems peculiar to her. She recalls her mother and her mother's friends asking their husbands for money and notes that Mike rarely throws his superior earning power—or her economic dependence on him—in her face, except when they fight. The reason the phone bill is so high—a constant source of friction between them—is that the phone is her main source of contact with her work friends and Biker Bob.

In the fall of 1990, Mike switched jobs at his plant. Responding to new environmental laws, his company had built its own water-purification system (taking on a responsibility that had rested with the local authorities), and Mike was one of four workers hired to oversee the new system. He loved this job, which chiefly required him to check gauges and make sure that everything was working properly. He liked being away from the chemicals that were everywhere in the rest of the plant; he liked being removed from the hubbub of the other buildings; he liked the solitude and the freedom from physical stress. Most of all, he liked the overtime. Soon after he started his new job, one of his four coworkers was hospitalized with heart problems and another went into a detox program (according to Mike, coworkers with drug and alcohol problems have become an increasing problem in the factories he has worked in), and he and the other man who had been trained to operate the new system had to fill in for the two absent workers. This meant that most of the time Mike was either working or sleeping. It also meant that he was working holidays and raking in a lot of extra money. That year, he expected to make

$48,000—the most he'd ever earned. On a few occasions, the only other worker fell ill, and Mike had to fill in for him, too, after sleeping for just a few hours. When that happened, he was paid triple time. Mike prided himself on his ability to maintain his backbreaking new schedule. During one of my visits in early winter, he pointed out with amusement a recent work log that, what with double and triple time, showed him working 176 hours in one seven-day period—more hours than there are in a week. Without this much overtime, he said, he would be unable to keep up with his monthly expenses—the mortgage payment, the disability and insurance payments, the house siding payments, and the utility, sewer, water, and food bills—which far exceeded his normal salary. Several times, he had even gotten behind on his mortgage payments, and on more than one occasion he had to borrow food stamps from Melissa. (Melissa received the stamps and three hundred dollars a month from the county because of her legal status as a single mother.)

During the era of Supreme Overtime, Mike saw Claire less often than ever, and he had almost no contact with Melissa or Willie, or anyone else, for that matter. At home, he was rarely awake. Aware of her mother's no-cooking policy, Melissa rose to the occasion by sending Daryl over every few nights with small portions of whatever she was cooking. Mike would sometimes say that things at home were "not bad"; at other times, he would complain that in the few moments he and Claire had with each other she ignored him and he felt invisible. But if Claire felt bitter about their nonexistent sex life, Mike seemed resigned to it. One afternoon, when the subject came up, he said he knew that things were not as they should be but attributed his lack of interest in Claire to the longevity of their alliance and the fact that they knew each other too well. From remarks people made, he thought that many couples just seemed to give up on sex after a while.

Did he count himself among their number, I asked.

"No," he said. "I think about it all the time."

The machinations of state and national politics held little interest for Mike or Claire. If politics were ever discussed around the house, it was when I wasn't there. Even in the hottest moments of the 1992 presidential election, Claire said that the election didn't interest her (though, ultimately, she did vote). Mike didn't like any of the candidates much, but in the end he voted for Bush. During the Gulf War, I had noticed a We Support Our Military in the Gulf sign taped to one of the windows, and had learned that Mike was an enthusiastic supporter of Operation Desert Storm. By the time we actually got around to talking about it, though, the Storm had passed, and Mike said that his only regret about the event was that Saddam Hussein had not been finished off. In general, he said, the world of politics seemed remote to him. Claire's parents had been Democrats, and she was a Democrat, too. Mike's parents had also been Democrats, but although he frequently voted for Democrats, he considered himself a Republican. He liked the Republicans better, he said, because, "it seems like every time I've been out of work, a Democrat has been president." (Actually, during the times he was out of work—1968, 1973, 1986, and 1987—a Democrat was in power only once, in 1968.) Like many of his coworkers, Mike said, he had come to believe that Democrats were head-in-the-clouds ideologues, oblivious of the needs of the white working-class man. The pitches made by Nixon, Reagan, and Bush to work-ethic values struck a responsive chord in him, and he found it gratifying to be voting with what he saw as the party of the successful. On the other hand, when he voted in local elections he mostly voted for Democrats.

IN early March of 1991, in a period when Claire seemed to be fighting with Mike almost daily, she received a telephone call from Matt Williams, the man who was supposed to have been their baby's godfather. Not long after the child died, Matt had been sent to prison for robbing three convenience stores in North Carolina and he now called to say that he was being paroled. He and Claire had been lovers shortly before she met Mike and the three of them had continued to be friends after Mike and Claire got together.

Later that month, Claire and I took a short drive along the Jersey shore, and she told me that she'd lost the baby exactly two weeks after Matt had lost his little boy in a house fire, under murky circumstances. The boy had been at home with his mother, who may or may not have been sober at the time. Claire and Matt had spent hours weeping together and trying to console each other, and basically Matt seemed to have just given up on life afterward. Mike acted rather cold and removed when their own baby died. "He can't help it; he is just not an affectionate person," she said. "I needed a lot of kindness, and he really couldn't give it to me. I couldn't even look at a baby for years." Not long afterward, Matt and his wife broke up, and he moved to the South. It was easy for him to get work anywhere, Claire said, with a certain degree of pride in her voice, because he was a licensed welder. After the move she had lost touch with him until she learned that he had been sent to prison. He had been sentenced to seven years for each store he'd robbed, so the full term of his incarceration was supposed to be twenty-one years, but he was being paroled after serving time for sixteen and a half years. While he was in prison, he and Claire corresponded, and Claire's dresser drawers were filled with his letters, and with carefully detailed paintings of flowers and delicate, romantic line drawings of, among other things, naked lovers, which he had made for her in prison.

Over the years, the idea, as yet untested, had evolved between Matt and Claire that, whatever their early history, each might well be the significant other that each had been waiting for, so as soon as Matt got out of prison he asked Claire to visit him in North Carolina. (He could not visit her, because of the terms of his parole.) Claire talked the whole thing over with Mike and decided to go, but to take Melissa along as a chaperone. Mike said it was plain that Claire had "itchy feet" and he would not try to stop her from "doing what she had to do."

The second time Matt telephoned, he told her, jokingly, that she had thirty days in which to make up her mind about visiting him. All his friends were trying to fix him up with women, he said, and so far he had resisted all temptation, but if she couldn't come down in that period, he wasn't sure that he could hold out. The next time he called, Claire said she'd be down with Melissa in three weeks. During the second telephone conversation, Matt also revealed to Claire the astounding news that he had become a born-again Christian while he was in prison, and told her that the couple he was staying with until he could find an apartment of his own were of a like mind. (Matt had gotten to know the husband—a former outlaw biker whose face once appeared on a poster featuring the federal Ten Most Wanted list—while both were in prison.) At first, Claire thought Matt was kidding—she had never heard him even *mention* God in the old days—but when she realized he was serious, it made her nervous, especially when he asked her to bring down something she could wear to church. At the time, there were only two reminders of the existence of the Deity in Claire's life, and they were two magnets on the refrigerator that read, "Grant me patience, God, but hurry" and "Bless this mess." Above the magnets was a photograph of Claire, wearing a leotard and striking a sexy pose, which had been taken some years ago when she worked briefly as an exercise instructor. The photograph was secured to the refrigerator with a magnetized clip bearing the words "The Boss."

Claire became even more nervous when she called Matt one afternoon and got his friend, Lamar, instead. Lamar expressed overwhelming joy at the prospect of her arrival, in the Southern way, but warned Claire that Matt was extremely jittery. Claire asked him why, and he said, "Well, he's afraid that you're going to be temptation and he knows that in the Lord's eyes he can't do anything outside marriage"—to which Claire replied, "Are we talking about the same person?" Lamar said, "He's changed. You'll see that he's changed."

Recalling this conversation as we drove by a boarded-up amusement park, Claire chuckled. "I said to myself, 'I'd better humor this nut.' So I said, 'Don't worry about me tempting him, Lamar. That's not going to be a problem.' I did *not* want this guy talking Matt out of letting me come down." A short time before Matt made his first call, Claire said, she and Mike had had a conversation about seeing a marriage counselor, but somehow they had never gotten around to it.

Naturally, it bothered Mike that Claire was contemplating getting involved with another man, but his position on the matter was that he thought it important to give Claire as much rope as she wanted. Perhaps he saw the whole business as a way out of their emotional gridlock, but, on the whole, I found his statesmanlike posture rather fishy. Reporting on a conversation she had with him about her coming trip, Claire said, "He says, 'If you've got itchy feet, you've got to find out. It's something you've been holding in for a long time. Maybe you'll go and be disappointed. Maybe you'll come back and tell me you're moving to North Carolina.' Of course, I wouldn't. I would never leave my grandson. Not for nobody, no man. If things went that way, he'd have to move up here."

Claire had recently dyed her hair a bright red, and, as she drove she gave herself worried looks in the rearview mirror from time to time. She didn't like the color, and she was sure Brother Matt would find it too brassy. "They're making fun of me at work because I've been a little absentminded. They say, 'Hey, you should be doing this requisition. Your mind's in North Carolina.' And it is. I worry about whether it's the right thing to do. But my friend Betty says, 'Go for it. Shoot for the stars. If it doesn't work out, what would you lose?' Mike's a good man, I know it. God, he's paying for my ticket. But our life is boring, boring, boring. Boring and sexless. Still, I know he's a little anxious about the trip, though he would never admit it. Last week, he said, 'You know, Matt's my friend, too. I never heard you ask me to go along.' So I said, 'Well, you know, this is my thing.' The only thing that's worrying me, really, is this religious stuff. What I don't need is anybody preaching to me. I mean, shit, if he starts preaching, I'm going to get on the next train and come right back. I don't care what time it is.'"

I asked Claire if she had mentioned her conversation with Lamar to Matt. She had. A few hours after she spoke with Lamar, Matt had called and had assured her that, while he agreed with Lamar about a great many things, he didn't agree with him about everything—and he had laughed in a way that Claire found reassuring.

While Claire was away in North Carolina, I met Mike on a bright Sunday afternoon, and we had lunch in a seafood restaurant near Matawan. It had struck me that neither he nor Claire had ever mentioned anything about their wedding, and as we began eating, I remarked on that. "Well," Mike said, looking straight at me, "to be honest with you, we never actually got around to marrying. But twenty-two years sure feels like a marriage. Most of the longtime couples we know are like us."

THE visit to North Carolina went well, and Claire returned there, without Melissa, in May. When she was there in March, Matt had still been living with Lamar and his wife. By the time of her second visit, he had an efficiency apartment of his own but had not yet gotten a phone installed. When he drove to work the first morning, Claire panicked—with no car and no phone, she felt isolated and cut off from her familiar world. But the next day Matt had a phone put in, and he got Claire to drop him off at work, so that she could use the car, and things improved.

From several conversations I had with Mike during that same period, I learned that one of the explanations for his remarkable broad-mindedness was that he himself had, as he put it, "gone gaga" over a woman some years ago. This, he explained, was not the young woman with whom he'd had the affair, which in truth amounted to a one-night stand in a motel. He had actually known this other woman for about ten years (she had been a neighbor

and used to work with Claire) and had been meeting her for coffee at a nearby diner before work with some regularity for years.
The woman was unhappily married, but she would not sleep with
Mike. She was reluctant to enter into a full-fledged affair. Mike
was always hoping that she would change her mind (her husband, he said, was "a jerk," who sometimes abused her), but he
suspected that she never would. She was the most beautiful
woman he'd ever known, he said, and she seemed to love to talk
to him as much as he loved to talk to her. Despite the current drift
of Claire's life, he hadn't shared this outside interest of his life
with her because he thought that she would "go nuts."

At the beginning of July, Matt got permission from his parole
officer to pay Claire a visit, and Mike and Claire went together to
find him a motel room. When she stayed overnight with Matt in
the room, however, Mike blew up. Even so, he wanted to see his
old friend, and, one afternoon Matt came over to the house and
he and Mike talked for about two hours. A few weeks later, just
before Mike was to go off on his annual fishing trip vacation to
Maine, Claire met a woman whose boyfriend had died recently.
This woman, Thelma, liked to fish. Since Claire knew that
Thelma was feeling lonely, she suggested to Mike that Thelma
might like to go to Maine with him. Claire had been on such ex-
peditions with Mike, and she didn't care for them, though she acknowledged that they had become an opportunity for her and
Mike to straighten out some of their problems and enjoy some degree of intimacy. Claire particularly did not want to go this year,
and Mike was not looking forward to making the trip alone, so he
agreed to invite Thelma along.

When I met him next, in early September, he said he had been
glad of the company and that he hadn't had a bad time with
Thelma, but that now the woman was driving him crazy: she telephoned *both* of them all the time; she arrived, uninvited, for
weeknight visits; and she constantly berated Claire for neglecting
her husband. Apparently, Mike and Thelma had gone to bed a
couple of times, but Mike insisted that he had made it clear that

they weren't going anywhere as a couple—that he only wanted to be friends. Thelma had other ideas. Much to Claire's annoyance, she was becoming a fixture in the house. Arriving in the early evening, she would settle herself on one of the living-room couches, or wherever Mike happened to be sitting, and hang around watching television for several hours.

Mike showed me some photographs of the place he stayed at in Maine—an expanse of deep blue water encircled with a feathery crown of pines. The lake was not easy to get to, because it was at the end of a loggers' road, he said, adding that it was his favorite place in the world. One of the photographs showed a hefty, grandmotherly looking woman with long graying hair thigh-deep in the light-filled water, and beaming.

One evening when the three of them were sitting in the living room, Thelma reached over and ruffled Mike's hair, and that gesture so infuriated Claire that she stomped out of the room, muttering.

For the next month or so, Thelma's designs on Mike and her general awfulness (from Claire's point of view) were a constant source of arguments. Despite the evident progress of her own extracurricular romantic life, Claire somehow felt constrained to act the outraged wife. Even when, after another November visit to North Carolina, she and Matt decided that they wanted to live together, Claire continued to object strenuously to Thelma's telephone calls and visits, which frequently occurred when Claire was home alone. She took to referring to Thelma as Fatso. Mike would find a note on the kitchen table saying "Fatso called," or "Fatso left something in a box."

Sometime in November, Claire began reading the Bible every night and attending church on Sundays. Whenever I visited them that month, Mike allowed himself a good number of cracks about Claire's newfound religiosity and said he had asked her if she was praying for forgiveness for her adultery. He looked depressed, but he said that the reason he looked that way had nothing to do with Claire. His domestic problems had for the moment been overshadowed by new developments at work. A few weeks before, he'd had to leave his job overseeing the water-treatment plant.

"The area manager, the man who hired us, couldn't stand the fact that, with all our overtime, we were making more money than he was," Mike told me. "So he combined the water-treatment and chemical operator's job, although it's a virtual impossibility to do the two jobs at the same time. You'd have to be running back and forth between two different buildings—and everybody turned it down. But they'll find someone who will do it, someone who's desperate. They always do, especially in bad times like these. Anyway, I went back to my old chemical operator's job. [Mike's plant manufactures petroleum by-products.] I'm making the same amount per hour, but there's much less overtime and I don't like the people I have to work with there. There's a lot of backbiting, and the supervisor treats us like dog meat. The supervisors at the water-treatment plant were great. It's not that the job is so bad, but this one guy is always creating problems. It's a real snake pit. I don't think I can stay there indefinitely. I don't see myself there five years from now, in fact. Sometimes I wish I'd stayed at the plant they left open at 3M—that's where the nicest people I ever worked with were. Of course, the money wasn't as good. You know, a couple of years ago, in 1987, I went back to high school. I just felt like it, and I completed everything but the last-year math. If I got that over with, I'd have a regular high school diploma—not a high-school-equivalency diploma but a normal one. I've been working since I was a kid—I had a paper route, and I worked at the local supermarket—and I still don't seem to be getting anywhere. Really, I was doing a lot better in 1960 than I am now. All the chemicals I've been around, like the solvents we used for the tape coating—sometimes I wonder what the hell they've done to us. Nobody told us these were toxic chemicals. I don't know. I'm even thinking of going back to school to get a boiler-room operator's license. But you know what I'd *really* like to do? I'd like to have a little store in Maine, a sportsmen's store."

That afternoon, Mike and I took the hour-long drive to North

Plainfield, his hometown. As we drove along, he spoke some more, and with considerable bitterness, about his work life, as he chain-smoked and sipped from a can of Pepsi that stood on the car's drink tray. When we reached North Plainfield, we dropped in on Mike's mother, a cheerful, youthful seventy-three-year-old woman who lived in the top-floor apartment of a converted private house that used to belong to a rich businessman.

Throughout our visit, Mike's stepfather, a kindly but beaten-down-looking man, stayed out on a small terrace with the family dog, a frenetic shih tzu. Mike's mother was afraid that the dog would yap too much if he were let in. From time to time, man and dog would peer into the room while Mike and his mother gossiped a bit about neighborhood people whom Mike had known all his life, and talked in a distant sort of way about Claire and Melissa. I got the impression that she did not know much about Mike's present life or anything about his state of mind, and, for the first time since I'd met him, Mike eventually fell utterly silent. When we left, he seemed relieved.

Afterward, we drove past a comfortable-looking two-story frame house, not far from where his mother now lived, and he told me that was where he grew up. He noted that the subsequent owner had spruced it up quite a bit. As we drove through the neighborhood, he told me all sorts of anecdotes about the past and present inhabitants of various houses. "There isn't a house here I haven't been in," he said. Graceful maples lined the street, and most of the houses were two and three stories tall and looked solidly built. The contrast between his old and his new neighborhoods was stunning.

Over lunch at a cavernous and schlockily fancy but inexpensive local restaurant called Pantagis Renaissance but referred to universally as Snuffie's (its name in an earlier, less pretentious era), Mike told me that he was planning a fishing trip with his son, whom he'd just talked to that morning. His son lived in a small town in Northern New Jersey, and in recent years he and Mike had made a point of seeing each other from time to time.

Mike said he had also tried to reestablish some sort of relationship with his daughter, but she wouldn't allow it. Over a plate of pasta, he fell silent again and then blurted out that he had finally realized that his marriage was probably coming to an end. Folding his hands over a little paunch that sloped out under a black "World's Best Grandpa" sweatshirt, he sighed and shook his head. He and Claire had been at each other's throats all week, he said, and, though he knew he'd always care for her, and couldn't really be happy unless she was happy, too, they seemed to have finally "burned each other out." The last time she went to visit Matt, Mike had said, "Why don't you ask me how I feel about this?" and she had responded with "I don't need to ask your permission, you're not my father." Recalling the exchange, Mike said, "I told her, 'That's our problem, we never really talk about anything.' But—you know—we're just not the same people we were when we met. I *need* to talk to someone. I realized that after I sobered up. I'm not interested in—you know—a Dolly Parton, but I need to really connect with someone. This woman I told you about that I meet with for coffee all the time—we don't seem to be getting anywhere sexually. Her husband's really awful, but she's afraid to leave him. Basically, what we do is talk. And we laugh a lot, too. I talk, she listens. She talks, I listen. It's never been that way with Claire and me. I don't know why. Claire would be out now if she could get a place. But I'll be damned if I'm going to help her with that. I had to put her name on the paper when I bought the house—to get the mortgage—but she hasn't put a cent into it, and now she's telling me that I should buy her out. That's ridiculous."

On the way back to Matawan we took a somewhat longer route so that Mike could show me where the rich people in the area lived—a place called Watchung Mountain. A number of the houses Mike wanted me to see were perched at angles on the mountainside and afforded a panoramic view that included Raritan Bay and, in the immediate foreground, the slums of black Plainfield. As we climbed a steep grade, passing grand old houses and showy new ones, Mike's voice rose with excitement. "This is real money!" he exclaimed. "You're in another league now, babe. We're talking millions of dollars here!"

The week before, Mike had been working the midnight shift, which ended at eight in the morning, and had also worked the shift from the 8:00 A.M. to 4:00 P.M. several times. The midnight shift began on Tuesday and was over the following Tuesday at 8:00 A.M. The Tuesday that he worked until 8:00 A.M. was considered a day off. His next shift began on Thursday at 4:00 A.M. and ended at midnight. The morning of our ride, a Saturday, he had left work at midnight, gone to sleep as soon as he got home, and driven to the train station to meet me at 11:00 A.M. Now, when we arrived back at the house at around 3:15, there was a message from his boss asking him to work overtime for a few hours, during the four o'clock and midnight shifts. He went in, worked from four to eight, went home, napped, and returned to work at midnight. The next time I saw him, a few weeks later, he was looking particularly pale and pinched. His already deeply lined face seemed to have a few new tracings. I asked him how his body adjusted to his constantly changing schedule.

"It doesn't," he said, shrugging. "But I wouldn't mind so much if they didn't work so hard at making it unpleasant. This particular part of the plant where I work is really dirty—filthy! Boy, I'd like to be out of there. Say I won the lottery, like this truck driver did recently—I'd buy some kind of property in Maine, where it's really *clean,* and maybe one down South somewhere, and I'd hire a pilot to fly me to wherever I'd like to go."

While Mike and I were sitting in the kitchen talking, Claire came in. She gave me a big smile, ignored Mike, and suggested that we go to the Shamrock Diner, a ten-minute drive, for a cup of coffee. Claire looked like a new woman. Her eyes were clearer, her brow was less furrowed, and she exuded an air of supreme well-being. She was wearing an off-the-shoulder blouse that revealed two new tattoos—one on each shoulder—which she had recently acquired down South. On her left shoulder was a small rose framing a lion's head, and on her right a dainty butterfly. As I was putting my coat on to go to the diner, I asked how Melissa was.

There was a moment of awkward silence before Claire responded, her voice heavy with disapproval: "She had another abortion. *He* helped her get it."

"Claire! She was sick again. She wasn't going to make it," Mike said.

I gathered that, though the doctor had strongly recommended that she wait at least a year before getting pregnant again, Melissa had ignored the warning. Almost immediately after becoming pregnant, she began vomiting violently and felt dizzy much of the time. For some reason, Claire was convinced that the sickness wasn't going to last long and that Melissa could bring the baby to term if she just held on. But in fact Melissa weakened every day and decided on an abortion again because her condition scared her. Mike accompanied her to the clinic.

Claire: "She should have held out a little longer."

Mike: "I think she did the right thing."

Silence.

As we drove to the diner, Claire said that for years she had been fearful of driving long distances alone. She was afraid of getting lost or breaking down or running into some kind of trouble that she couldn't get out of. But the last time she visited Matt she had driven all the way down herself instead of taking the train and had found the experience exhilarating. She told Matt when she got there that, while she was happy to be with him, she felt sad about Mike, sad about Melissa's abortion, and sad about a lot of things in her life that seemed to pass out of her mind before she even had a chance to name them. Matt suggested that she read the Bible—in particular, Acts and Romans—and, to her amazement, she had found reading it a comfort. In North Carolina, she had accompanied Matt to the Baptist church he attended, but the Bible-thumping style of its minister had alarmed her. ("I thought the guy was going to have a heart attack.") Back home, attending the local Presbyterian church, she had begun to find the minister's sermons interesting and (with some prompting from Matt) had attempted to pray for the people who got her mad, instead of cursing them out.

"I even tried praying for Fatso—though that didn't work out too well," she said. "But I've started feeling better, no doubt about it. They finally offered me a new job, as senior technician. I'd been hoping to get that for a long time. I still don't know what the money's going to be. They don't tell you that right away. But I'm feeling a lot more confident. There's this guy at work who's been giving me a hard time for a couple of months now. Matt said, 'Say a prayer for him,' and, son of a bitch if I didn't find this little passage, in a book of prayers called *The Upper Room* that they had at the hospital chapel about getting along with your coworkers. The passage was about a woman who hated a guy in her office, just like me. Well, I prayed and I prayed, but finally I said, 'What's needed here is a staff meeting.' I was a little nervous, because I'm sort of on trial in my new job. But I thought to myself, I'm not going to be able to go the rest of my life saying prayers for this son of a bitch. So we met, and guess what? He pulled the same stupid stuff with the head of the department that he pulls with me—insulting her, and everything. He made a complete ass of himself. She really got mad and told him he'd better not bother me again."

Over apple pie and coffee at the Shamrock, Claire's favorite local diner, she talked about her hopes for a new life with Matt, her ambivalent feelings about Mike, and her desire to find an apartment of her own. She had offered to relinquish all claims to her share of the house if Mike would just give her $2,000 toward expenses for a new place. New Jersey does not recognize consensual marriage, and Claire was not intending to explore the matter of her legal rights (or lack thereof)—all she knew, she said with considerable agitation, was that she wanted to get out. She pushed the last crumbs of the apple pie around on her plate with her fork and sighed. She wasn't completely confident that things would work out with Matt. He was a moody man, she said, and she wasn't good at dealing with his moodiness. But she was hopeful. "He's a really *attentive* guy—look at this," she said, and she held out her hand. On each of her fingernails, Matt had painted an intricate Art Deco design over her nail polish. Later on, after we drove back to the house, she showed me more examples of Matt's handiwork: elaborate flower designs painted on scores of letters, on a denim jacket, and on a cigarette lighter. She also produced a photograph of a remarkably happy-looking Claire standing in front of an equally happy-looking burly, bearded middle-aged man, whose arms were wrapped around her.

Late one night the following week, Claire telephoned to say that she and Mike had had some terrible rows and she was afraid that he might hit her. She sounded scared. They were arguing about everything, she said, but they had had a particularly bad fight about a mysterious bounced check for eighty-eight dollars, which she swore she had never written, and which she believed had been written by Thelma, who she was convinced had been poking around the house in her absence and had thus had access to her checkbook. Claire asked me to talk to Mike because he seemed to "act calmer" after our meetings. Feeling the full weight of the peculiarity of my role in the Robbinses' lives, and with the utmost reluctance, I waited while Claire passed the telephone receiver to Mike, who said that Claire "exaggerated everything," but added that her fussing about Thelma did infuriate him, since he didn't give a damn about Thelma—she was just a sad person who was lonely, like a lot of other people, and, if anybody should be fussing, he was the one. "I just wish I could sell the goddam house and move somewhere else," he said. But he added that if he did sell it he'd lose money. He'd bought it when the market was inflated, and he'd have to pay the real-estate agent a large amount of money he didn't have. "On the other hand," he said, "I always did want a home, and, though this isn't the Taj Mahal, I've got one."

Over the next few weeks, I received regular phone calls from Mike and Claire. In periods of great stress, most people that I knew, in circumstances not very dissimilar from those of the Robbinses, drew on therapists, friends, relatives, and a whole range of complex emotional self-rescue techniques. These techniques were like some form of stored body fat that got them through bad times. Claire and Mike had a meaner, cleaner way of proceeding, and they had no answers to most of their woes, only painful questions. Even Claire's newfound religion got her only so far, as did Mike's amazing native optimism and doggedness.

The week before Thanksgiving, Claire telephoned again to tell me that, for the first time since they'd been together, Mike was refusing to celebrate Thanksgiving with her—the one day a year when she cooked. His factory gave out free turkeys, but he was turning over his turkey to Melissa, who, she added, was pregnant again. She sounded pleased. She thought she might work on Thanksgiving. Things had quieted down at home. In fact, an icy silence prevailed. She and Mike didn't speak to each other unless they had to. There had been a few more evening visits from Thelma, and—ominously, she thought, a gift of a bed for Mike, who had taken to sleeping on the couch. There was a closet-size second bedroom in the house, which used to be Melissa's room, but the only bed in it now was a small Ninja Turtle bed that Willie slept in. Mike had begun to think about trying to find a roommate to help him with the bills after Claire left, but he did not want the roommate to be Thelma. He agreed to accept the bed only after she asked him to think of it as an early Christmas present and a quid pro quo for the Maine trip (for which he had footed the bills).

In the post-bed period, however, Thelma seemed to be showing up more often, and sometimes she hinted at the broader role she might play in Mike's future. When it became clear that there was no feasible way for the relationship to continue along the lines Mike envisaged, he told Thelma that she had better not come over.

Claire was still certain that Thelma had forged a check and made off with some other money as well, but Mike did not believe any of that. He was sure that Claire had overspent, as she often did, and was trying to weasel out of her responsibility for the bounced check by blaming Thelma. Somehow, the greater part of Mike's current feeling of loss was usually translated into financial terms. He was incensed because in recent months Claire had run up regular monthly telephone bills of five, or even six, hundred dollars talking to Matt in North Carolina and had gotten so far behind on her payments that she'd had to make a special arrangement with the telephone company to pay something every week. Since she was paid every two weeks, she had asked Mike to advance her some money to help pay the bill. He had, and she had yet to pay him back. A few days later, he'd had to help Melissa with some extra money, because Claire had also made an extravagant number of calls on Melissa's phone, and the phone company was threatening to shut it off. (Claire subsequently denied that Melissa's problems with the phone company were related to "just a few calls" she'd made on Melissa's phone.)

In late November, Mike's this-is-probably-all-for-the-best-anyway attitude deserted him briefly, and he began to sound more like an injured party. "Whenever she's needed anything, I've bought it for her," he complained. "We've been in this house four years. The first year, I bought the house and paid for whatever we needed to put into it. The second year, I bought her a car. The third year, she wanted a deck, so I paid for a deck; and last year I bought her a bedroom set. I'm still paying the bills for it all, and now she's walking out into the sunset."

Actually, Claire felt as if she were drifting out into a choppy sea. And, while it was true that Mike paid most of the major expenses in their lives, his characterization of Claire as a ditsy spendthrift hardly jibed with the reality of her life. She was determined to get her own apartment, but so far, she couldn't afford to; the salary hike that she'd assumed would come along with her new job had still not materialized, so, like Mike, she had been volunteering for many hours of overtime. She had also taken a second job, as a sterile-instrument dispenser in the operating room at the hospital. A mandatory daily two-hour job-training session came along with the O. R. job, so Claire was getting up at five, working at her regular job, training for her new job from three to five, then returning to her office to work late, often until about nine. She called one night, sounding exhausted and on the verge of tears. Mike had threatened to take her car away, she said. "He used to say, 'We have such a long history—twenty-three years. No matter what, we care about each other. I don't think either of us can be happy if the other isn't.' And that's right, really. I love two people. I don't want him to be miserable. But he's becoming a maniac."

It seemed to Claire that Mike ought somehow to be giving his blessing to her plans. "Why can't he say, 'Go ahead. If things work out good, OK; if not, just come home in two or three months.'"

When I ventured to suggest that perhaps that was asking an awful lot from a rejected mate, she sighed. "You know, he's never actually said 'Don't go.' Not once."

THE already frigid emotional temperature of the Robbins household plummeted even lower the following week when, in the course of yet another argument, it came out that for some time Mike had been regularly meeting the woman he was smitten with, whose name was June Cowan. Mike told me about it on the telephone one afternoon in early December. He'd insisted to Claire that he was not having an "affair," but at some point in the conversation the word "love" was spoken. Mike explained that he needed someone to talk to—someone who would listen to him. Apparently, June and Claire still occasionally talked on the telephone. Claire was skeptical about Mike's claim that they weren't sleeping together and accused him of having an affair with her "best friend." Mike told me he'd replied, "I wish I were, I wish I were."

Mike and Claire had this discussion just after he'd gotten home from the 8:00 P.M. to 4:00 A.M. shift, and "She insisted I go straight over to June's and bring her back so she could talk to her," he told me. "June doesn't have a phone. I said, 'You're crazy. ' But she said, 'You'll see that this is a good thing.' So, like a fool, I went and got her, and they had their powwow, and, after June drove back home, Claire said, very matter-of-factly, 'This is a mistake. She's going to hurt you.' I told her I could take care of myself, and then, somehow, we both lost it and started screaming at each other, and we've been screaming ever since. You know, she has never acknowledged that what she was doing with Matt was wrong. But somehow she feels justified in being completely indignant about my relationship with this woman. At one point, we made an agreement to just leave each other alone, but Claire cannot do that. She was at me all the time about what a heel I was. Finally, I just totally flipped out. It was like she couldn't give me any space at all. I just couldn't take it. I was emotionally and physically finished. I felt like I was going nuts. I don't know how I got there, but I drove to a diner and just sat there for a couple of hours. Eventually, I mellowed out, and I just said to myself, 'I quit.' I realized that I just can't deal with her.

"When I went home, I said to her, 'OK. Go to Matt. You've got my blessing. Don't stay with me.' Then she starts the whole business up again, saying, 'You just want to get rid of me because you have a guilty conscience.' Then I said, 'You want to keep me and Matt, too. It can't be done.' And she said, 'I still have feelings for you.' So I said, 'OK. Go call Matt and tell him good-bye, and I'll drive over to June's and say good-bye.' Of course, she wouldn't. After that, I was pretty calm, but I could see that Claire couldn't stand the idea that I had strong feelings for another woman. I think what she really wants is for me to beg her to stay. Maybe a year from now I might, but there is no way that's going to happen now. We've got to get away from each other. She just has no conception of any of my feelings. I mean, Matt's moving up here, and the apartment she's trying to get is just around the corner. Can you believe that? Like I said to her, 'I've got to go to the store and run into you and Matt? That's not going to be easy.' And all she can say is 'Just let me do my thing.' Now the deal is that she wants me not to see June until she goes down to North Carolina for Christmas. I said, 'What the hell, OK'—though it seems really ludicrous to me. At least, now she's talking to me. For weeks—hell, years, really—I'd come home and she just wouldn't react at all to me. The only time I get a reaction from this woman is when she's totally pissed. Today, she called me at work. She *knows* that I can't talk at work—my boss is three feet away from me, for Christ's sake. So all I can do is 'yes' her. Why does she do that?"

While Mike was talking on the phone, I could hear Melissa moaning in the background. She was in the third month of her pregnancy now, and once again she wasn't holding her food down and felt nauseated most of the time. Several days before, Mike had taken her to the hospital, and they had hooked her up to an I.V. She had been vomiting all morning, and Mike was worried about her.

Although the Robbinses' house is small, it has two telephones—one in the living room, where Melissa was resting, and the other in the kitchen, on the wall next to the bathroom door. Anyone who wants to carry on a private telephone conversation walks into the bathroom with the phone and talks from there, and that was apparently what Mike had done, because our call was interrupted by a sharp cry of "Daddy!" and the sounds of violent retching. Melissa had rushed past him, Mike said, and it looked to him as if they'd be heading for the hospital again soon.

Several days later, however, Melissa began to feel better. Though she was still far from strong, she was determined to keep this baby, Mike said, because she thought that it might make Daryl love her more if they had a child together.

IN mid-January, Matt drove up from North Carolina. He and Claire had agreed to live together, so he gave up his job, put a few things in his car, and headed north. Mike had again come around to thinking that it was probably all for the best. He and Claire would be better off living apart, and he felt hopeful that in time he might meet an available woman with whom he would fight less and "communicate" more. But, as the day of Matt's arrival approached, Claire began to have misgivings. She was tired of fighting with Mike but not really that sure she was ready to throw her lot in with Matt. By the first of February, however, she and Matt had moved into a small efficiency apartment that was about a five-minute drive from the house.

Mike's attitude toward Matt was amazingly fraternal. In fact, the two of them had had several good, if circumspect, talks together, according to Mike. Sounding more like a thoughtful grandpa than like a wronged mate, Mike pointed out when I visited him about a week after Claire had moved out that he and Claire were the only people Matt knew in town, that Matt had lost touch with most of the friends he'd had while he was in prison, that he was pretty isolated in general, and that prison life had seriously "beaten him down in a lot of ways, mental and physical." In truth, Mike felt sorry for Matt—so sorry that he had actually moved in with a friend for two weeks and let Matt stay at the house with Claire while they looked for an apartment.

Though the scene had shifted, the scenario of the Robbinses' life in some ways remained the same. Claire was calling Mike from work as often as she always had; she came over to the house regularly to do her laundry and stayed to talk, and a few days before, Mike said, she had blurted out in the course of one of these conversations that she'd discovered that she really liked him. "Imagine that. Twenty-three years and she's just discovered that she likes me. Jesus Christ. 'Isn't life strange?' as the Moody Blues would say." It also emerged that since Matt hadn't brought much money into the picture and hadn't yet been able to find a job, Mike was still doling out money for Claire's bills. Claire's new job had thus far proved to be only slightly more rewarding financially—she was now making $14,000 a year—and her habit of asking Mike for out-of-pocket expenses hadn't ceased with her departure. The week before, Mike had paid for a new starter motor for her car. The day before, the exhaust had fallen off his own car. On the day of my visit, in fact, we drove to the office of the Aberdeen Township clerk so that he could pay his sewer bill (something he was supposed to have done the day before but hadn't, because of his car problems).

Back at the house, which showed no signs of having fallen into bachelor disarray, Mike expressed the opinion that Claire "already wanted out" but would stay with Matt for the time being, because she felt she had to. Apart from all other considerations, Matt's blood pressure was high, and he had some lesser health problems as well. Mike thought he might have difficulty passing a union physical if a job required one. As always, Mike looked tired, but he was in good spirits, which were apparently fueled by a considerable degree of Schadenfreude. He sipped black coffee from a large plastic mug and speculated about the source of Claire's dissatisfaction in her new situation. "She's complaining that he's acting like her shadow. With us, she came and went as she pleased. I mean, we were really like two single people living together. You'd probably find this hard to believe, but sometimes I'd walk in the house after work, and she'd be on the phone in the kitchen, and when I grabbed something to eat she would make another call in the living room, and then we'd switch places again, and I'd go to sleep and she'd be on the phone again, and in all that time we wouldn't say one word to each other. Matt expects her to be *with* him—that's what she's not used to. She's uncomfortable with that."

A few minutes later, the dogs started barking, and somewhat to his surprise, Mike discovered Matt at the front door. He had come to pick up a broken vacuum cleaner of Melissa's that he said he'd take to the repair shop. After it was found, he lingered at the door, as if he wanted to talk to Mike, but, seeing me, he fell silent and looked uncomfortable. Like Mike, Matt had deeply creased pouches under his eyes and a kind of trammeled but alert demeanor. In some subtle way, he seemed more approachable than Mike, and a longish, slightly upturned mustache, carefully trimmed beard, and a modish blue polo shirt with a contrasting aqua collar gave him a more modern self-presentation. You could never imagine Mike playing on anyone's bowling team. Matt didn't look like a bowler, either, but you could at least imagine him *inside* a bowling alley, hanging out. Mike introduced us and invited Matt into the kitchen. It turned out that Matt had come by to ask Mike about the job market. At the time he went to prison, there had been jobs for the asking. Now, even for a skilled worker, there seemed to be none. He told Mike that he had put in two job applications earlier that day but was not feeling optimistic about either of them. There were fifty applicants for one position and a thousand for the other. At the first place, they would eventually be hiring two people, and, at the second, six or seven. Matt asked Mike how long the job market had been so tough. Mike shrugged and shook his head. "Jesus, for a long time, Matt—eight or nine years," he said. Matt looked down at his work boots and said that he might have to switch tactics and try to find work in "food management"—a subject he had studied in prison. "I don't know," Mike said. "The pay scale for that kind of work is lousy." Matt nodded. Both men punctuated their sentences with long drags on their cigarettes. They seemed like—in fact they were—two old pals, commiserating. Matt talks a lot more slowly than Mike. Both Claire and Mike had characterized him as "mellow," but the mellowness seemed to rest on a base of caution, and there was a dreamy, reflective look in his eyes, which were a pale blue, that softened his general appearance considerably.

When Matt had left, Mike asked me if I'd ever heard the full story of Matt's arrest, and I said I hadn't. "Well, after his son died, Matt really began to drink and he did a lot of drugs," Mike began. "When he went down to North Carolina, he just sort of went off the deep end. He began hanging out with bad guys. One of them was a real wacko. Some kind of heavy-duty druggie. This guy cheated and stole—whatever—to keep himself on drugs. So one day the guy asks Matt to drive him to a couple of 7-Eleven stores, and he runs in and runs out of them, and then he asks him to drive to another 7-Eleven, only this time, the guy not only robs the store but comes out with this girl, and the girl is terrified. Matt didn't know what the hell was going on, but he knew enough to know that it was bad. So this guy says, 'Just drive!' and they pull off. But the girl starts screaming, so after a mile or so, Matt slams on the brakes and walks around and opens the door and tells the girl to get out. Now the guy starts screaming at him, but Matt just jumps in and drives off, leaving the girl on the road. Well, it turns out that, Jesus, the girl is the daughter of the local judge, and when the cops catch Matt and this guy they beat the shit out of them—pardon my French—in jail and they're ready to throw everything in the book at them, including attempted rape. In the end, the girl testified that Matt saved her from being raped, and maybe even saved her life, but they still sent him up for twenty-one years. He was lucky to get paroled in sixteen."

As Mike concluded his story, the frenzied barking of the dogs announced another visitor. It was Claire. She was on her way from the supermarket to her new apartment and was stopping by to pick up some clothes. The new place was so small, she explained to me, that she still kept a lot of her stuff in her old closet. Claire also asked Mike if he knew where an old kitchen table of hers was—she wanted to use it for a TV table in the new place. Mike thought he might have thrown it out but said he'd look for it later on. Claire had left almost all the furniture where it was—even the living-room chairs and couches, which had belonged to her sister—and that seemed a little odd to me. On her way out, she said she'd drive by later and take me over to see the new place.

"Get me some milk, Mike," she said over her shoulder as she reached the front door, "I'm not going to have time to go to the store again." We were going out, too, to catch some lunch.

"Jesus, why don't you get Matt to get it? Oh, never mind. All right."

After we slid into Mike's car, and Claire pulled out, Mike said, "You see? She's not really gone. Last night she called me up before she went to sleep—she's done that almost every night—and I said, 'Look, Claire, you can't be doing this.' She's calling me three, four times a day, and she's dumping on him, and I'm telling her it's not right. It's funny, when we were together she always seemed to have something more important to do than talk to me. Now she's talking to me all the time. I gotta find someone I can share things with. That's what Matt wants from Claire, and that's what's getting on her nerves. I want the same thing, but I'm realistic. I'm not ever going to get it from her." Over lunch, it became clear that though Mike had no idea where he might meet a new woman, he assumed he would. "It will happen when it happens," he said. It had taken him a long time, he added, to realize that Matt was not really the problem. "Even if things don't work out," he said firmly, "I don't want her back." But, final as this sounded, a future Mike-Claire reunion was not entirely ruled out. As we were driving back to the house, Mike articulated what definitely sounded like an altered version of his position—one in which Claire was allowed to return via the back door. Regretting the absence of a wide circle of friends in his present life, he began reminiscing about the old days at the Smithfield Tavern, his former drinking haunt. The only thing that ever came even close to this tavern in terms of communal feeling and warmth, he said, was the AA meetings he attended when he was sobering up. But that was more than ten years ago, and the AA meeting place was more than an hour's drive from Matawan. There was no place in his present life where he could expect to see a constellation of familiar faces, no place where he could "shoot the bull" as he used to with Matt and the other people at the tavern. Mike had been a pallbearer at Matt's son's funeral, and when his own baby died in the hospital Mike had gone to Matt's house and cried. He needed to let go like that, he said, but he didn't want Claire to see him crying.

It was ironic that Matt had come to talk to him about jobs that day, Mike said, because the night before, when Claire called to say good night, she'd said she didn't think Matt was looking hard enough for a job. "I said, 'Jesus, Claire, he's looking, he's just do-ing it at his own pace, and it's bad out there.' Claire wants every-body to do everything immediately. She cares a lot about people, but she wants everything to happen right away. Maybe she doesn't have the *patience* to see this thing with Matt through. She was even hinting the other day about coming back, but I said, 'I don't want you back unless Matt goes back to North Carolina. I don't want to see anybody hurt.' I shouldn't have said that, because no way are we ever going to be different with each other."

At four-fifteen that afternoon, Claire arrived to pick me up. She wanted to go to a consignment shop near her new apartment to look for a bathroom shelf. Mike had forgotten to get the milk, and she said "Jeez!" and rolled her eyes. Mike shook his head, but while she was changing her clothes, he drove to a market around the corner for the milk and a few things for himself. When he re-turned, Claire said she needed a five-dollar loan for incidental ex-penses, and he reached into his pocket and wordlessly handed her the money.

Claire looked less tense than she used to, but seemed dis-tracted and soon confirmed what Mike had said: she was already unhappy in her new situation, though she hadn't ruled out the possibility that things might improve. It had all happened too fast, she said. Matt traipsed after her too much. He was moody. When she snapped at him, he didn't just ignore her the way Mike did. He sulked. And he was cheap. She understood that he'd come north with only a limited amount of money and he still didn't have a job, but she couldn't stand the way he hovered over her at the supermarket and asked her whether certain items were really necessary. She was furious that she didn't make enough money to simply pay for everything she needed herself, but she had somehow never seriously questioned the idea that "the man" was supposed to supply her basic needs automatically and uncomplainingly. Thus, when Matt met her at the consign-ment shop and she found not only a small wicker shelf for the bathroom but several porcelain animal miniatures, some paper flowers, a plastic tablecloth, and a painted bowl, the bill came to more than thirty-five dollars in all, and Claire handed over her five dollars to the woman who ran the store, then looked inquiringly at Matt, and he, with a pained but resigned expression, forked over the rest.

The new apartment was on the second floor of a converted private house in a somewhat upscale neighborhood of Matawan called Keyport. Generously built houses dominated the block, and the nearby food and clothing shops catered to middle-class tastes. The apartment itself was bright and cheerful, but held so little furniture at the moment that it had the appearance of a stage set. Living room: convertible pale blue velvet couch, TV, and a six-gallon jug filled with paper flowers; kitchen: gray Formica table and two chairs; bathroom: a startling embryonic version of Claire's old bathroom, with a profusion of blue and pink paper flowers, soap-filled straw baskets; animal print towels; and matching blue toilet-seat cover and scatter rugs.

Neither resident of the apartment seemed entirely comfortable with it. Matt kept opening and shutting the refrigerator door and peering inquisitively inside, as if it might hold some secret. Claire paced back and forth, and three times in the span of half an hour she asked Matt when he was going to put up the wicker shelf. Matt wanted to talk to Claire about his job interviews that day, and, as he had with Mike, to somehow establish for the record that there had been a palmier time, when a welder did not have to look far to find a good job. Claire gazed at Matt with a sympathetic expression as he recited his woes, but said nothing. She seemed to have no vocabulary for commiseration. Her fondness for him, which was obvious to anyone who knew her, was demonstrated mainly by her forbearance.

MATT never did find a job, and by March he and Claire had split up and she had moved back in with Mike. The most tangible reminder of the time she had spent away was the blue convertible sofa, which she had brought with her. After Matt returned to North Carolina, he was operated on for a tumor in his stomach that proved to be benign, though his health was still far from good. Claire had remained friends with him and had visited him several times during his recuperation, but sex was no longer part of their relationship. One day in July, Matt showed up at their doorstep, looking as white as a sheet, and fainted. They put him on the blue couch and let him stay with them for a few weeks. He did not seem well but claimed that nothing was seriously wrong.

Mike did not really know why Claire had left Matt. "She needed some romance and she got it for a while," he ventured. "But she said he drank too much and that he didn't have any ambition. When she came back, she said, 'Maybe we can work things out.' But we can't. Basically, I guess I welcomed her because the bottom line was I didn't want her in a bad situation. But we can't get along."

On July 31, 1992, Melissa gave birth to her second child, another boy, and told Mike several times in the weeks that followed that she was thinking of going back to school. Claire was still trying to pay off the telephone bills she had incurred during the period when she and Matt were talking long-distance so much, and she had agreed to go with Mike to Maine in late August. In early August, as Claire's birthday approached, Mike was planning a sort of celebratory few days. He would go to the beach with her, and then they would drive together to a truck stop in northern New Jersey that was reputed to have the kind of Indian jewelry she liked. They did make it to the truck stop, but Mike had to work the day they were supposed to go to the beach, and Claire backed out of the Maine trip at the last minute. They were getting along "pretty well," Mike said when I talked to him by phone, but they had started to fight again, and he feared that things weren't ever going to be right between them.

"We have finally decided to go our own ways," he said tensely. "We'll sell the house next summer, or declare bankruptcy if we can't sell it, and I'll get myself a little apartment. Claire will get herself one, too. I'd like to find someone else, really. But, you know, I believe what will be, will be."

When I spoke to him last winter, Mike was no longer so sure that he and Claire would split up. Claire told me that things weren't so bad, and neither of them could remember the last time they had thought about moving, or leaving.

$\mathscr{W}$ORKING RELATIONSHIPS

THOUGH MORE AND MORE WOMEN WENT TO WORK BE-
tween 1900 and 1920, and the twenties brought a dramatic loosening up of the nation's sexual habits, there was a paradoxical
shift in interest away from social reform and toward psychology
and consumerism. A well-known curious fact of American history is that American women's getting the vote did not kick off an
era of enthusiastic female participation in politics, bring about
any radical new reforms in women's situations, or lead to large
changes in the workplace. Few businessmen were willing to train
women for management positions, and most women therefore
had fairly low-paying jobs. Three out of four women who started
careers in the twenties and thirties became nurses or teachers,
and the number of female lawyers and doctors did not increase
significantly. "The highest profession a woman can engage in,"
one businessman of the 1920s wrote in an article in a women's
magazine, "is that of charming wife and wise mother."

The Depression made women's entry into the marketplace
more urgent, and, in fact, the number of married women with

jobs went up 50 percent in the 1930s, but there was also a renewed emphasis on the solace of home and hearth in those hard
times, and the general prejudice against hiring married women—
who were now seen as competitors for scarce jobs—was acute. In
1930, a survey of fifteen hundred U.S. school systems revealed
that 77 percent of them did not hire wives and 63 percent made a
practice of firing any female teachers who married. A good number of city, county, and state governments took similar stands,
and the federal government declared that a husband and wife
could not be in its employ at the same time. The Depression was
a period of growing social innovation and also of renewed domestic conservatism. When the pollster George Gallup asked people
in 1936 whether wives should get a job if their husbands were already working, 82 percent of those questioned said no.

The resistance to the idea of married women working was in
part a product of economic anxiety, but it also reflected, as it still
does, an unwillingness to contemplate rearrangements in domestic life—specifically, the sharing of child rearing, cooking, and
daily chores. Even today, with 75 percent of all married women
with children working, though men help out in the home far
more than their fathers did, the help they offer is too often woe-
fully inadequate. The women's magazines of the twenties and
thirties derided the very idea of women's "careers," and linked
them, once again, to dark forces imperiling the family. "No matter
how successful, the office woman is a transplanted posy," one social critic opined in *The Ladies Home Journal* of October 1930.
"Just as a rose comes to its fullest beauty in its own appropriate
soil, so does a home woman come to her fairest blooming when
her roots are stuck deep in the daily and hourly affairs of her own
dearly beloved."

The Second World War brought married and unmarried
women into the paid labor force in unprecedented numbers, and
the attitudes of both men and women were permanently affected
by the contributions that working women made during the war.
Between 1941 and 1945, six and a half million women took jobs

as, among other things, grease monkeys, baggage loaders, riveters, precision toolmakers, lumberjacks, and heavy machine operators, not to mention their service in the army, navy, and coast guard, an increase of 57 percent in the total female labor force. Before 1940, most women who worked were young and single, but during the war 75 percent of all new female employees were married, and by far the greatest number of them were middle aged. The sudden, dramatic shift in employment patterns (one California aircraft company, which employed no women at all before 1941, had hired 13,000 by 1942) and the opening up of jobs never before thought possible for women changed women's thinking permanently—and the thinking of many men as well.

After the war, despite another revival of conservative family patterns, women kept on entering the workplace in impressive numbers, and the overall number of working women did not decline from the wartime levels; on the contrary, by 1960 the figure was increasing at a rate four times that of men, and by 1975 50 percent of all married women were employed. Moreover, if in the thirties most working women were single and poor, by the seventies the labor force included women of every class, married and single.

The steady increase in women's employment over the last several decades has made for a new kind of marriage and a new marital paradigm that reflects a growing interest in psychology, self-development, and an open attitude toward sex. American wives and husbands have changed in the way they regard each other, and though the relationship between women's work and marital mores is still evolving, the expansion of women's horizons and the inevitable rethinking of the needs of men and women have come to be taken for granted by more and more couples.

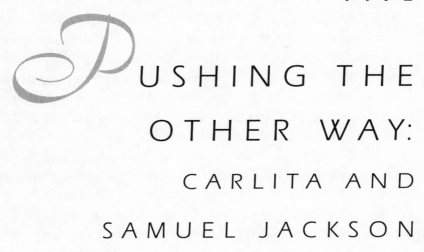

PUSHING THE OTHER WAY:

CARLITA AND

SAMUEL JACKSON

FROM A CERTAIN POINT OF VIEW, IT IS HARDLY SURPRIS-
ing that Carlita Bailey and Samuel Jackson discovered each other
and found reasons to get married. They were born a few months
apart in the late forties in small black communities in the rural
South and later moved north. They came from similar backgrounds: their families were religious Baptists who were strict
about manners and morals; as children they were similarly sheltered from white society; and they had a similar zest for life and
ambitions for themselves. But after childhood their lives followed
remarkably divergent paths. In part because hers was a more
"striving" family, as they say in the South, and in part because of
the times they lived in, Carlita's life progressed like an arrow
from a bow drawn by a brilliant marksman; Samuel's moved
more like one of those wobbly children's balls that are weighted
to keep them from ever rolling in a straight line. The milieus they
moved in at the time of their first encounter were so different, in
fact, that to some of their friends their marriage, in 1983, seemed
to be a triumph of affection over social destiny.

Two weeks after Carlita was born, on a wet, stormy day in late December 1948, her father, George Bailey, died. He was forty-two. The Baileys lived in Sunflower County, Mississippi, where there was a plantation owned by Senator James O. Eastland, the country's arch segregationist, and another that was the workplace and home of Fannie Lou Hamer, who eventually became one of the heroines of the civil-rights movement. Carlita's father, driving home from a Masons' meeting with a friend, skidded into a ditch and, as he was getting out of his car, tripped over a live wire felled by a storm and died. Because this was Mississippi, where violence against blacks occurred all too frequently, his death nearly sparked a race riot. Word of his death first reached his relatives and friends in the form of a rumor that he had been run off the road by a white mob, so they went for their shotguns and vowed to find his killers. But, before anything could happen, Carlita's mother, Rose, learned from her brother-in-law, who had spoken with the other man who was in the car, that it had been an accident, and the posse was told to put its guns away.

Carlita was the tenth child, and eighth daughter, born to the Baileys. Rose was then thirty-nine and her oldest, Mary, was twenty-one. The family was poor but was well respected in the community. George Bailey had taught math at the local black technical high school; and, like almost all his neighbors, he grew cotton on a small plot of land he rented from a white landowner. Rose had met George when she was a student at his school, and they married when she was eighteen and he was twenty-three. She later attended cosmetology school and worked briefly in a beauty salon, then stopped working to concentrate on raising her family. George Bailey quit teaching not long after their marriage, in order to farm full time, and he sometimes rented his services and tractor out to other farmers. Neither Rose nor George had attended college, but they strongly encouraged their children to do so, and urged them to apply for scholarships, and most of them followed their parents' advice and earned undergraduate degrees.

The Bailey children grew up in a small, tightly knit community where a small army of teachers, relatives, family friends, and fellow parishioners constantly inspired them to do well in school. When Carlita was born, Mary was a student at Jackson State, a black college. The rest of the children were in high school or elementary school, and some of the older ones had part-time jobs. At school, the Baileys were known as polite children and hard workers, but the school system for black students in Sunflower County was a poor one. In that era, Mississippi spent less on the education of its black students than any other state. There were few four-year black high schools, and few publicly funded school buildings for blacks (classes were often held in stores, sharecroppers' cabins, or churches), and the school year was sometimes run more for the benefit of the local economy than for the education of the children. In some places, classes began in December, when the cotton picking was over; kept going through March, when the children would be let out for the planting and weeding season, then reconvened in summer for two additional excruciatingly hot months. Years later, Carlita once remarked to her mother that she thought picking might be fun. But Rose, who had grown up picking cotton and pricking her fingers on the thorny stems, assured her that it wasn't. Still, Rose continued to grow a cash cotton crop and vegetables for the family table after her husband's death.

Sunflower was a fairly typical rural Mississippi county. Its population was largely black, but whites ran it. Dirt roads connected its houses and its towns, the water fountains and restrooms were labeled White and Colored, and whites wrote and enforced the laws. Two years after her husband's death, Rose Bailey decided to move to Memphis, Tennessee. Memphis was governed by the same Jim Crow laws that prevailed in Mississippi, but Rose's older sister lived there, and it was the Emerald City compared to Sunflower County. Memphis had long been a magnet for uprooted rural Mississippians. It offered better educational opportunities for children, it had a large black middle-class population (made up partly of the old mulatto elite and partly of a rising group of professionals who served their own community), and it had movies and theaters, shops, and parks, though all of them were as strictly segregated as the schools. The house that Rose moved into with her children was on a street bordered on one side by tidy, middle-income private houses and on the other by a low-income project called Lemoyne Gardens, and Carlita grew up knowing children in the very different social worlds that existed on the two streets. She played with children from both neighborhoods, but almost as early as she learned to talk, she understood that she was expected to avoid the children in either world who were likely to get into trouble.

After the tragic death of her father, which marked her infancy, Carlita's life was notable mainly for calm cohesiveness. In Memphis, she attended a neighborhood black elementary school, where she was an eager and diligent pupil; she spent four after-school afternoons and all day Sunday at the local Baptist church; and she joined the Girl Scouts. After the accident her family, who had always been close-knit, drew even closer together. Like many southern blacks of that era who decided to remain in the South rather than join the mass migration to Chicago or New York, they dug down into their private lives, found affirmation in the church, and buttressed themselves against racial injury by shunning the white world as much as possible. Keeping clear of whites wasn't particularly difficult for Rose and her children, because they rarely ventured outside the triangle of church, school, and home.

Carlita could not remember a time when all her brothers and sisters were living in the house together, but there were usually at least four or five around. The older ones left for college, or married, or worked in other cities and lived on their own. Those who had jobs helped Rose out with money. There had also been a small amount of life-insurance money. (One of the chief functions, if not the chief function, of black fraternal organizations like the Masons and the Elks was to provide life insurance and burial funds for the widows and orphans of members, and even for the poor dependents of deceased nonmembers.) Even so, most years the Baileys' income was below the poverty line. But Carlie, as her family and friends called her, didn't really think of herself as poor. Her mother was a good seamstress, so Carlie had nice clothes; there was always food on the table; and an older sister's husband owned a neighborhood candy store, so the Bailey children were never short of sweets. In Memphis, too, the Baileys were an admired family. One childless couple at church liked Carlita so much and were so taken with her air of quiet determination that they offered to adopt her. More than once, Rose had to tell them that she couldn't spare her. Rose was a strong-willed woman who set high standards of behavior for her children and relied on the teachings of the church for moral backup. She was strict but good humored, and tender toward her children. Even after they grew older, when she prayed for them they felt protected by her prayers.

Rose had pretty much a single standard for her sons and daughters (unlike most white parents of the era). She wanted them to be good Christians, to acquire an education, to be able to earn a decent living, to choose as mates people with similar values, and to feel that they were as good as anyone else, despite any signals to the contrary they might pick up from the white world. And this set of goals was by and large shared by the Baileys' neighbors.

The black middle class that George and Rose Bailey wanted their children to find a foothold in has probably been the least scrutinized group in the United States, largely because until recently it represented such a small slice of the population. That a black middle class developed at all is something of a miracle, or, as the sociologist Bart Landry has put it, "a fluke, an accident running counter to the historical norms and trends of American society, which attempted to restrict all blacks to the unskilled working class." The emergence of a black middle class of any size is traceable largely to the passage of the National Origins Quota Act of 1924, which limited the numbers of immigrants allowed into the country in any year to 150,000 and discriminated against eastern and southern European immigrants. Deprived of a sufficient pool of workers, the owners of northern factories, mills, and stockyards reluctantly began hiring blacks, and the opportunities offered by these new hiring practices were the stimulus for the mass migration to northern industrial cities that began in the second and third decades of the century and lasted until the 1960s. Since most white professionals of that period were unwilling to address the needs of the growing northern black urban communities, a new middle class soon developed, composed of doctors, dentists, undertakers, ministers, teachers, and small businessmen who eagerly seized the opportunity. Ever since that epoch, though, gaining and keeping a place in the American center has continued to be a struggle for most blacks.

When Carlie was born, 40 percent of America's workers were skilled laborers or held white-collar jobs, but only about 10 percent of all employed blacks held jobs that could be considered middle class. The very term "middle class" is defined far more fluidly in black society than outside it. Since no degree of success or attainment has ever truly given many blacks equal status in the white world, they have traditionally been generous in widening the doors of their own middle-class club. This was true even at the beginning of the century, when the number of middle-class blacks was minuscule. *The Bright Side of Memphis* (1908), a book written by C. P. Hamilton, who was a local high-school principal, combines black pride, boosterism, Memphis history, and extravagantly admiring biographical sketches covering every black doctor, lawyer, minister, teacher, bicycle repairer, boilermaker, butcher, candy maker, coffee roaster, cooper, glazier, blacksmith, mailman, janitor, undertaker, plumber, and pressman in town. In fact, the author conveys the impression that anyone fortunate enough to get out from behind a mule was considered eminently deserving of middle-class status. A similar book, written by a local mail carrier, was published privately in 1965. Even at that late date—and in the midst of the strongest protest against civil-rights injustices—the author strikes a determined note of how-our-black-citizens-have-moved-from-success-to-success. Memphis, of course, had a better record than a lot of other cities, and it had Beale Street, which provided black residents with jobs and drew musicians and tourists from all over the country. But Beale Street had fallen on hard times by the time Carlie was growing up, and the city was still strictly segregated.

In the fifties, Memphis blacks still weren't allowed to try on clothes in some of the downtown department stores, could visit the zoo only one day a week, had to drink at separate public water fountains and ride in the back of the bus, and, when they went to a movie at the Malco Theater, had to enter through a side door and sit in the balcony, but these things rarely impinged on Carlie's consciousness because she saw so little of the white world. She ran into direct racism only once, when she was about eleven. While she was downtown shopping one afternoon with a friend, an old woman spoke sharply to the friend for crossing the color line by sitting on a store chair. The girl leaped out of the chair, and Carlie froze with humiliation. Later on, at college in the Midwest and working in New York City, she encountered racism, too, but of a far subtler kind.

SAMUEL Jackson was born into an environment that was even more sheltered than Carlie's. He and two older sisters spent their early years in deep rural South Carolina on a prosperous sixty-acre farm owned by Henry Jackson, their paternal grandfather. Jackson augmented the income from his cotton and corn crops with a thriving crystal-ball-reading business. The reliability of Henry Jackson's predictions was acknowledged throughout the county. People sought him out for advice about crops, livestock, family troubles, and romantic problems. So prized were Jackson's powers that whites, too, sometimes appeared on his doorstep to avail themselves of his services.

In 1948, when Samuel was born, the farm was worked by

Henry Jackson and his two sons, who lived, with their families, in their own small houses on the property; the elder son was Samuel's father. The farm was situated in a hollow that was about a quarter of a mile from the nearest narrow dirt road, which, in turn, was several miles off the local main road. The Jacksons rarely left the farm. On the edge of the property were a cemetery and a small Baptist church, which they attended on Sundays, and five miles away there was a grocery store, which Samuel sometimes walked to, usually with one of his sisters, when the family needed breakfast cereal or white bread. The family raised all the other food they needed, and they ate their meals together around Samuel's grandparents' kitchen table. Except for the occasional advice-seeking farmer, they rarely saw a white face. The adults spent their free time with each other or with relatives who lived nearby, and Samuel and his sisters and four cousins, when they weren't doing chores, roamed around the lush backwoods.

Samuel's mother, Lucy, and his father, James, had met in church, and Lucy's large family lived nearby. James and Lucy had strong ties to their families, but they had for years listened with longing to stories about the opportunities that awaited blacks in New York and Chicago. They never told Samuel exactly what had motivated their decision to move north, but in 1953, when he was five years old, the couple boarded a train to New York, and until they found a place to live they left him and his sisters with their grandparents. That same year, Samuel's grandmother died, and not long afterward his grandfather married a woman with six children of her own who came to live on the farm. Ten months later, Samuel and his sisters left South Carolina to join their parents in New York, but until they were teenagers they returned to the farm every year for summer vacations. Eventually, most of Samuel's uncles, aunts, and cousins followed his parents north (most moved to Chicago or Washington), and after his grandfather died, in the mid-sixties, the land was sold, except for the patch that the church and cemetery stood on. Henry Jackson had stipulated in his will that the church land could never be sold.

If Samuel's father hoped for less drudgery in his work in the North than he'd had on the farm, he was to be disappointed; the only job he could find was that of a dock worker on the New York waterfront, and, after Samuel and his sisters were settled in school, his mother, who had had a great deal of practice at cooking for large numbers of people, was hired as a cook for a restaurant in the Schrafft's chain, on Fifty-second Street. At first, the Jacksons lived in Washington Heights. Then they moved to a larger apartment on 164th Street, and eventually they settled down in a third place a block away from that apartment, not far from Sugar Hill, the home of the most prosperous residents of Harlem. At the time, the neighborhood was racially mixed, and so was the elementary school Samuel attended. Today, it is largely Dominican. Samuel's friends were black, Puerto Rican, and German Jewish. Most of them had two working parents who lived together, and the children rarely got into trouble. Samuel liked school, but he didn't have good study habits and was only an average student. He excelled at sports, though, and he dreamed of becoming a professional baseball player. Both his parents showed him affection, but they didn't talk much, especially about sensitive issues. Samuel learned from his mother at one point, for example, that he'd had an older brother, named William, who died, but neither she nor his father was ever willing to tell him anything further about the brother. Academically, he was on his own. His father had been needed on the farm even when he was a small boy, so he had never attended school and couldn't read or write. His mother had dropped out of school in her teens, and she rarely questioned him about his studies or helped with his homework.

In his early school years, he felt that his teachers, who were mostly white, were free of racial prejudice. As he got older, however, he began to sense that the teachers' attitude toward their black students differed subtly from their attitude toward white students. They didn't seem to push their black pupils as hard as they pushed the white ones, and they also seemed to expect less from them. His first personal encounter with what he felt to be racial prejudice occurred when he was in the fifth grade and had stayed up all night to write a book report. His teacher returned the paper with a poor grade. Calling him aside, she told him that his essay was excellent, even outstanding, but that she was certain he could not have written it himself. Samuel stoutly asserted that the work was all his, but failed to convince her that he hadn't had help.

In 1959, when Samuel was eleven, his parents separated. They hadn't been fighting, and Samuel didn't know that they weren't getting along, but at a certain point, his father just stopped living at home. At first, Samuel was afraid that his father might disappear, but he moved to an apartment only five blocks away, visited the family almost daily, and continued to provide for them as he always had. Two years later, however, when Samuel was thirteen, his father died. There was some Social Security insurance money, because his parents had never actually divorced, but the next years were lean ones.

BY the time Carlita met Samuel, in 1980, she was thirty-two. She had been through college, had earned an M.B.A. at Columbia, and had already held several good financial-management jobs at blue-chip corporations. Like many black women who came of age in the post-civil-rights-laws 1960s, Carlie had found the business world hospitable to her, though her upward progress always stalled at the middle-management level. She had done well in college and emerged with a strong sense of her own abilities, and, after overcoming an initial aversion to the North in general and city life in particular, she had become an enthusiastic New Yorker. She was working at that point for a thriving, internationally known cosmetics company, she had a wide circle of friends, and she spent many hours each week as a volunteer youth leader for teenage girls in a Harlem church. She had been hard hit when her mother died, in 1976, from a cerebral hemorrhage, but her family, though they were by then scattered around the country, and her friends had given her a lot of support. She was particularly close to two of her old graduate-school classmates, Patricia Walcott and Gwen Lewis, and was sharing an apartment in the West Seventies with them. They liked going to the theater together and trying out new restaurants, and recently the three of them had taken up tennis.

Carlie had had a number of suitors, but, except for one early boyfriend, they hadn't captured her heart. The pool of educated black men she came in contact with seemed to be radically shrinking every year, and, at some point, she had decided that she was going to concentrate on aims other than finding a husband. By the time she turned thirty, in fact, she had no serious expectation of ever marrying, and her initial encounter with Samuel Jackson did nothing to alter that expectation, when they met on a public tennis court at Crotona Park, in the Bronx.

Carlie and some of her friends belonged to a sort of peripatetic tennis club; it had no real clubhouse, but the members gathered regularly at the Crotona Park courts. Samuel, an exceptionally good player, often played with the pro who gave the three roommates lessons, and he frequently turned up at the courts at the same time they did. When someone introduced Carlie and Samuel, she thought he was likable, but a bit rough around the edges. He was usually dressed in a grubby T-shirt and old shorts; his speech bore unmistakable signs of his rural roots (he used *d*'s for *th*'s, and his grammar was by no means perfect); and he was a lot less polished than most of her friends. Months passed before Carlie discovered the intelligent, good-humored inner man concealed by the rural accent and unprepossessing clothes.

Just one generation ago, the proportion of black women who married was higher than the proportion of white women who did. Although, according to most surveys, few women, black or white, choose to remain single all their lives, demographers have recently estimated that 25 percent of black women will never marry. According to the 1990 census, black women outnumber black men by a million and a half, and, as everyone who reads a newspaper must know, the pool of eligible potential husbands is diminished every year by drugs, incarceration, chronic unemployment, and crime-related death. Educated black women are more likely to marry than poor ones, but as the college enrollment of black men has declined in the last decades so has the number of suitable partners. All in all, these changes have created for blacks formidable challenges to the institution of marriage.

SAMUEL was well liked by nearly everyone who knew him and had been in most ways a happy boy, but his passage to adulthood had been marked by far more frustration and self-doubt than Carlie's. Despite the civil-rights breakthroughs of the 1960s, he had not found the academic or corporate worlds particularly eager to help or advance him, and, unlike Carlie, he had no one at home nudging him toward college or urging him to think in any kind of focused way about his future.

At some point in his junior year in high school, his boyhood dream of becoming a professional athlete began to seem unrealistic. At about the same time, he developed an ambition to be a psychiatrist. He got along well with people; he liked to think about what made them tick; and he'd heard that psychiatrists made a good living. He wasn't sure he knew exactly what psychiatrists did, and he had no idea of how to go about becoming one, but he assumed that a liberal-arts college degree was essential, so he approached his school guidance counselor, a middle-aged white woman, to inquire about colleges that he might attend. An awkward conversation ensued; they seemed to be talking at cross-purposes until Samuel realized that his adviser had rejected out of hand the possibility of his becoming any kind of professional and was intent on throwing cold water on his plan to attend a liberal-arts college, urging him instead to consider a more "realistic" option, such as a technical or two-year college.

Samuel left school that day feeling depressed, but by the time he arrived at his front stoop he had decided to go ahead and apply to a few colleges just to try his luck. When he told his mother about his meeting with his adviser that evening at dinner, however, she sided with the teacher. The teacher probably knew best, she said. He sent away for college catalogues anyway. But when they began filling the mailbox he saw that he had no way of figuring out whether he had a prayer of being admitted to any of the idyllic-sounding, expensive institutions they described. Still confident that he was a strong enough athlete to do well in college sports, he decided to try for scholarships at schools that had football teams. He hoped that Syracuse University or the University of Illinois might take him and bravely telephoned Syracuse's then well known football coach, Ben Schwartzwalder, to discuss his chances with him. It was not a fruitless call; the coach was kind to him. But Samuel got scared off when Schwartzwalder asked him to mail him a game film (he had none) and, afterward, by the complexities of the application process. The paperwork daunted him so much, in fact, that he ended up abandoning the idea of college altogether.

After his high-school graduation in 1966, he worked for a year in the mailroom of a television station and then tried to combine study at a local community college with part-time work at the station. He found it hard to concentrate, though, and didn't connect much with his courses, so in 1970 he left school and began working full time as a postal clerk. Over the next decade, he tried his hand at quite a number of jobs, including narcotics counseling, and picked up enough college credits to get a two-year degree at Bronx Community College. He still hoped that he could one day acquire a B.A. In 1978, he began working for the state police, first as a guard in a state prison—a job he loathed—and later as a night security guard in a state mental institution. That was the job he held when he met Carlie, and still holds.

WHEN Carlie entered a small midwestern liberal-arts college, she planned to major in science. She was seriously considering becoming a doctor and had been encouraged by the teachers at the all-black high school she attended to think that she might make a good one. But after a few months at college, she found that she wasn't doing particularly well in her science courses, so she decided to switch her major to economics. After that, she did quite well.

Despite her academic success, however, Carlie was not happy. She missed her high-school boyfriend, who was a student at Yale, and she felt lonely. There were fourteen thousand students at the college, but only seven of them were black. She was there because the school had offered her a bigger scholarship than any of the other schools she had applied to; she had really wanted to go to Spelman, an all-black, all-female college in Atlanta, but Spelman hadn't been able to offer her enough money. The students at her college were conservative and were utterly uninterested in the civil-rights movement that was attracting so many students, white and black, at more liberal colleges around the country. Venturing beyond the college gates one day, she found that the college was surrounded by an all-black neighborhood, and after that she attended church across the street from the campus every Sunday. But in the neighborhoods that stretched out beyond the college environs there were no blacks, except for the little painted jockeys that dotted a good number of the lawns. The college had no black professors or administrators, no black speakers, and no black sororities or fraternities.

Carlie did not consider herself particularly political. Her mother belonged to the Memphis chapter of the NAACP, but Carlie had never succeeded in finding out from her exactly what happened at its meetings. Now, however, Carlie began growing an Afro; she signed a petition asking for a black faculty member (it was ignored, but a lower-management black administrator was hired the year she graduated); and she joined the six other black students in a sit-in organized to put pressure on the college to meet their demands.

When she became an economics major, Carlie gained a strong booster at the college—her accounting professor. She was glad to have a professor rooting for her, but his interest in her proved less than helpful on a weekend when she decided to visit her boyfriend in New Haven. To stretch her time in New Haven out a bit, Carlie had told the authorities that her maternal grandmother had died and that she would be cutting a few classes to attend the funeral. All of Carlie's grandparents had in fact died long before Carlie was born. As ill luck would have it, among those who happened to hear the news was her friendly accounting professor, and he telephoned her mother at once to offer his condolences. The call set in motion an elaborate operettalike series of events involving Carlie's mother and the boyfriend's grandmother. Carlie was routed from her boyfriend's room, many recriminations flew across the Mason-Dixon line, and the weekend ended earlier than had been planned.

Carlie was then twenty years old, and that was the first time she had become sexually involved with anyone. She hadn't liked getting caught, but she didn't regret the weekend, either, except that she dreaded offending her mother. She considered her sex life her own business. She thought of herself as a good Christian and accepted most of the tenets of the Baptist Church, but, as a modern woman, she took a dim view of its sexual prohibitions.

Just before Carlie left for college, a teenager who was about three years younger than Carlie and was active in her church had become pregnant. The girl decided to keep the baby. Few girls Carlie knew who got into trouble had abortions; the babies were simply folded into the girls' families. Instead of offering the girl support, however, the minister of their church forced her to stand in front of the entire congregation and apologize—an act that enraged Carlie to the point where she angrily confronted the minister after the service. When he lamely explained that the congregants had pressured him into doing what he did, she mentally wrote him off as a hypocrite.

A FEW months after Samuel and Carlie met, he won the club's tennis tournament, and not long afterward he began giving Carlie lessons. In time, they began dating, and in the summer of 1983 they married. It was a small church wedding attended mostly by their friends and those few members of Samuel's family who lived in New York. By the end of 1990, when I met them, they had two children, a boy, Derek, who was born in 1985, and a girl, Corinne, born in 1987. The Jacksons were the busiest people I knew. Samuel was holding down two jobs, and Carlie, who had by then left the corporate world to work (at a substantial pay cut) for a large, community-minded, activist Harlem church she had done volunteer work for since she had come to New York, was attempting a kind of high-wire act in trying to balance the demands of her job and her children.

The Jacksons live in a solidly built prewar co-op apartment house on Amsterdam Avenue on the Upper West Side. The building has a doorman, but the hallways have seen better days. When Carlie first met Samuel, she was still sharing an apartment farther downtown with Patricia and Gwen. She moved into her present apartment about a year after she started going out with Samuel, and he moved in with her not long afterward. He had been living uptown, not far from where he had lived with his family. But his roommate's brother had a serious drug problem and was stealing things and generally making life around the apartment unbearable. Carlie refused to visit Samuel there and wasn't all that happy about his living in that situation, so their two households merged somewhat by default.

Samuel was away at his night security guard job when I first visited the Jacksons' apartment—a cheerful, sparsely furnished, toy-littered, two-bedroom place—on a weekday evening in the winter of 1990. Carlie was (as I would discover she usually is) doing three or four things at once: keeping an eye on her son and daughter, then five and three; mending a pair of shorts; and taking late-night work calls. Derek is plump and sweet natured, and Corinne is a mischievous live wire. They are unusually open, friendly children and accepted my presence as a sort of mysterious form of entertainment. A tape I made that evening is about 70 percent giggles and inquiries about the recorder and 30 percent grown-up conversation.

Carlie has a high forehead, large, inquisitive eyes, framed by oversized glasses, and a pale, freckled, copper-colored complexion. She laughs easily and speaks slowly, in a voice that sounds like cream poured on honey. The turn her life took when she met Samuel still surprises her. "At that point, the male-female relationships were not great," she said. The only person I ever thought I was definitely going to marry was my Yale boyfriend, and he called me up shortly after I arrived at graduate school to tell me he was seeing somebody else. Yale had just started admitting women and she was one of them. It floored me. But I had a lot of hard work to do in school. I had exams, I had papers, and I just decided to throw myself into all that. It took me a long time to get over him, but I was lucky—I had great friends at school. I had three serious boyfriends over the next ten years but, by the time I met Samuel I had pretty well settled into single life."

At first, Carlie said, their courtship was fairly one sided. "I really didn't get to know Samuel at all until he began giving me tennis lessons. Before that, I had run into him on and off for about six months, and things were—you know—friendly. But he asked me out once, and I said no. I think I made up some excuse." Carlie interrupted herself several times as she talked to clean up a mess Corinne had made by emptying two full bottles of dressing over a salad Carlie had made for her and to prevent Derek from using a sharp knife to open a ketchup bottle. She dealt with these matters good humoredly, but there was a note of steel in her voice that both children quickly responded to.

"What changed your mind about Samuel?" I asked.

"Well, he just sort of coaxed me into dating him, but after a while I basically began to find out that he was a fine man. At first, though I really shouldn't admit it, the way he looked made me think there would be too many gaps between us. But, getting to know him, I saw how smart he was, and that he was a person of depth. It took me about four months to see that this was something serious and I was falling in love—but—you know—it's kind of hard to define those feelings. It wasn't a whole lot of heart pounding. It was more like 'I think he's wonderful.' We were both in our thirties. He had a life. I had a life. At some point, we decided to live together, but the idea was that I wouldn't interfere with things that he enjoyed, like all his sports and coaching activities, and he wouldn't interfere with the things I enjoyed, like my working for organizations that supported black professionals, which took me away from home a lot, and the youth groups I've always run that meant a lot to me. I was surprised to find myself in love. I was sure I wouldn't marry. But we got along so well that when the subject of marriage came up I felt that it was the right thing to do. Samuel brought it up. He didn't like just living together. He said, 'I'm too old for this.' I didn't exactly rush right into it, but it seemed like a good idea. I'd say my attitude was 'What the heck!'"

At one point, Carlie mentioned that they didn't have a regular baby-sitter. As she straightened a Miss Piggy nose on Corinne's face, I asked her how she managed the job, the kids, and her various other commitments.

"I don't manage," she said, laughing. It was a kind of low-pitched laugh that seemed to draw her whole being along with it. As I soon learned, you get to hear Carlie's laugh at least once in every five minutes of conversation, and you get to look forward to it. "I began working full time at the church in 1989, but for quite a few years before that I was involved with a teen-pregnancy prevention program there. We didn't call it that. We called it a youth group, because if you're with a church organization it kind of turns young people off if you sound too preachy. I also became involved with a group called Elakiko—that's an African term that means women's initiations. It's basically a big sister–little sister group. I'm still leading that on the first and third Saturday mornings of every month. During the week, my mother-in-law takes the kids after school—I leave work, pick them up at school in the car, drop them off at her apartment in the Bronx, then go back to Harlem to work, and pick them up again after work. On Wednesday evenings, I have choir rehearsal. Ours is a very active choir, and we sometimes travel. We used to do a lot more of that than we do now. We sang with Zubin Mehta for five or six years, and we still have a lot of standing engagements. I have pretty much stopped all the things like meetings with the Council of Concerned Black Executives—that sort of thing—but there are still a lot of extra meetings related to my work that I have to go to. Samuel's great about helping, but, since he works two jobs, he just can't be around to help with the kids a lot of the time."

I asked Carlie how they had worked out their responsibilities at home. "Before we got married, we sat down and talked about how we were going to handle things, and we agreed that everything would be fifty-fifty, even down to cooking. He had certain days, and I had certain days, and certain days we ate out. Saturdays were sort of junk-food days. But that arrangement didn't last long. I used to love eating out in nice restaurants, and I still do. We did quite a bit of that. But Samuel wasn't used to it. Once we went to brunch and I ordered bacon and eggs and hash browns—a big breakfast—and he said, 'I just don't understand why you go out and order bacon and eggs when you could be eating the same thing at home.' Anyway, when the kids came along I was working, but the job I had at the time, working as the financial person for a company that provided home care for the elderly, was the kind of thing that I could mostly do at home. So, since I was here all the time and Samuel was always off at his jobs, I tended to do a little more, and gradually our arrangement became more traditional. But we're always talking about the way things are going. Samuel is a great one for sitting down and talking. I'm more of a brooder. But he's always saying, 'We need to talk.' He loves to get things out in the open."

One of the things that the Jacksons got out in the open early was the likelihood of problems arising because of the difference in their job status. So much has been made of the ego deflation of black men supposedly caused by what has sometimes been referred to as the black matriarchy that black men and women alike have become painfully aware of a whole range of potential misunderstandings, resentments, and fears that await the black couple of unequal professional status. Since 85 percent of all American black college students are women, according to recent estimates, this has become a far from uncommon problem. Until Samuel took a second job, in 1985, Carlie regularly brought home about twice as much money as he did. Today, they each earn approximately the same amount—just under $50,000 a year.

"Samuel's best friend actually told him that the marriage wouldn't work because I made more money than he did, and things like that. But he's been proved wrong. I never even thought about it."

IN the fall of 1991, Samuel's mother died after suffering a heart attack; she was sixty-three years old and had been ill for some months. At about the same time, Samuel left his daytime guard job to work at their church as its after-school-program director and to supervise the launching of a vastly expanded athletic program. For several years, he had been volunteering his services, coordinating many of the church's after-school athletic programs—the basketball, football, and double-dutch programs were particularly popular—so when the church was given enough money to expand its recreation program, they offered the job to him. Samuel, like Carlie, puts in many hours every week working without pay—in his case, with teens and preteens. Every Saturday during the football season, right after he leaves his night job, Samuel heads for a playing field at 138th Street and Third Avenue in Manhattan. Usually, he arrives about 8:00 A.M. and, until sundown, supervises the players in a football league he organized in 1986.

I met Samuel for the first time at the apartment on a non-football-season Saturday afternoon when Carlie and the children were at the movies. Then, and at all our subsequent meetings, Samuel seemed a little uncomfortable around me, but he was never less than polite and manfully tried to work up some enthusiasm for our conversations. From his point of view, the structure of his marriage and of the rest of his life were so tightly interwoven that they were nearly impossible to talk about as discrete subjects—especially, perhaps, to a white stranger. Among the first things he told me was that he rarely got more than four hours' sleep a night but that those few hours seemed to suffice. A dignified, slightly portly man with round features, dark skin, and an athletic gait, Samuel radiates a kind of grave sweetness and an almost Roman solidity. He told me that the rhythms of his childhood, like Carlie's, had been greatly influenced by the rules and demands of an old-fashioned Baptist upbringing.

"After I came to New York, I was at my Aunt Ruby's every Sunday. She's my mother's sister. During the week, she had a job cleaning house—she had that until she was seventy—and every weekend my two sisters and I went out to Rockaway to stay with her. My brother, Roger— He's not really my brother, he's my oldest sister's boy, but she wasn't married when she had him. She was only twenty, and my mom raised him, so I call him my brother. He went out to Ruby's, too, later on. Ruby came and picked us up after school on Fridays, and we were on the train by four. She cooked us wonderful food and often bought us clothes—she never had any kids of her own—and she would take us to the beach and that kind of thing. It was sort of like we had two mothers. Sunday mornings, we went to Sunday school and then to church. One or two o'clock, we'd be back on the train, and my mother would be there at the train station waiting to pick us up. Summers, we'd go back to the South. I did that until I was about fourteen, and then I decided I might miss something if I left the city, so I stopped going, and not long after they sold all that land."

When he was growing up, Samuel went on to say, the system his parents devised for keeping the kids out of trouble after school was simple: you had to stay home until someone arrived home from work. In the warm weather, when the days were long, the kids went out to play after dinner. In the winter months, they went home after school and stayed there. "Minding" and "behaving" and "discipline" were the key words of Samuel's upbringing, and, to a large extent, they are the ones he uses to characterize his own children's upbringing (which includes spankings as threat and punishment), although Derek and Corinne are clearly given a lot more rope than he was. "We weren't angels," Samuel said. "We'd make snowballs and throw them at the bus; we'd call Chicken Delight and place a phony order and that kind of thing. But the kids who were into trouble—we didn't socialize with them, we stayed away from them. And trouble in those days was *nothing* like it is now. Trouble was smoking an occasional reefer or drinking a glass of wine, or stealing some fruit from the grocery store. Actually, some friends of mine and I did chip in and smoke a joint together once, but there were so many of us sharing it that we didn't feel a thing."

When Samuel got older, a number of the neighborhood bloods joined gangs—the Young Lords and the Savage Skulls were two that boys he knew gravitated toward—but he had no interest in them; baseball, football, and basketball occupied his thoughts and all his free time, and in between seasons he played stickball. Like Carlie, he dreaded causing his family any trouble. His father's labors on the docks and his mother's job in the restaurant kitchen took a lot out of them; they both came home bone tired, and, early on, Samuel came to feel that he shouldn't do anything that might add to their burdens. His parents obviously felt the same way. There was a lot of hugging around the Jackson household, but there were stiff spankings and sometimes strappings with his father's belt when he or either of his sisters got out of line. Carlie can remember her mother spanking her older brothers, even when they were teenagers, and both she and Samuel accept this physical form of punishment as fair, and they feel justified in meting it out to their children when they think it necessary.

Initially, the Jacksons' old-fashioned child-raising views bothered me. Their strictness seemed so out of synch with the times, so hidebound. I sometimes wished, too, that they would be willing to discuss with me some of the more difficult struggles of their marriage that they, like any couple, have had to grapple with. But in time I came to understand that their insistence on a rigorously defined code of behavior was inseparable from their sense of vulnerability and pride—a way of shoring things up in an often disappointing and unreliable world.

The persistence of black families in sticking together during the nineteenth century despite every obstacle put before them by the slave culture has been well established by the historian Herbert Gutman. But in modern times, when the survival of the black family is indeed in question, keeping to the straight and narrow—following a well-marked path of propriety, respectability, and faith—may still look to many blacks like the only lifeline to a sane existence. The price paid for a way of life in which rules and discipline override personal choice is, of course, often a certain degree of old-fashioned distance between parent and child. Carlie adored her mother but could not discuss sticky personal matters with her; when she needed to talk about her problems, she sought counsel from her oldest sister. Samuel know that his father and mother loved him, and recalls with pleasure scenes like those in a family album, scenes of emotional warmth—picnics in Central Park and crowded annual Thanksgiving and Christmas dinners—but he wouldn't have dreamed of taking any of his anxieties to either of his parents. "Those types of things we did not discuss in the house," he said.

"I think I just matured earlier than most people," he went on by way of explaining some of his early feelings of isolation. "When everyone was listening to loud rock, I would listen to jazz and classical music. When I found out that my father had passed away, I never cried. I had gotten out of school and I was on my way home and everybody in the neighborhood was looking at me. I couldn't understand why they were staring, but it was because they knew. Everybody always knew everything that was going on. That's another reason why it was hard to do anything wrong. There would be our neighbor—Mr. Rodriguez, or whoever—and he knew you, he knew your parents, someone was always at the window, watching. Anyway, when I got home, I found out, but nobody ever did tell me why he died. He was only forty-two. Later on, I heard that it might have had something to do with his liver. He might have been ill for a while, but I didn't know it. He didn't miss any work. The strange thing was I *never* cried. I didn't cry at his funeral, or ever. All my father's friends and my friends, and my best friend's father asked me why I didn't cry. I mean, I was only thirteen. Everyone thought that was kind of strange, and they thought my not knowing why he died was strange."

Samuel's family lost a lot, he believes, when they left their rural way of life in the South and became dispersed in various northern cities, and he is pretty sure that they lost out financially, too, when they sold their land for not very much money. He has the impression that his parents weren't really prepared for city life.

Unpreparedness is a big subject in general for Samuel. The vast majority of black men, he says, have so few guideposts in terms of professional goals that they usually don't figure out what they should be doing with their lives until they're quite mature, and by then it's too late. The hippie phenomenon fascinated him. He was amazed that young white kids could check out of the system, then casually check back in three or four years later, getting a little help from their parents (as he sees it), or their parents' friends, to proceed full speed ahead with conventional middle-class lives. Black kids, he says, could never behave like that.

Carlie characterizes her husband as "a determined man" who wants badly to succeed. More than once, he told me that he planned to be a millionaire by the time he reached fifty. He would like to open a vast sports complex in Harlem someday that would be a combination of recreation hall, sports center, and counseling resource—a place where he and others could help kids to understand "the system" and receive the kind of encouragement they need to "get through it." But he has also been thinking about a less ambitious project, which he actually hopes to realize in the next few years: a van service for black tourists who come to New York City.

"There's a market for it," he said. "You come into the city with a bunch of people and you try to rent a van and you can't get one. I was thinking of getting a van—maybe several, eventually—and using it for a tour service. A lot of people can't drive; and a lot of people want to go places and just not bother with driving. So I came up with this idea. You'd take people on shopping tours, maybe out of the city, in the city—whatever. I figure I would make two trips a day, and it would run seven days a week. I could get the van now, but the question is: Is it the right move to make now? The question is when to jump into the water: We're a little overextended now. We own a car, we're struggling to pay back our plastic debts and keep up with the mortgage payments and paying the kids' school bills—they both attend private church schools—so there's a lot going out now." As soon as they got their heads above water on their bills, Samuel said, he was going to try to start this business or another.

"You *have* to be in business for yourself," he said. "You have to be prepared for the opportunity when it comes along. I'm *always* alert for any opportunity. Carlie can never believe how many job interviews I go to. I go to all kinds of interviews just to see what the job is going to be like. I'm basically always job hunting. I never stop looking."

Samuel is an enthusiastic reader of books about how America is run, of business-success-story books, and of self-help books written for black readers. Among the books that have made a strong impression on him are *The Power Elite* (1916), by C. Wright Mills; *The Miseducation of the Negro* (1933), by Carter C. Woodson; *Black Capitalism: Strategy for Business in the Ghetto* (1969), by Theodore L. Cross; *Think and Grow Rich* (1972), by Napoleon Hill; and *Power: How to Get It and How to Use It* (1975), by Michael Korda. One book of this genre whose title and author he had forgotten divided the lives of black men into twenty-year segments and advised them not to lose hope if they arrived at middle age, as Samuel has, and had not yet achieved what they would like to.

"I don't know if a white person can understand this, but we make so many mistakes," he said. "I mean, what with drugs and school screwups and crime deaths and war deaths, I'd estimate that only about a quarter of the kids I grew up with are even alive now. And those who do survive have it really tough. The average black man doesn't even begin to *start* to achieve success, they say, until he's at least thirty-five. It's because they've usually made so many mistakes in terms of getting an education, and doing different jobs, and not understanding the structure of the system. They often haven't gotten the right advice, or had anyone to point them in the right direction and say, 'Hey, when you get to such-and-such a point, this is what you do.' If your parents are not middle class, they can't do those things, and basically by the time a black man begins to sort all this out he's been on a job for a long period of time, and it's too late to start all over."

I asked Samuel if he was worried that that would happen to him.

"No," he said, a little too quickly. "Of course, it's true that I've often thought about going back to school. But I don't think that's realistic now. My first concern is my family—providing Corinne and Derek with a good environment and giving them the best education they can have—so I can't really start all over. I can't afford to make a real mistake or a big wrong move. It would be too costly. We thought of this apartment as future security—for the kids, eventually. But the maintenance is high, real high, and then I'm always laying out more of my own money than I should for uniforms and all kinds of things—trophies, banquets—for the league. It adds up, and I don't always get it back. And Carlie is impetuous; she is not a good planner. Even though she does what she does for a living, she tends not to apply what she learned in school to our own finances."

While we were talking, Carlie and the children came back from the movies, and shortly afterward, Samuel's twenty-six-year-old "brother," Roger, showed up with his eight-year-old daughter, Charlayne, to drop her off. Charlayne was going to be staying with them for a while, Carlie said, because her mother was having "mental problems," and at the moment, was staying in a hospital. Samuel greeted Carlie with a kiss and a pat on the shoulder, hugged Derek and Corinne, approved of Derek's new haircut, and laughed obligingly when Corinne rushed out of the room, then rushed back wearing her Miss Piggy nose.

Carlie, Corinne, and Charlayne went to the bedroom to change. They were going to the park. Derek, who was ready to leave, lingered for a minute in the hall and then came back into the living room and climbed into his father's lap.

"How're you doin', partner? You ready for the park?" Samuel asked him.

Derek nodded shyly, then pulled his father's sleeve to activate Samuel's own park-readiness mechanism, and everybody headed for the door.

ON a warm day not long afterward, I attended a special Sunday musical service at the Jacksons' church, at which, in addition to the resident choir, a number of visiting groups from around the city were performing. The neighborhood around the church bears all the marks of entrenched Harlem poverty—long stretches of boarded-up, abandoned buildings, littered streets, too many people at loose ends, too few signs of human well-being. The church itself is a vast, dark Gothic structure built in the early 1920s that has been well maintained by a large, predominantly middle-class congregation, most of whom now live in distant neighborhoods. The church's ministers have traditionally been politically active, and under the direction of its current minister, it has become deeply involved during the last decade in scores of projects designed to improve the life of neighborhood residents— providing low- and middle-income housing, providing health information and referral services, and helping people with educational and job programs. Finding the money to finance these enterprises is a major part of Carlie's job.

Carlie was already inside and lined up with the choir when I arrived at the church, but Samuel, dressed in a dark blue suit and a crisp white shirt, was waiting outside to escort me in. The children had been at church earlier, he said, but were staying with his sister in the Bronx for the afternoon.

The pews were filled to capacity, mostly by women past their youth—some fashionably outfitted, many more swathed in rather old-fashioned light-colored and intricately draped dresses and elaborate hats. Quite a few of the women were fanning themselves with small paper fans. A fair number of dignified older men in dark suits filled the interstices of this pastel tapestry, and, here and there, a few younger men and women were visible. From the outset, the program rolled along with fluidity and grace. When the Church Sanctuary Choir opened up the program with a tremulous version of "Didn't It Rain," a good number of the congregants stood up and began waving at the singers and shouting exclamations of approval. Carlita, her mouth open in a wide O, her head tilted slightly, was in the second row of a four-tier group of maroon-robed choristers surrounded by banks of flowers. She looked happy. The hymn singing of various city church choirs alternated with presentations of service awards and some speeches, and great bursts of applause greeted the announcement of almost every name. As the glossy white-and-purple program revealed, Carlie and many other church members had put in many hours to make the event a success.

By about the midpoint of the program, the congregants were rising to their feet so regularly that the line between performers and audience became very fine indeed. After the last choir sang its last note and the minister gave his benediction, the musical feast was followed by a real one in the basement. The people the Jacksons know at church aren't intimate friends, but there is a warm connection between them. Carrying plates of fried chicken, salad, and hot rolls, Carlie and Samuel wandered around greeting people and chatting and, in Carlie's case, tying up loose ends of church business. Usually, the children attend Sunday school before the service begins, and the whole family eats lunch at the church afterward. More often than not, there are church functions or meetings scheduled for Sunday afternoons, so, what with one thing and another, the Jacksons often don't get home until early evening, and laundry, shopping, mending, and the hundred-odd details of everyday life that have been left for Sunday tend to get done on the fly or just pile up.

But if in the organizing principles of their marriage the Jacksons seem firmly wedded to tradition, closer examination of the actual texture of their lives reveals definite signs of modern adjustments. Even if you did not know that Carlie frequently introduced herself as Carlita Bailey-Jackson (she tried using it at the church, but the women there never assimilated the Bailey part) or that Samuel did most of the food shopping because they both consider him better at it, you would probably notice various fundamental updates in the marital script that had been familiar to the Jacksons from childhood.

In Samuel's family, all domestic chores were shouldered by women. Neither he nor his father nor any of his uncles or male cousins ever washed a dish, made a bed, or picked up a sock. Nowadays, even though Carlie's share of the domestic chores and the child rearing has ballooned considerably from the long-ago-agreed-upon fifty-fifty, Samuel washes dishes, straightens up, and generally tries to help ease Carlie's burden wherever he can.

One afternoon over lunch after a particularly difficult week, Carlie said that Samuel's basic sense of fairness was what made their present crazy life endurable. "He knows what's got to get done, and if he sees I can't handle it he'll step in and help. Of course, he hasn't got all that much free time, because of the two jobs. But he makes sure that he spends some time with the children every day after work, and he'll always try to take them to the park on the weekends. Whenever Samuel thinks there's any kind of problem, he makes sure we talk about it. He is far more adamant about good communication than I am—and I think that is kind of rare."

After Samuel's mother died, the Jacksons no longer had anyone to leave the children with after school, and Carlie didn't like the idea of leaving them with anyone who wasn't a relative. Unfortunately, the children's after-school programs now ended at different times. Carlie thus had to leave work in the late afternoon to pick up Corinne at one school, then return to work, then leave again a few hours later (with Corinne in tow) to pick up Derek at his school; after that she returned to work again, and continued working while the children played in the church nursery. Carlie accepted a substantial salary cut when she left the corporate world to take her present job, but she has no regrets about the move. In fact, she sees it as predestined.

"You know, you try to decide what your purpose is in life, and I think that I was supposed to be where I am now," she remarked as we were served our coffee at the restaurant. "In a way, marriage helped me focus on what the priorities were in my life. I believe that all the things that happened to me have led to my being here. I know I can contribute a whole lot where I am. That will be my reward—just seeing some of the things I'm involved in come to fruition. We are really trying to do whatever we can to revitalize the community. You feel that so many things in society are pushing things in a bad way, and you are pushing the other way. Doing that, you feel you're really doing something for people. Working for a corporation, you're getting a salary and it's benefiting you, but what's your contribution to the world? The trouble with a job like mine, though, is you always feel that there's more to do. And there is! So the hours keep expanding and expanding. Our minister is great. I'm absolutely autonomous in my job, and I don't mind at all not having to deal with the subtle race problems that were part of everyday life in the white corporate world, but, heck, I wish there were more time."

With a notable lack of rancor, Carlie began to elaborate on some of the pressures of her life. "Corinne is a night owl, and I usually have to go to sleep with her to get her to go to sleep. I get into bed with her at around ten, intending to get up as soon as she falls asleep, but often I end up waking up at one and I still have work to do. For a while, I was working until three and then getting up at six. Sometimes I think it's not possible to do what I'm doing. Especially the cooking. The time just came when Samuel couldn't be there to get dinner ready, so I did it, even though I am *not* a good cook. And things keep going along that way. Certain things he still does, though he hasn't done them in a while. He cooks very good fish, and sometimes he'll cook breakfast on the weekend. But we always eat together. That's important to both of us. When I lived with Gwen and Patricia, we three always had our meals together. They were from strong Southern families, like mine. That's the way we were brought up, so I just kind of carried that habit forward into my own living arrangements."

I asked Carlie if they ever had any ordinary free time to spend together. She told me that, though they hadn't been to a movie together in two years, they tried hard to do as much as they could together. "Recently, Samuel has been taking the kids to tennis at a park uptown that they call the Jungle," she said. "But we're both exhausted all the time. I wish Samuel could work a little less, but I know that right now, since we have so many bills, he can't. I understand that. Maybe in the next couple of years he can ease up a little. I'm lucky, actually, to have the kind of job I have, because, for now, it's like 'Have Kids, Will Travel.' They're almost always with me when they're not in school, even though I'm busy. I just fill a backpack with Legos and coloring stuff and park them in the church nursery room, and they do pretty well. I don't know what I'd do if I couldn't do that."

When Carlie and Samuel first met, in the early eighties, Samuel understood quite well that Carlie had misgivings about him. But he was attracted to her from the start. He liked the way she carried herself, he liked the southern cadences of her voice, and he loved her long, tapering fingers. Samuel is a hands man. "I look at a woman's hands right away, and hers were nice, real nice," he told me. He had already lived with several women (one of whom was white) for various lengths of time, but, for one reason or another, things had not worked out—mainly, he thought, because there had been a real clash of values. He felt confident as he watched Carlie standing around with her friends that the two of them were basically cut from the same cloth. He was sure that they would get along well if only he could get through what he thought of as her "bougie-bougie" prejudices.

But overcoming her resistance had not been easy. One afternoon in his office at the church, Samuel recalled the early days of their courtship in the manner of an old soldier who has waged a successful campaign in a particularly difficult theater of war.

"For a long time, I got nowhere at all, mainly because I could never get near her," he said. "She and Gwen and Patricia would get to the tennis court at eight or nine in the morning, play, and then leave for brunch, then they'd shoot over to the beauty parlor. They did that *all* the time. It was crazy. I mean, every Saturday. They'd play for two hours, rarely spend any time socializing, then—boom—down to Sylvia's or somewhere else for brunch. I think they ate at every restaurant in the city. I don't believe they missed one."

"Did you try to talk to her?" I asked.

"I had no chance to. They'd come right in and shoot right out. I never had a chance to say *anything*. It was all so rigid. I mean, this was the *weekend*. Brunch, hair, nails, then out to a play, and back to work on Monday morning. Even when she finally agreed to go out with me, it was, 'Well, call me before you come.'" Samuel folded his hands across his stomach and shot me a look of sly pleasure. "I didn't. That's what you say when you want to get out of something. So I just showed up at her apartment that night."

Samuel had got it right about Carlie's intentions for that evening. She planned to call it off. When Samuel arrived at her apartment, he found Gwen there, but Carlie was still at the office. Although she shared Carlie's reservations about Samuel, Gwen was embarrassed and telephoned Carlie, insisting that she come home.

"We kind of circled around each other for the rest of the evening, you know. We just sat around and talked, and that was that," Samuel went on to say. "But the next time we met I took her to an uptown restaurant I like called Flash Inn, and things clicked right away. We were holding hands before the evening was over. That group of friends of hers—there are about twenty of them, and they're my friends now, too—you won't find a nicer bunch. About half of them Carlie met at Columbia. Only two of them are married, though. As a group, they have big male-female problems. They're like a family to us: we celebrate Thanksgiving, Christmas, and Easter together, and we get together for rap sessions whenever we can. I *know* the women are ruling out guys they might well get together with—for superficial reasons. I say to them, 'Try to look beyond the surface. Give these guys a chance.' I mean, Carlita was surprised that I'd taken modern dance in high school and college, but I did. Granted,"—he smiled—"I started out with it because I read articles about football players taking modern dance to make them more mobile. I said to myself, 'OK, they won't think I'm a sissy.' *And* a whole lot of nice-looking women were in those classes. But I really got to enjoy it. The point is, you got to look beyond the superficial things to what's important. Out there in the world, white people are ready to judge blacks too quickly. They're *afraid* of black people. I mean, I don't care how I dress; even if I have a business suit on and I walk along past a white woman, she will grab her bag. No matter how I'm dressed, it doesn't make any difference. So it's really stupid for us to do basically the same thing—to think about our own people in stereotypes. But it happens, it happens."

ABOUT a month later, I met Carlie at the East Harlem field where Samuel spends his fall Saturday with his football league. It was a chilly October day, and dry leaves were swirling in gusts

on the hard dirt field. Recently, Carlie and the children had begun hanging around at the games on Saturdays, too, just so that
the family could spend a little extra time together, however fleet-
ing. More and more, the Jacksons' work and other obligations
seemed to be sucking up all their waking hours, so, even though
they didn't get to say much to each other when Samuel was out
on the field, they were glad to be able to be in the same general
space at the same moment. Samuel had left his night job at 7:00
A.M., as he did each week during the season, and by eight he was
on the field, alone, marking the yard lines with chalk. At about
10:30, Carlie and the kids, wearing many layers of clothes,
showed up in a secondhand blue van that the Jacksons had just
bought from an old friend of Samuel's with the idea of using it
for transporting sports equipment and for general family needs.
Later on, Samuel thought it might perhaps be used for the tour
business. But the van broke down all the time and was costing
them a lot to repair (they had already sunk $5,000 in it), so its fu-
ture as a flagship for the Jackson van flotilla seemed in doubt.

The football field was close to the FDR Drive, and cars whizzed
by noisily as several dozen young teenagers in red football uniforms tossed a football around or stood in little knots near a small
crowd of parents, older brothers, and one elderly couple who
lived next door to one of the players and had come, they said, to
lend the boy moral support, because neither of his parents
seemed much interested in him. The red team had arrived
promptly at nine o'clock. The other team was late and at eleven
still hadn't shown up. Samuel, dressed in a heavy gray sweatshirt
and sweatpants, was doing his best to calm the red team's pep-
pery assistant coach, who was demanding that the other team for-
feit the game. But the latecomers were driving in from New
Jersey, so Samuel argued for forbearance, saying they'd probably
run into traffic problems. The assistant coach didn't look like a
man who could be easily persuaded of anything, but Samuel kept
talking to him in a reassuring tone, exercising what from six feet
away looked like complex diplomatic skills, and finally he pre-

vailed upon him to wait a bit longer. Sure enough, just as the assistant coach, kicking dirt, was about to rejoin his team, the New Jersey kids arrived. Dressed in uniforms of bright yellow and black and far outweighing the reds, they soon began to score heavily, to the delight of their own modest cheering section—hefty middle-aged men, who high-fived and pummeled each other after every good move on the field.

While Derek and Corinne played along the sidelines, supervised by a young girl from the church who had come along to help watch them, Carlie and I retreated to the van to warm up. She had dark circles under her eyes and looked exhausted. An as yet unsatisfactorily diagnosed condition affecting the left side of her jaw was giving her trouble. Several doctors thought that the problem was trigeminal neuralgia, a painful recurring condition that afflicts portions of the face served by the trigeminal nerve. Carlie thought that the problem had something to do with her teeth. Whatever it was, it flared up intermittently and gave her such severe pain that she always carried medicine around just in case an attack might occur. She had been looking so tired at work recently, she told me, that when she had jokingly said in passing that she needed a vacation from her kids and husband a coworker had phoned a ticket agent she knew on the spot and booked her on a flight to Jamaica. She wasn't going, but she'd been tempted.

"I don't know what I'd do if Samuel was like some of the other husbands I hear about" she said. "I have a girlfriend whose husband didn't even know how to change a diaper—and wouldn't learn. Really! Now, Samuel never had anything whatsoever against diapering, and he bathes the kids, and he dresses them. I know from my sisters that my mother never expected my father to do anything around the house. You know—he was the breadwinner and she took care of the house. That was the deal. But we have an *entirely* different sort of life, so we have to divvy things up. We share expenses, the raising of the children—you name it and I think he would take part in it. But I'd say it sort of comes naturally to him, even though he wasn't raised that way. He's not the sort of man who will walk past a pile of dishes in the sink and think, She'll do it. He'll stop and do them. If I'm running late, he'll say, 'You just worry about yourself. I'll take care of the kids.' Except for hair combing. I have to do that. But he's rather unusual, I gather. Just like his insistence on our always talking about the things that are on our minds."

Early in their marriage, one of the things the Jacksons found themselves talking about was their sexual relationship. Carlie is pleased that these discussions took place and pleased that Samuel's attitude toward sex, like her's, has always been fairly straightforward and open, she says. Historically, the prim and proper mien of churchgoing black men and women offered a rebuke and challenge to a nineteenth-century stereotype: that of the loose, hot-blooded black woman and the potent, sexually obsessed black man. In the era when white women were intent on climbing down from the Victorian pedestal, black women were steadfastly climbing up the steps of the church to find solace and a firm social structure. But being "proper" in churchy black society has not necessarily precluded a more flexible view of sexual relations than has generally been tolerated in similarly conservative white religious circles. Of her own premarital sexual relations, for example, Carlie said, as we sat in the van, "I don't think I ever felt guilty about them. I never had sex with anybody that I didn't really care about or that I might not potentially marry, so it wasn't as if I was out there sleeping around. I mean I can count the number of guys I've slept with on the fingers of one hand. To me, there wasn't anything to feel guilty about. Of course, I'd never have let my mother know that that was so."

She takes a modern view of divorce, too. "I'm a romantic to a certain extent, but then I'm a realist, too," she said. "I'm here because I want to be and not because I have to be. But if things started going wrong, or if we were just bringing each other down instead of encouraging each other, then there'd be no reason for us to be together. So I'd have no qualms about divorce if it came to that. But I still think that two people—two parents—are better in a home."

In an earlier conversation, Samuel, who tends to draw on impersonal language to describe the personal aspects of his life, cited "good communication, good sex, and good finances" as the cornerstones of his marriage. Carlie tended to characterize the central concerns of her marriage in a more fluid way. At different times, she said, different needs had preoccupied her. At the moment, domestic survival and child-raising cooperation were the key issues in her life. Sex was up there in importance, but, as time had passed, other concerns had occasionally pushed it backstage—especially when she'd been working hard and late. Somehow, she added, they had always found a way to work out to the satisfaction of both of them whatever difficulties emerged from their different needs.

As we watched the players cheering on the field, Carlie observed that Samuel's acknowledgment of the issues that were important to her meant a good deal to her, though she'd noticed that some of the things that changed in her life after she married had kind of crept up on her. "I lost some of my independence. Definitely. But it was really because I kept falling into weird patterns I never would have anticipated. I noticed I was waiting for Samuel to do things I would normally have done myself before I got married. Little things like changing lightbulbs. Instead of getting a new bulb and putting it in myself, I heard myself saying, 'Oh, the bulb blew out in the kitchen,' and asking Samuel to change it. A lot of little things like that. I'm also kind of impulsive, and Samuel *really* likes to plan things. I might decide in the morning that I'd like to go somewhere that evening and I'll say, 'You know, Samuel, I'd really like to do x, y or z tonight,' and he'll invariably say that I should have told him about it earlier. And, of course, I'll say, 'I just thought of it—you know—right now.' Sometimes we might be invited somewhere, and I'd tell him four or five days before it was to happen, and he'd say, 'Why did you tell me about this at the last minute?' I don't think that's the last minute—not by my definition—but that's how he is."

• • •

IN the next few months the Jacksons and I kept trying to get together, but their workloads were so heavy that they rarely had any spare time. Toward the end of January, a few uncommitted hours opened up in their schedules, and the three of us arranged to meet for a weekday lunch. I suggested a number of midtown places, but Samuel has a strong preference for uptown restaurants, and we ended up meeting at Flash Inn—the site of the Jacksons' first meal together. A signless old restaurant beloved of black politicians and longtime Harlem residents, Flash Inn hugs the edge of Manhattan, on Macombs Place, just across the river from Yankee Stadium. It is spacious, dark, and comfortable, and at the time of our visit it was fairly deserted. Most of its customers show up in the evening. The only waiter in sight was a small, alert-looking man with a permanently amused expression on his face who looked as if he might have served his waiter apprenticeship under Fiorello La Guardia. Carlie said that she and Samuel ate at this restaurant frequently, though they hadn't been there for lunch in years.

The waiter recognized them, greeted them as if they were young relatives, and gazed at them approvingly as we settled down at a big table near the window. After Carlie and I ordered, Samuel said, "I believe I'll take the roast prime rib."

"No, suh," the waiter shot back, staring at Samuel with a fixed neutral expression.

"'No, suh?'" A small silence. "OK, what should I have?"

"Take the skillet steak."

"The skillet steak. OK. Give me the skillet steak."

"How would you like it?"

"Medium."

"That's fine, just fine."

During lunch, Carlie and Samuel got into a prolonged discussion of a problem that had come up recently at Derek's school. Derek, an exceptionally sweet, unaggressive boy, had been getting into fights recently with the class bad boy, who was white. Despite the fact that the other boy had a long history as a trouble-maker, the teacher seemed to assume that Derek was out for trouble, too, and suggested that the Jacksons get the boys together for a play date so that they could come to know each other better and "get friendlier." The Jacksons had great misgivings about the idea, but they duly arranged the play date. It had not turned out well. Samuel had objected to the plan on principle. He thought the other boy should have simply been told to behave, and he bristled at what he believed was the teacher's underlying assumption—that all black males are aggressive, so Derek probably started the trouble. Carlie disagreed. She thought that the teacher had merely been trying to approach the problem neutrally.

"Well, I think that she found a foolish solution," Samuel said. "The idea that two little boys could settle their differences that way! Hey, lots of adults can't do that. These are seven-year-old kids. The original fight happened during recess. The monitor was busy *reading*. She said she can't watch them all the time."

When the Jacksons showed up at the school to discuss the still ongoing fights, Samuel said to the teacher, "Derek doesn't start fights." And the teacher told him she knew that.

"So my question was 'Why am I here?'" Samuel recalled. "They know this other kid is a troublemaker."

"Even on the play date," Carlie added, "he made some racial slurs."

A discussion ensued of the subtle racism both Jacksons had experienced at the liberal Upper West Side school Derek attended. "Racism is an accepted part of life for blacks," Carlie said. "You know that it exists everywhere. Even here. Maybe it's even stronger here than in Memphis. I still am aware of it. For example, if you look at the *Today Show*, you never get to see a black guest except if they're discussing crime. But I am not affected by it personally anymore, because of the environment I work in now. I'm not in midtown working in a corporate structure. The only time I run across racism is at the kids' schools. There are parents I sit with on committees at school. During the meetings, they may be very friendly, but there are some who if they see you outside the school building don't even smile. It's like, 'Well, who are you?' That kind of thing. I just know it's there, and you should be prepared to cope with it."

"I think I'm more willing to cope with it head-on than Carlie may be," Samuel said, "especially when it comes to the kids. I don't think Carlie always recognizes racism when it's there. For instance, when Derek was tested a while ago part of the test was oral, and the tester was a white lady and Derek couldn't understand some of the terminology she used, and he got confused. Later, he and I discussed some of the questions and he knew the answers. It was just that the way she put things confused him. I think that there ought to be black teachers around for testing black children. You get the idea, too, that even now the expectations are lower for black kids. After Derek took the E.R.B.s recently at his school, we never received the results of the test, though we knew that the other parents did. Did they just forget, or did they think we weren't interested? I've had the same experience that Carlie had at that school. You make contact with people, but it doesn't hold up. Same thing with the people in our building. I was president of the co-op board for a while. You sit there, you know, and talk to these people, white people, month in month out, and they live in the same building. There's one guy who's even on my floor, and he's the treasurer. But they get out on the street and they don't talk to you."

Carlie shook her head and asked, "What does it cost them to smile?" Recently, she went on to say, she had come to feel that the strong social connectedness they had with her friends was an extension of the world that they'd left behind in the South and that the white people she knew had no experience of.

"Do you feel you've gained more than you've lost by leaving the South?" I asked.

"We've definitely gained more," Carlie said, "in terms of opportunity and richness of life. But there are big challenges for raising a family. I talk to kids at the church who are really troubled. I'm worried that when these kids leave home they're going to get lost. They seem not to have any kind of strong value system to fall back on. I don't know if it's the fault of their families or their lack of connectedness with the church or a combination of both those things, but they're just so materialistic. They don't even *think* about a value system. Recently, on a retreat we went on, the kids from the neighborhood said that they believed in God, but many of the church kids said they didn't. I mean, what's going on here?"

"Carlie's right—there's no comparison in terms of opportunity," Samuel said. "But there's a kind of crazy focus on living fast. If I'd started out in the city, I don't think I'd be here today. I don't think the city kids get the same foundation that we had; they're not having family reunions, or big social celebrations, or holidays. They're isolated. On the other hand, what would I have done down South? Race relations are saner at least on the surface here. Down there, I might have become a successful farmer but little else. The women down there, even those with education, a lot of them are still working in restaurants."

"There's no question but that we have a better life up here," Carlie said, sipping some iced tea. "But sometimes I wonder when I'm going to get to enjoy it. I'm working now till eight-thirty, nine almost every evening. I have to finish up all the things I didn't get done earlier, because of picking up the kids at different times. But next year the kids will be in the same program after school, so things should ease up."

Since Samuel started working at the church, his schedule had become tighter, too, and he was usually asleep at the time when he used to be doing the marketing.

I asked the Jacksons when the shopping got done.

"Shopping? Forget shopping," Carlie said. "Weeknights, we're eating takeout: Kentucky Fried Chicken, Chinese. But we've been looking at the budget and we really cannot afford to go on this way."

In the past year, Samuel had read more books about successful businessmen and had become even more convinced that after a period of trials and tribulations, he will join their ranks. In another year and a half, he said, things were surely going to ease up.

Carlie laughed, not unkindly. "He thinks we'll have paid off our major debts by then. We have slightly different ideas of success. Mine is not needing to use plastic all the time, not living from check to check." Samuel mentioned that they thought there might well be a stash of money hidden away in his Aunt Ruby's house. Ruby had died not long ago, and a few thousand dollars were found tucked away in the house after her death; the Jacksons believed that there was more squirreled away somewhere. "Samuel's mother actually told me that Ruby was trying to tell her something about money right before she died. But she didn't want to listen, because Ruby was talking about death, and she didn't want to hear about her dying."

Roger was staying at Ruby's house now, but neither he nor anyone else in the family had had time to search the house really thoroughly. Samuel thought there could be as much as $50,000 hidden away. Ruby had been a big saver. They had meant to drive out to Rockaway themselves to look for the money but hadn't yet gotten around to it. Still, even if there was no secret inheritance, Samuel said, with the emphasis of a man trying hard to convince himself of something, he was certain that they would surely be better off in the next period of their lives. "It's just a process of learning to wheel and deal in this society in terms of finance," he went on. "We're making plenty of money. Once we get rid of the bills, we'll be on a roller coaster, flying."

When Samuel talked in this vein, as he did often, Carlie never actually contradicted him. She just kept silent. I asked her once if she shared Samuel's optimistic financial vision of the future. She laughed somewhat ruefully and shrugged. "Well, it's possible, though right now it just seems hard to stay on top of the bills. Anyway, it's nice to dream."

But when Samuel swallowed the last of his coffee and folded his hands on the table and said, "Whatever happens, Derek and Corinne will not make the same mistakes I did, because Carlie and I will guide them and help them find a good course."

"Yes, that's right," she said, and put her hand down on his.

"I always tell Carlie, I wish I'd met her sooner," Samuel went on. "I try to think sometimes who would I be if I hadn't met her. She's so kindhearted. I believe that she is the person who was meant for me. At one of the job interviews I went to, there was a white psychiatrist who asked me did I hit her. Hit her! You know, that's the way he thought it was with all black men and women. He couldn't actually believe I didn't. Really. The truth is, I used to pray that I would have somebody that would care for me and that I would care for, and it happened."

SIX

BODY AND SOUL

LONGER LIFE EXPECTANCY, IMPROVED HEALTH, AND A radical decline in childbirth deaths have all affected the tenor of marriage, but few phenomena have so thoroughly changed the tone of modern married life as our growing national preoccupation with therapy and therapeutic ways of thinking—our "psychological gentrification," as one contemporary observer has put it. A more psychological approach to experience was, in fact, found to be one of the principal changes observed in a group of Americans of all classes interviewed in 1956 and again in 1976 by a team of sociologists from the University of Michigan's Institute of Social Research. (The others were a greater number of happy marriages and a greater willingness to admit to emotional problems.) Beginning as an experimental exercise for the few, therapy has become a part of our culture.

Some ten million Americans a year consult psychiatrists, psychologists, or social workers. (Untold millions more get help from pastoral counselors, healers, imaging experts, and so on.) Therapeutic thinking has made its presence known in every stratum of society and has been accompanied by firm belief in the right to optimal sexual and spiritual happiness—self-actualization, as it is known—which has become virtually an unwritten clause of the marriage vow. An ongoing national debate rages over whether this is good or bad, the argument focusing on the supposedly insidious effect on the national cast of mind of a population too self-absorbed versus the supposedly beneficent effect of increased consciousness and more relaxed relations between the sexes. And rarely does the debate glide quickly past Americans' attitudes toward sex.

Alfred C. Kinsey's initially scandalizing works, *Sexual Behavior in the Human Male*, published in 1948, and *Sexual Behavior in the Human Female*, published in 1953, were based on 12,000 interviews, and, though his subjects (like the respondents in most surveys) were mostly white, middle-class, and college-educated, Kinsey gave his sampling a scientific aura that went far to gain the survey wide acceptance. Kinsey's methods and his sampling have been questioned, but even his critics concede that, at the very least, he established it as a fact that there was a great deal more premarital sex around in the generations born after 1900 than there had been hitherto. Kinsey was also the first American to advance a popularly accepted view of sexuality that was divorced from religious and moral imperatives. It has been noted that probably more people talked about the Kinsey reports than read them, but they were said to be better known to the general population in their day than the Marshall Plan. By the time Kinsey's spiritual descendants, Masters and Johnson, produced *Human Sexual Response* (in 1966) and *Human Sexual Inadequacy* (in 1970), sex research was no longer a form of exotica but a field, and a more mechanistic view of sex, along with the gung-ho therapeutic mood of the time, assured the authors a wide and enthusiastic readership. The Masters and Johnson books sat on the bedside table beside the glass of warm milk.

The Kinsey reports demonstrated that many of the modern era's changes in sexual and psychological outlook had actually been evolving since the first decade of the century. Indeed, the 1920s have come in retrospect to seem like our national teens. To some observers in that era, it seemed that sex and psychology were being elevated to a quasi-religious status and were shunting aside the old verities. A multitude of books with titles like *The Psychology of Golf, The Psychology of Selling Life Insurance,* and *Psychology of the Poet Shelley* came out, and terms like "repression," "libido," "defense mechanism," "fixation," "subconscious," and "unconscious" found a permanent place in the language. Even away from the urban centers, the popularizing of Freudian ideas was heightened by a steady outpouring of self-help books such as *Psychoanalysis by Mail, Psychoanalysis Self-Applied, Ten Thousand Dreams Interpreted,* and *Sex Problems Solved,* which could be ordered through the Sears, Roebuck catalogue. So high pitched was the therapy obsession for a while that, according to historian William E. Leuchtenberg, the psychoanalyst Karl Menninger found himself "badgered at parties to perform analyses of the personalities of guests as if he were a fortune-teller."

If one of the tenets of the Freudian cosmography—that women's destinies were shaped in large part by their biological makeup—sounded remarkably like a reprise of an old nineteenth-century tune, it was countered by the jazzy emergence of the androgynous, irreverent, energetic, not particularly domestic, and often vampy flapper, and, though most American women were neither flappers nor analysands, neither die-hard career women nor St. Theresas of the Stove, these warring stereotypes and sundry variations on them fought it out over the next few decades in stories, novels, and—most influentially, perhaps—in movies, *The Women, Alice Adams, Pat and Mike, June Bride,* and *Baby Face,* among them. Movies made plain the rapidly changing relationship between men and women and the resulting confusions; they served (and still serve) as a kind of bravura rendering of emotions and modes of behavior already well established in people's lives. But, whatever the underlying currents affecting marriage, by and large the old formula—Mom cooks, Dad works—continued to be the rule until the 1960s, which, like the post-Depression years, were a watershed era for domestic relations. During that decade, all the expressive, individualistic aspects of personal relations that had been in the air since the century's first decade went, or at least seemed to have permission to go, into overdrive, inspiring first a big, sloppy national grin and then, beginning in the seventies, a wave of dolorous second thoughts.

By the eighties, it had become apparent that many people felt unsure about the rules and roles that applied to their marriages. A vocal group of critics has suggested that the nation began a catastrophic downward slide when parents—particularly fathers —lost their authority, and, to judge from the popularity of Robert Bly and his male-identity-confirming woodland hug-ins, an unknown number of men felt an absence of solid ground beneath their feet. But it's obvious that a good part of the confusion endemic to contemporary marriage derives from the inevitable clash between old, deeply ingrained fantasies of the roles of "husband" and "wife" and our rather more shakily defined individualistic modern notions of them. In every class, the old moral rigidities and patriarchal verities have lost their hold without any standards of comparable solidity emerging to replace them. The flags of mutuality, free expression, and feeling nice fly high over marriage, but there is less than complete agreement on the parameters and limits of these ideals. As far back as the 1970s, the sociologist Jesse Bernard observed that marriage had "not caught up with our thinking about it."

Public rhetoric on the subject has done its share of adding to the confusion. Bernard herself, in *The Future of Marriage,* published in 1972, wrote about men's traditional resistance to the economic burden that marriage imposed on them and about what was then alleged to be their greater need for sexual variety. She assured her readers that these issues could be easily resolved if men received more financial help from working wives (as she rightly predicted they would) and if "sexual varietism" became more feasible. The shift toward two-income families has, in fact, gone far to relieve many men of their former dray-horse burdens, but what about Bernard's assurance that "a conception of marriage which tolerates, if it is not actually sympathetic with, extramarital relations is on its way, provision for sexual varietism is almost standard in male blueprints for the future" and that "the time is not far when this desideratum of husbands' marriages may also be achieved."

What can one say to that except In which galaxy?

The latest survey of sexual mores in this country, published in 1994 by the University of Chicago, suggests that people have sex less frequently and are more faithful to their spouses than was commonly assumed.

In a recent study of husbands and wives that downgraded practical help as "instrumental behavior" and classified direct verbal expressions of sympathy as "affectionate behavior," a researcher felt compelled to tell one of the husbands that he ought to show his wife more real affection. Taking the advice in good faith, the man trotted outside and washed the family car, and was genuinely dismayed to learn that neither his wife nor the researcher considered this a gesture of affection.

Still, a false interpretation that sterotypes women as given to feeling, and men as given to action, a number of feminist scholars argue, is at the root of a great deal of marital friction. They would like to see a more androgynous (their word) identity that unites the masculine and feminine spheres—and a definition of love that would encompass, in the words of one, "affection, material help and routine cooperation." More poetically, as Rilke put it in *Letter to a Young Poet,* "Perhaps the sexes are more related than we think, and the great renewal of the world will perhaps consist in this, that man and maid, freed from all false feeling and aversion, will seek each other not as opposites, but as brother and sister, as neighbors, and will come together as *human beings.*"

OF all the changes that have occurred in the last several hundred years of marriage, the shift in sexual attitudes probably has been the most seismic. In a famous study of the erotic life and beliefs of forty-five married middle-class women, conducted between 1892 and 1920, Dr. Clelia Duel Mosher, who began her career as a zoologist and later became a doctor and a lecturer on

personal hygiene, found that 20 percent of her subjects still believed that "the true purpose of intercourse" was procreation, but
the rest firmly acknowledged the importance of the sexual pleasure principle in their lives. Only two of Dr. Mosher's respondents believed what doctors had been telling them for a
century—that sex was a necessity only for men—and more than a
third reported that they reached orgasm "always" or "usually."
Although there was to be no comparable scientific scrutiny of
men's erotic lives until the Kinsey Report, Mosher's study affords
a limited and salutary view of the respondents' husbands. A good
number of the women indicated that, in the course of their married lives, there had been considerable variation in the rhythms of
their own and their husbands' sexuality, and that their husbands'
patience and consideration had been helpful. In its day, the
Mosher Survey was an anomaly and a curiosity—a rare look beyond the bedroom door. At the turn of the century, which was
when most of the women interviewed in the survey came of age,
sex was rarely discussed in public, and, also, if the diaries of that
era are to be believed, rarely discussed in private by husbands
and wives, before or after they married. By the 1920s, however,
the degree to which the public seemed to be obsessed with the
topic of sex dismayed some members of the older generation, including Clelia Mosher. Her interest in sex was keen but purely
scientific, and, having never been married herself, she objected to
what she believed was an unwholesome focus on sexual matters.
The new national obsession "disgusts and revolts me," she declared. "I like to keep away—sex has its place but not for constant
contemplation. There are so much more interesting things." She
did not elaborate.

After the turn of the century, marriage manuals began to mention favorably (if obliquely) the idea of sex for fun, and by 1920
they were recommending freer expression of emotion (within the
bounds of marriage) and a generally more recreational attitude
toward the subject. The real origins of the sexual revolution can
surely be traced to the growing interest in talking about sexual
matters that developed after the First World War. In his memoirs,

Sherwood Anderson remarks on the relief that people felt in that period when they grasped the fact that they could articulate their secret fears and doubts about sex. "A kind of healthy new frankness was in the talk between men and women," he notes, "at least an admission that we were all at times torn and harried by the same hurts."

By the late sixties, Anderson's "healthy new frankness" had been catechized by therapy, and the traditional pattern of courtship, then engagement, and then marriage gave way to a pattern of dating, followed by breaking up, followed by more of the same and, increasingly, trial cohabitation (or, as an older generation nervously called it, "shacking up"), sometimes leading to marriage, sometimes not. Many of the 1960s couples living this way (or in the even more experimental communes) shocked their families, even though they tended to form little marriages for however short a time they stayed together, and, unsurprisingly, experienced the same problems that married couples did. Nonetheless, the contemporary sociologist who observed that "marriage no longer seemed to occupy its place as the dividing line between socially approved and socially disapproved sexual intimacy" was not just whistling Dixie.

In the next two decades, premarital sex began to be taken for granted, sex counseling became a growth industry, and new sexual customs and ethics evolved, though no one can say with certainty what they are today, in the age of AIDS. Since the number of unmarried couples living together tripled between 1970 and 1982, and the divorce rate has generally kept going up, the viability of marriage itself is often cited as one of the prominent social uncertainties of our era. Yet people keep marrying as frequently as ever, and it is probably safe to say that, for the most part, the end-of-marriage predictions are merely taking their place in a long line of alarmist critiques, stretching back to the eighteenth century. Also, while Americans may be divorcing more than they were thirty years ago, they are expressing greater satisfaction with marriage than they did then. And when they are unhappy, those who can afford it seek some kind of outside help. For the middle class, therapists—particularly couples-therapists—have become the new family ministers. So great has been the demand for their services that membership in the American Association for Marriage and Family Therapy has gone from 9,000 to 19,000 in the last decade.

Theoretically, there need be no real opposition between marriage and work for women or between working husbands and working wives, but there frequently seems to be such opposition, in no small part because there is an undeclared war between a public that in the last thirty years has moved toward a new economic system requiring both husbands and wives to work, and government policies that barely acknowledge this change.

In an age of increased self-awareness, men and women certainly have a greater chance of leading less rigid lives, but, in another sense, we have "only recently emerged from the mists of original consciousness," as Jung wrote in a 1925 essay called "Marriage as a Psychological Relationship," adding that "we constantly overestimate the existing content of consciousness." To some extent, consciousness is a luxury, coaxed into being by the widening of experience and of reading and by exchanges that are part of a reasonably decent education. To those whose lives appear to be governed by psychological, economic, and social forces beyond their control, marriage too often seems to be yet another predestined, inexorable force. The proliferation of experts offering advice on everything from family budgets to orgasm management attests to a general loss of moorings. That there is a widespread desire to escape "false feeling" and the straitjacket of the expected, and that men and women alike long for more egalitarian marriages, is fairly clear to anyone who watches TV or goes to the movies. But, inescapably, powerful traditional ideas play havoc with this latest and fondest of American dreams, and even the most forward-looking couples must grapple with forces surviving from their own misty past.

SEVEN

O PIONEERS:
NEAL AND
VERA CLARK

YOU COULD NOT SAY THAT EITHER NEAL OR VERA Clark had approached the day of their marriage, now thirty years old, in a glow of rosy optimism. Particularly Neal. In 1965, the year they married, Neal was living in Paris, taking the second half of his junior year at college abroad. He had not yet quite revived from a kind of swoon that overcame him as he first began walking along the Paris streets, and had just landed a job at a Left Bank art gallery with the help of a family friend, when Vera, her voice low and tense, called him from the States to announce that she was pregnant. Neal had just turned twenty. He had met Vera Hammond, who was a few years older than he was, the previous fall, at her mother and stepfather's house, in Amherst, Massachusetts. Vera's stepfather taught history at the college, and Neal was a classmate of Vera's younger brother. Vera had recently returned from London, where she had been studying design, and during that fall she was living with a friend in an apartment not far from her family's house and was unsure about her future plans. One bright October afternoon, she stopped by the house to pick up some clothes and found Neal there, playing a Beethoven sonata on the piano. It was a scene that might have been an illustration in a nineteenth-century romance, though both Vera and Neal were in fact enthusiastically modern people, whose way of looking at the world was strongly influenced by the then gusting social and political winds of the 1960s.

Vera and Neal liked each other from the start and discovered fairly soon that they had a lot in common: a strong interest in books, music, and art (Neal was a budding painter); major difficulties with a powerful, self-absorbed parent (his father, her mother); and, perhaps most important of all, a deep desire to live creatively rich lives. Before long, they became a couple. Neal was a bit shy and was prone to pessimism; Vera had a degree of reserve, but was more outgoing and optimistic. Both were slim, tall, angular, and intense looking. Neal had long blond hair, Vera's hair was dark, and they both tended to wear loose-fitting, richly textured, unpreppie clothing. Oblivious, ardent, and sweet looking, when they walked along the college paths, they surely attracted admiring glances.

Over the next few months, their romance bloomed. They were together almost constantly, until Neal left for Europe, in early February. Neal had missed Vera in Paris and had been glad that she was planning to visit him as soon as she had saved up enough money, but he felt crushed by her news. They had both been reading and discussing *Ulysses* for several months, and Neal had been carrying on the discussion by writing to her every day. Now, when he thought about it, he realized that he obviously had strong feelings for Vera, but these feelings had never coalesced either into the word "love" or into a mental picture of any future life with her. After a lot of soul-searching and transatlantic discussion, they decided that Vera should keep the baby and that they would marry; Neal was sure that it was the right thing to do, but, more often than not, this conviction was overwhelmed by urgent feelings of panic and dread. Neal's own father had left home when Neal was nine and had remarried not long afterward, and somehow Neal had found himself ever since in the role of the Great Compensator—the always dutiful, always thoughtful son (he had a difficult older sister who had a barely perceptible sense of filial duty)—and he was just beginning to grasp how difficult it was going to be to free himself from the long shadow of his father, a brilliant and widely admired historian.

Neal spent his boyhood in a small Greenwich Village walk-up crammed with books, paintings, and elegant, if chipped, crockery. His parents were radical intellectuals who had grown up in comfortable circumstances. His mother drew a small income from a trust fund that just kept her (and more than a few radical causes) going, but his father's family's modest fortune had dwindled away in the previous generation, and the high regard in which he was held as a historian was not reflected in his income. They tended to live frugally. Neal's parents' circle was ambitious, contentious, sexually adventurous, more interested in ideas and work than in personal relations, and not particularly focused on children, even their own; many of them were more than a little childish themselves. Neal and his older sister were reared in an adamantly "progressive" atmosphere with few parental directives. They were taught from the onset to address their parents by their first names, to reduce the socially imposed barriers that supposedly impeded free discourse between parent and child, and, like children of an earlier, less liberated era, they were generally treated like miniature adults. Though these attitudes deprived them of quite a few of the pleasures of childhood, theirs was nonetheless a lively, buzzing household. Neal could not actually remember much about his parents' relationship or *anything* about the predivorce years, but friends of the family told him that before his parents split up he had been a lively, outgoing boy and afterward he had become shy and withdrawn. Whatever the trials of Neal's boyhood, he grew up to be a gentle, likable young man with a quick intelligence, considerable artistic talent, and a warm, engaging manner. At the time he and Vera met, he was working hard in college and spent most of his free time sketching.

Often, he was at his desk until the small hours of the morning, bent over a drawing, his long blond braid trailing down his back.

In their first months together, Vera found herself smiling whenever she saw Neal or thought about him. Her first impression of him was a topic of an early conversation we had one fall afternoon several years ago in the Clarks' apartment—a cheerful book-, memento-, and painting-crammed walkup railroad flat in the Fort Greene section of Brooklyn. When she was in London, Vera said, she had made a list of all the attributes she considered desirable in a man. "It was an impossible list," she added, as she served me tea and cookies. We were sitting at a sturdy oak dining table in a cozy, pocket-sized living-dining room whose door opened directly on to the building's peeling hallway. "He had to be a comfortable sort of person and talented, bright, funny, and nice looking. He was also supposed to play the piano, draw, and love me exclusively, poor guy. Well Neal was it—the walking realization of my list."

Vera speaks with a soft, quicksilver intensity. She radiates a fairly high degree of energy even when she's not moving, and when she is in motion she moves like a well-built sailboat sheering along on a good wind. She has studied dance on and off for most of her life, and when she was eight, she announced to a great-uncle that she intended to be a dancer. "And that," she said, smiling ruefully, "was the only surging flame of a career idea I ever had." Vera's family lived in Manhattan when she was young, and she attended a number of different schools. After her parents divorced in 1945, when Vera was five, she moved around quite a lot as one or the other parent settled in a different residence. Both her parents had been raised in strict religious households. Her paternal grandfather was a Southern Baptist minister, and his wife, according to Vera's father, took to her bed with a migraine at the very mention of cards, whiskey, or dancing. Vera's mother had had an equally strict Catholic upbringing. Vera's maternal grandmother was an icily stern woman whose strictness her mother resented so deeply that her whole life had been built in defiance of her. Whenever she made an important decision, she told Vera, she would ask herself, "What would my mother do?" Then she would do the opposite. Vera and her brother, four years younger, were thus raised without religion, yet even so their upbringing was fairly puritanical.

In the months after the breakup of her parents' marriage, Vera's mother moved to Chicago, and for two years Vera rarely saw her father, who taught law at one of the city colleges in New York. In 1947, he remarried and moved to Connecticut, where he found a new job in a small liberal arts college, and by then Vera and her mother and brother had moved back to New York. She began to visit him once a month. She was seven. After each of these too-infrequent visits, she felt sad and usually departed in tears. But not long afterward, because her mother was having health problems, Vera and her brother went to live temporarily with their father and stepmother—a good-humored, even-tempered woman, who won Vera's heart by showering her with intricately detailed hand-sewn doll clothes and lavishly designed ballet costumes. Her own mother, by contrast, rarely focused on her. Once, in a sort of take-it-or-leave-it way, she had told Vera that she much preferred little boys to little girls. She worked hard at various administrative jobs at colleges and foundations, and occasionally dabbled in writing, but she didn't seem to enjoy being in the company of her daughter. "She's a putting-down kind of person," Vera told me, shrugging. "Even today, she's on the other side of any point I make."

Eventually, Vera's mother made a good second marriage to a professor of history. He was a kind, thoughtful man, and he delighted Vera, who was nine years old at the time the wedding plans were announced, by assuring her that they were "all getting married up together." However, the good second marriage didn't alter the strained relationship between mother and daughter. When Vera needed advice or support, she turned to her father. "It's odd," she said, "but my father was always interested in what I was feeling and thinking—even though he was shy with women;

my mother was more interested in surface things. She was always striking flamboyant poses and wanting terribly to be considered an intellectual, always conscious of 'important' people. I guess I've spent a good part of my life searching for her love."

When Vera was in her early twenties, she set off on the first leg of what proved to be a long venture into psychotherapy. She was seeing a psychiatrist in Amherst when she met Neal, and, except for a hiatus of eight years in the 1970s, she has been actively examining her problems and concerns with professionals—five of them in all—most of her adult life. Her current therapist, she told me, has been the most satisfactory. Vera also credits a women's group she joined in the early seventies with providing revelations that helped her understand herself as much as, or perhaps even more than, most of her therapists. After I'd been meeting with her for a while, Vera told me that when she was eight, a teenage baby-sitter, a boy—"horrible creature"—had fooled around with her sexually one day, and nearly two decades later when, with considerable embarrassment, she brought up the incident at her women's group, she was astonished to learn that every one of the twelve participants (and it was a fairly diverse group of women rich and poor, black and white) had some similar childhood incident to report.

When Vera was growing up, it bothered her that, though she was more gifted artistically than her brother, he was a far better student. In a feckless attempt to show him up, she applied to only a handful of top colleges, but she was rejected by every one. She ended up in London at design school more or less by default but thrived there, leaving after four years, she told me, only because she felt there was no niche in English society for a young, free-floating American woman. "If you're not English, you're not really accepted," she said. "I felt I had to take out citizenship papers or leave." Back in Amherst, she attended a few art classes, and a local art gallery mounted a one-woman show of her furniture designs. But a certain torpor seemed to overcome her. When, because of the show, she received an offer of a good job working for a New York designer, she turned it down. She thought at the time that it was because she preferred living in the country, but years later she came to wonder if she hadn't just lost her nerve and sense of direction, as so many women of earlier generations had done once they left school.

By the time she met Neal, she had been working for about a year in a college science lab; she had been sitting in on a few academic classes and had been feeling increasingly frazzled around her mother. She was fascinated by the way Neal looked at the world and by the intellectual verve and the radical politics of his family. "I thought you couldn't get further to the left than Roosevelt," she told me, on another afternoon, as she poured two mugs of pale mint tea in her kitchen, a bright but bumpily plastered, somewhat decrepit room. "I was absolutely knocked off my feet by Neal's ideas," she said. Neal then considered himself an anarchist, and he still does. "He's not the bomb-throwing sort—Neal's not violent at all." Vera said. "But you know, he grew up in an anarchist circle. His mother still thinks of herself, at eighty-one, as an anarchist. In a way, both of us, when we first met, were only repeating the political views we heard. Neither of us really connected with politics in a meaningful way until later on. Neal has almost never voted—that's been a considerable source of grief to me. I wish he would. Anyway, I felt differently about him than I had about anyone else I'd ever met—quite dramatically different. I don't like to use terms like falling in love. I know I felt dubious about the conventions of marriage and quite separate from the husband-hunting crowd—though I always wanted to have children and vaguely assumed I'd be with someone."

To her old list of ideal characteristics she might desire in a mate, Vera now found herself adding the appealing attributes of Neal Clark. These included "his passion," "his particular kind of humor and laugh," "the way his hair grew," and the fact that "he was far and away more interesting than any of the men I'd gone out with before." In some mysterious way, she said, his whole being seemed to complement hers. "For example," she went on, "I panic easily, and he is a sort of let's-step-back-and-see-what's-go-ing-on sort of person. We were an amazing fit." About halfway through our conversation, Vera excused herself to feed a pair of gerbils that were clamoring for attention from some hidden fast-ness on the kitchen floor. For some years now, she has been work-ing as a nursery school teacher at a small, progressive school in Brooklyn Heights and, though the Clarks' crowded apartment does not have much extra space, it has nonetheless domiciled a wide variety of creatures—rabbits, guinea pigs, an iguana, mice, chameleons, and even, at one point, some chickens that Vera lugged home in crates from school because she was the only teacher willing to be saddled with them. The chickens eventually ended up at a farm, but for the year they called Fort Greene home they regularly repaid the Clarks' hospitality with beautiful white breakfast eggs.

In 1965, when Vera learned that she was pregnant, she seri-ously considered keeping the news from Neal. A not particularly well-defined picture formed in her mind of going off somewhere to have the baby on her own. "I saw myself starting a new life in the Southwest. I just didn't want to involve him. And, in fact, he was speechless with horror when I finally told him."

After Neal and Vera decided to marry, they broke the news to their families. Neal's father was too preoccupied to react much, but his mother, Mary, who had initially not warmed to Vera (Vera speculates that it was because of her beehive hairdo, four-inch spike heels, and girdle), rallied around and offered to help them financially, and in the next weeks she telephoned Vera every night from New York City, where she lived. Mary Clark also ac-companied Vera around Paris, where, for about six weeks, while Neal was at work, Vera wrestled with the intricacies of the vast amount of paperwork inflicted on foreigners who wished to marry in France. "I could never have done it without the help of a friend of Mary's who knew the ropes in Paris," Vera says. "*Every-thing* had to be stamped twice and submitted in triplicate to le-gions of bureaucrats." Mary also helped Neal and Vera arrange a small wedding. The guests were mainly expatriate friends of the Clarks whom Neal was fond of; one of them was a celebrated woman novelist, who volunteered her house for a small reception. By the time the event took place, Vera and Mary had become friends.

Vera's mother reacted to the announcement of her daughter's pregnancy and impending marriage by giving her a withering look, then turning around and walking out of the room. Her father was sympathetic. "It was his finest hour, in a way," Vera said. "I kept putting off telling him, and then, at four o'clock one morning after we'd been talking about everything else, I finally told him. He was extraordinarily supportive."

Vera was in the fourth month of her pregnancy when she and Neal were married at the *mairie* of the sixth arrondissement, across the street from Saint-Sulpice. Afterward they traveled around France for a while, then returned to Amherst just before the beginning of the fall semester. After Neal registered for his classes, they left for New York. Neal had strong feelings about having their child born away from Amherst. He hated college. He'd gone to Amherst primarily because his father thought it was a "first-rate school," but he had never adjusted to the preppiness of the place. Vera agreed to move to the city temporarily, and they settled in with Mary in her long, narrow West Village apartment in early September. The baby was due at the end of the month. Neal returned to Amherst to be on hand for the first week of school, then went back to New York, cutting classes, so that he could be with Vera until the baby's arrival. But her due date came and went, and the school was making unpleasant noises about his absence, so when the first week of October was drawing to a close and the baby still hadn't arrived, Neal said that he would have to leave by the ninth. The baby, a boy, obligingly arrived on the eighth. They named him William, and by the end of the following week the three of them were back in Vera's old apartment.

The happy arrival of a bright-eyed grandson had little effect on Vera's relations with her mother. Mrs. Eakins (she had taken the name of her second husband, the history professor) was irritated with Vera and Neal for deciding to marry in Paris and for having the baby in New York. About six months after they returned to Amherst, however, she told them that, despite her misgivings, she had decided to throw a party for them. It was to be rather a formal affair; she was planning on sending out printed invitations until Vera prevailed upon her not to. Neither Neal nor Vera knew most of the people she was inviting. Vera's mother also told Neal that he would be expected to wear a tie, but he pointed out that he *never* wore ties and didn't really like them. "Well, then don't come," she responded. In the end, they attended the party but stayed upstairs most of the time. Neal remained tieless.

But if the party issue and some other minor dramas of Neal's life at that time still had the familiar ring of adolescent sparring, the major ones were bringing him quickly into adulthood. For one thing, William's arrival made him feel a lot more enthusiastic about his marriage. "Although the decision to marry had always seemed like the right thing," Neal told me one evening at the apartment, "I felt that my life was coming to an end. Vera says she fell in love with me immediately, but with me it was different. I had been in love with someone else not long before I met her, so there was an imbalance—a real difference in our attitudes from the beginning. The marriage really started out on uncertain terms. To complicate matters, I had this sort of fatal predisposition to suppress my own interests and focus on doing things for other people, which often left me feeling depressed. I never really rebelled when I was a teenager, never even yelled at my parents. I was always so *dutiful*. Mary was always looking for a father—hers died when she was one. I instinctively filled that role, and here I was taking on a family before I even finished college. It was all a little unreal: there I was, this grind, still writing papers and going to class, doing all my assignments, and still in shock that I was married."

When Bill was born, however, Neal found that he loved looking after him and found fatherhood in general so absorbing that he no longer felt trapped. His painting was also going well, and he was getting good feedback about it, and his relationship with Vera seemed to give him more pleasure all the time. "I saw that we were really well matched," he said. "We're both nonconformists and we're interested in the creative aspects of life. We both sort of felt like outsiders and were both introspective. Bill forced me to grow up much faster than I might have, but in many ways I was still pretty childish."

I asked Neal what he meant.

"Well, after I finished school we rented another small apartment outside Amherst for a while, and then in 1967 we moved to New York. We found this apartment fairly soon, and we've been living in it ever since. From the start, we agreed to share things at home as much as possible, including caring for Bill. Vera began taking courses at N.Y.U.—she felt she had to work toward getting a B.A.—and I had a few odd jobs here and there. But, basically, until 1970, when I was twenty-six, we were being supported by Mary. That was a bad mistake. I had no idea how to make money. You could live on very little money back then, and we lived fairly close to the bone, but the truth is I hardly ever thought about money matters. I had this idea that my father was famous and I would be, too. A fantasy world. I never actually talked to anyone about any of this. I didn't have close, confiding friendships. Most of my friends were people I knew through my parents—older people. I was really unsophisticated about the world. I wasn't interested in therapy. Mary went to a therapist for years, but, like my dad, I thought I should solve my own problems. Even in the years she wasn't in therapy, Vera was always much more aware of her emotional confusions—and able to talk about them—than I was. I was very closed off. Actually, we were both so needy in those early years that it was hard for us to give each other much support. At the beginning, I'm sure that Bill kept us together."

In 1969, the Clarks' second child, Susanna, was born. Bill had always been a quiet, easy child, but Susanna was colicky and far more demanding; she never actually slept through the night until she was eight years old. The Clarks' egalitarian household arrangements continued. Neal didn't like to cook, so Vera prepared their meals, but Neal did all the dishwashing and a lot of the housekeeping, and after a number of fights about Vera's unbuttoned practices with the checkbook he started doing most of the bill paying and paperwork. A good many of the Clarks' male friends who were married gave lip service to egalitarian principles, but their domestic lives were actually not much different from their fathers'. Neal probably did as much as Vera around the house. He approved of what he called their "democratic" sharing of child-rearing obligations and never doubted that it was the way to go, especially since there was never enough money for baby-sitters, or the kind of expensive day-care arrangements that some of their slightly more affluent friends could afford. But as the years went by he seemed to find less and less time for getting into the small back room that served as his studio.

In 1970, Vera began her teaching job and Neal began working at an international human rights organization run by one of his aunts. Because his hours were far more flexible than Vera's, he found himself spending even more time with the children—TV-less time, since the Clarks, on principle, didn't own a television set. For a while, a cooperatively run day-care center in the neighborhood provided some relief, but "a lot of the parents were sort of hippie, off-the-wall types, and their children were pretty wild, so it was hectic and it didn't last long," Neal said. "Luckily, we eventually found a more established, better-run co-op a few blocks away. I wasn't getting much painting done, but I still believed that success would somehow come to me. Eventually it would all work out in some kind of vague way. You know—son of great man, I'm surely going to follow in his footsteps."

I asked Neal if he thought his diffident attitude toward his career had anything to do with the general sixties distrust of traditional careerism.

"Well, I suppose I agreed with all that. But I was not a real sixties person. I never took drugs. I didn't much like rock and roll."

"You never experimented with pot?" It was difficult to imagine someone like Neal not dipping into the readily available drug pharmacopoeia of the sixties.

"I smoked it a couple of times. But I mean it wasn't a part of my culture at all, and Vera was even less in tune with that part of the sixties, though we were totally involved in the politics. The Vietnam War and the general tenor of sixties politics had a big effect on us. We went to every demonstration. It was an incredibly vibrant time. You really felt that you were making a difference—you felt swept up by a kind of ongoing energy. You'd go to parties and have huge political arguments. All that had a solidifying effect on our marriage. There was one demonstration in Washington when John Mitchell stood on a balcony and said that it looked like the Russian Revolution—and it did. It was pretty heady. I have a feeling that if we'd married in the eighties it would have been harder. The sixties allowed you to get psychologically outside yourself, and there were a lot of big issues to focus on. I turned in my draft card at one point, to a minister in Brooklyn. But about six months later, when my case was being reviewed, I discussed my options with a lot of people and decided that I'd take my card back. I knew that I would get a deferment, because I was a father, and I wasn't ready—especially in terms of Bill—to go to jail. I didn't think I could take it—and it seemed like too small a personal gesture. But I definitely wouldn't have gone into the army then, no matter what. Of course it was an easy thing to say, because I wasn't in any imminent danger."

I asked Neal how attuned he and Vera were to other counterculture ideals of the sixties.

"Well, neither of us was into free love or a lot of sex—that sort of thing. In that sense we were totally square, totally out of tune with a lot that was going on. We used to drink vodka-and-tonics; we were drinkers, not smokers. I did have long hair and dressed sort of sloppily. My father was upset by the way I dressed, though he was a terribly messy dresser himself."

I mentioned having encountered Neal's father in public from time to time, always in suits.

"Yes, but they usually had big stains on them; he often didn't wash, and stuff. Anyway, he was really upset with me at one point for wearing an army jacket that was all ragged. But at least part of it was economics. I was like him that way. Most of the time, he lived on very little money, and so did we. I didn't like spending money on clothes, so I would wear the same thing till it practically dropped off. I still don't care about what I wear. I buy clothes at the Salvation Army. They usually don't fit me all that well but as long as they're passable I'll wear them. Bill and Susanna are totally different. They're choosy about their clothes and they care a lot about how they look."

At one of our early meetings (we met intermittently over several years), Neal mentioned that he had been keeping a diary since 1972. Since then, he had filled twenty-two spiral-bound notebooks with observations about his daily life, his marriage, his work, and his children, and he offered to let me look at several of them—an offer I enthusiastically accepted. One of the notebooks he gave me covered the years 1974 and 1975, and another was written fifteen years later. Together, they provided a riveting view of Neal's ongoing struggles and preoccupations.

Most of the subjects the diaries touch on also came up, naturally, in our conversations, but the unedited emotions of the diaries provided a more naked and, ultimately, a richer version of them. You could not know Neal for long without knowing that he consistently disapproved of the old, rigid roles for men and women, or that, though he was a passionate sports fan and a highly competitive tennis and basketball player, he rarely identified with the Hemingway aspect of American masculine society. He took pride, for example, in being a rather radically nonsexist husband, and if he happened to mention in conversation the domestic arrangements of his marriage he tended to downplay the incredibly time-consuming aspects of liberated fatherhood. But the diaries bear witness to enormous frustration as he attempts to balance his domestic and creative life. As his studio hours dwindled, he began to feel that he was drifting out of the artistic swing of things.

In fact, Neal's diary in that period resembles nothing so much as the confessions of the nineteenth-century feminists: their journals and diaries are rife with similar descriptions of the numbing effect of their domestic duties and their struggles with guilt and resentment. On April 19, 1975, Neal writes that he has been feeling increasingly "fragmented . . . a terrible anguish, as if nothing mattered . . . and the piles of projects sit there untouched . . . Depression—no time to do my work . . . Am I destroying myself by the way I've set up my life?" Earlier, he confesses, "Every minute spent with the kids registers as a minute lost from . . . getting something done." Like many a harried mother who longs for a break from her children but feels uneasy when she's away from them, he notes, "When I do get down to work, I feel negligent as a father. . . . I love B. and S., and this is my time to be with them, to show them that love. They need it—and I need it. But always the pull to work is there." In May of that year, he complains about Susanna's tantrums and middle-of-the-night alarms but also berates himself for lack of patience. Lately, Vera, who is a doting, imaginative mother, has been overwhelmed with the papers and reports she has had to bring home from school nearly every night, and Neal has offered to take care of the kids longer for a few weeks, to give her some extra time. She has done the same for him often, he writes, so he thinks he ought to feel resigned to the additional bite into his time. But he doesn't. On the contrary, the less he works, the more he feels himself succumbing to a kind of insidious lethargy.

Certain omnipresent themes float, cloudlike, over the years: Neal's ongoing struggle with his brilliant, self-centered father (he died in the early eighties) and with his thoughtful but somewhat remote mother, whose life he continues to feel overinvolved in; his struggle to lead a less fantasy-ruled existence; his concern about his stalled career (he has a few shows but their reception is mixed, and his limited public recognition is unchanged by them); and his love for and interest in his children and increasing happiness with Vera—despite important disagreements about their sex life.

Most of the problems that Neal writes about are like small demons that are kept at bay by the basic solidity of the Clarks' marriage, but the sexual dissonance is a source of serious marital strain. Neal pretty much wanted to make love every night, and for years Vera did not refuse him, though they sometimes had arguments when Vera seemed less than enthusiastic about this schedule. When Vera joined her women's group, in 1971, however, she learned that no one else in it had a comparably epical sexual life, and as time went by she began to feel more justified in sometimes rejecting Neal's advances. At about the same time, Neal began to notice that he was often quite strongly attracted to other women, and one evening he told Vera that that was the case, adding that he was sure their marriage was strong enough to withstand the diversion of an occasional affair. To Vera, the idea of having such an affair had about as much appeal as kissing a cobra, and she emphatically said as much, but nothing was resolved. They had long since agreed that they would always be honest about whatever was on their minds, so, even after Vera strongly protested the idea of sexual experimentation, it did not occur to Neal to keep his further thoughts on the subject to himself. Neal had first broached the issue in 1973; the following year, the phrase "open marriage" fell from his lips. But however many times Neal brought the subject up, or whatever vocabulary he used in referring to it, Vera refused to discuss it.

"Vera was convinced that I'd find someone else and run off and that would be the end of our marriage," Neal told me as we walked along the rundown streets of his neighborhood on a windy winter afternoon. "And I was sure that it wouldn't. I felt that an affair would be totally separate; it usually has nothing to do with love anyway. I know there are cases when it does, but I felt that our marriage was too strong for that to happen. If anything, I saw it as strengthening the marriage, because it would show that we could be independent and still love each other. Anyway, the subject kept coming up, off and on, all that year."

Neither of Neal's parents had been known to talk much about their emotions. His father's intellectual concerns, not his personal life, absorbed most of his thoughts and his energies as well, and Neal's mother shied away from any direct talk about delicate subjects. But Neal's diary returns again and again to his struggle to articulate his feelings to Vera and to his hope that Vera will feel free to articulate hers. He rejoices when her participation in the women's group enables her to say what is on her mind more directly, but he can't quite understand why neither of them seems to be able to discuss anything related to sex without getting into an argument.

In early December of 1974, during a period when he has been "feeling annoyed with every little thing that comes up with *V.,* every little conflict," they go to see a double bill of *The Sting* and *Slaughterhouse Five* one evening, and afterward, he notes, "we started talking about the movies and that led . . . to a good talk about our relationship and even about sex—one of the most open and frank talks," he adds. "And that led to very good sex as well."

Nowadays, Neal feels that his restlessness in the mid-seventies was at least partly related to his stalled career and his unresolved feelings about having married too young. The changing political climate of the mid-seventies, he believes, also contributed to his state of mind at the time. "Around 1973, politics just seemed to die, and I think I went into a kind of trance," he told me. "Suddenly there was none of the old vitality in the air; nothing seemed to happen. Everything just seemed so quiet. In 1974, there had been Nixon's resignation, and after that—nothing. In the early seventies, there had been Attica, Watergate, and all that. And there has been this *hopeful* feeling in the air. And then everything seemed to go on the back burner, and maybe it was a coincidence, but I felt that my life kind of went on the back burner at the same time."

Neal's job at his aunt's office, soliciting money for victims of repressive regimes, was, despite its worthiness, not terribly demanding, and it bothered him that he still hadn't pushed beyond the family orbit to earn his living. By 1973 he had been producing strong paintings for quite a while, which critics he respected responded to enthusiastically, but he rarely accumulated enough for a show. In his diary of that period he is restlessly self-critical, especially about his immaturity and his tendency to lapse into sexual fantasy. No outside observer could be more unsparingly critical than he is. When a woman brushes by him in a movie theater, for example, and excuses herself, he self-mockingly observes that he assumes "not that she *might* be attracted to me but that she is." He berates himself for his all-too-frequent Walter Mitty–like mental cruising and vows to try harder to live in the present.

EVERY summer, Neal and his family join Mary at her summer place—a small cedar-shingled house with three pocket-size bedrooms facing a salt marsh on the Maine coast. Mary has had the house since the early fifties, and Neal has spent part of almost every summer of his life there. In the surrounding woods live many artists, writers, and assorted intellectuals whom Mary has known since she was a young woman; like her, they usually migrate to that area of Maine in August, after the July renters who help foot the tax bill have departed. Neal and Vera have their own circle of friends there, too (some of them are children of Mary's friends), and sometimes Neal's sister appears briefly. For several summers I visited the Clarks during their stay in Maine and was struck at each visit by the rare sense of timelessness of the place. Architecturally, Mary's house is not much more than an overgrown shack, ringed by a small stand of white pines and sweet pepper bushes. A tattered volleyball net sways near a small deck that provides a sparkling view of the marsh. Various parts of the house are badly in need of repair and these days Mary, who is in her mid-eighties and suffers from several chronic ailments, cannot, even with the help of a visiting nurse, travel to any point more distant than the deck chair outside her front door. But all the Clarks eagerly anticipate their visits there and always regret having to leave. Mary's septuagenarian and octogenarian friends regularly make their way slowly down the bumpy unpaved road that leads to her steep sand driveway, and most evenings, one or two of them can be found with her on the deck, jiggling the ice in their mixed drinks and immersed in deep reminiscence. Except for a summer when Neal, Vera, and the children made a cross-country tour (they stayed in a motel only once; the rest of the time, Neal, Bill, and Susanna slept on the ground in sleeping bags, and Vera slept on picnic tables) they haven't missed a Maine summer in thirty years. Neal's ongoing anxieties about his too close relationship with his parents' world also take a vacation in the summer, when Mary's friends, Neal and Vera's friends, and Susanna and Bill's friends (both children are now in their twenties) are often thrown together. In fact, a pleasant multigenerational hubbub is one of the hallmarks of the place and adds to the Chekhovian tone of the late-afternoon deck scene. When the visitors are gone, Mary and Vera, who have become intimates over the years, can often be found, heads buried in books, tea mugs steaming, in the shawl-strewn, mildew-scented living room of the house.

BACK in the mid-seventies, the more Neal kept pressing Vera to accept the idea of an open marriage, the more she began to suspect that Neal's preoccupation with the subject meant that their marriage was edging toward failure. But, curiously, even in the pages of his diary there is no suggestion that Neal thinks his interest in sexual experimentation is related to any weakness in his marriage. Even when the subject is most on his mind, he writes appreciatively of Vera. After an afternoon of cross-country skiing in Vermont, on April 5, 1975, for example, he remarks that while he was skiing it had gone through his mind that "marriage to Vera was a stroke of luck. Of all the possible trails in the world, I seem to have hit on the perfect one for me (and not just sexually)." Of course, he goes on to say, that does not necessarily rule out the possibility of exploring "new trails" for enjoyment and a sense of renewal.

Much to Neal's astonishment, about mid year in 1975 Vera said she would go along with the open-marriage idea—though she did so, she told him, with great misgivings. At the time, she was reading Emma Goldman's autobiography, and Goldman's radical leanings and spirit had inspired her. Perhaps she had it in her, she told Neal, to rethink her ideas about what might be possible in her life. She did not tell him that she had also become weary of what she once referred to as "a steady drip of pressure" from him about the subject. She had just begun night school and perhaps, too, the sense of purpose that her academic progress was giving her made her feel brave. She and Neal had been having a lot of arguments about sex—he always wanted more than she did—and though he was an extremely sensitive husband, they were too often oddly out of synch in bed.

Neal's sexual-experimentation musings, at least as they are reflected in his diary, appear to be above all ideological, and they actually seem rather innocent and touching. It does not seem to have occurred to him to fool around secretly, for example. Neal hated the idea of lying, and part of his tell-all deal with Vera was that they would always confide in each another when or if one of them was having an affair. Both prized their growing ability to speak about difficult personal matters, and a discreet affair, all the more erotic for its clandestineness, was not their style. Still, reading the diary entry that Neal wrote just after Vera agreed to the possibility of an open marriage, I was struck by how important to him her gesture was. The pleasure in having *permission* to dally seemed almost to outweigh the prospect of an actual affair. On May 30, 1975, he wrote, "Vera's changed consciousness about sexual experiences has not only lifted a small weight, a constriction, but has brought me even closer to her. In the last two months, our relationship has gotten much stronger and physically closer. Last night she said that she could understand that our relationship was deep—we had ten years of shared experiences and personal attitudes—and she could see how outside sexual experiences would be different now, not so threatening. And she said that if I had an affair she no longer felt that she would leave me (her statement last summer/fall). We had a long talk about our feelings about affairs and our fantasies—a maturing openness to sex, which has always been difficult for both of us, repressed each in our own way about sex." Reading this and other, similar entries, one cannot help wondering whether Neal's fervent wish to be granted freedom might not be related to his frustration in not being altogether successful at launching himself away from his mother's orbit, and whether it didn't represent, in fact, a sort of symbolic side-door resolution of that problem.

The upshot of their agreement, the irony of which has not been lost on Neal, was that, like a character in an O. Henry story, Vera acted on it first—and, as it turned out, most. Since the day of their sexual accord, Neal has actually had only one affair (fewer, surely, than a great many men with no particular "principles" about sexual experimentation); Vera has had five. Her lovers included the head of the day-care center, an antiques dealer, an actor, an editor, and a teacher. Two of her lovers were women. Her first affair, with the actor, took place in 1975 and was brief. Neal claims not to have felt a single pang of jealousy ("I must be missing the jealousy gene"), but admits that he was somewhat taken aback by the speed with which she had gotten with the program.

"She had been so nervous about the whole idea," he said one evening, "I guess both of us assumed I would be the one who would act first. She was so worried about the threat of our breaking up that I was actually quite surprised when she agreed to it. But I was so shy. I had probably been secretly relieved when she resisted the whole idea. But that first affair only enhanced her attractiveness for me. I know it sounds strange, but that's how I felt. The idea that one person possesses another denies individuality."

Four years after her first affair, Vera had a one-night stand, and several years later, she had a liaison of longer duration. This third affair, which was with a woman, overlapped with Neal's lone foray into the world of extramarital experimentation. When Neal told Vera that he was seeing someone, idealistic principles notwithstanding, Vera became nearly apoplectic—especially when she happened one evening to catch a glimpse of Neal and the woman as they were leaving a restaurant. According to Neal, however, "she acted like a trouper." The fact that she had a woman for a lover did not bother him unduly, he says. On the contrary, he claims that the *slight* edge of "competition" he felt, despite himself, with her male lovers was entirely absent when her partners were women. In fact, he was "sort of turned on by the idea."

His own affair lasted about four months. It was the woman who broke it off. "She had just gone through a divorce and was still bitter about it," he said. "I liked her. She really enjoyed sex; she was actually more sexual than I was. We had good times together, and I was upset when she said we couldn't see each other anymore. She said she didn't think it was right—because of my being married—and it was also the wrong time in her life for her."

The intermittent redistribution of Vera's and Neal's sexual energy may have expanded their horizons, but it did not much change the character of their bedroom strains, and, unsurprisingly, it created new sources of stress. While they were having affairs, their own sex life went on, but several times when Vera refused Neal he asked her if perhaps she was not merely bisexual, as they had both come to believe, but more deeply lesbian. Bitter words were exchanged. Often, they went to sleep back to back, and Vera was beginning to wonder if they would *ever* make sexual peace. But, unlike many couples whose sexual frustrations inevitably fuel brush fires in the rest of their lives, both Neal and Vera continued to consider themselves signally blessed in having each other, and they shared the belief that their marriage had gone from strength to strength over the years. They agreed about most child-raising issues and loved doing things with their children; they agreed about money issues (together, they earned less—about $50,000 a year—than any of the other couples I had talked to, but rarely focused on money issues and never mentioned money as a source of marital stress); they usually liked the same movies, paintings, plays, music, and people; and, increasingly over the years they felt that it was because of their unshakable compatibility that their marriage had succeeded when so many of their friends' marriages had not. The sex issue was somehow in a special category—a sort of ongoing Great Unsolved Mystery.

Neal's diary records long periods when he feels isolated and blocked in his work, angry and confused about his father's seeming lack of interest in him, or his mother's remoteness and passivity, and frustrated with his own ongoing bouts of low spirits. His creative juices dry up for long periods, and he worries that his career might have become permanently stalled. Often he feels he is struggling just to keep going: "Except for Vera, no feedback or support. . . . I feel . . . unappreciated . . . unfulfilled. I am always trying to do the right thing and feeling that I'm cut off from living my life. Some of it may be my own fault but only Vera makes me feel really good."

In 1982, at Vera's urging, he began to visit a therapist, a woman, and he still sees her. Neal feels that therapy has helped him a lot, but until a few years ago he was convinced that whatever sexual problems he and Vera had could be attributed largely to her unresolved psychological problems—especially the trauma caused by the abusive baby-sitter. He suspected, too, that the puritanical atmosphere of Vera's home strongly influenced her attitude toward sex. Actually, the only conventional view that Neal ever expressed to me about male-female roles came up in his assessment of their differing attitudes toward sex. "She's changed over the last few years," he said not long ago. "She really is adapting. But often I sense her being very tense about what happens when we make love. She has this whole male-female thing—that sex is love, caring, it's not a physical thing as much as a spiritual one, which I feel partly, too, but I enjoy the purely physical side as much. It's an expression of love. There are times when you're not feeling as close and you still have sex. It's not always the perfect romantic thing, and Vera is aiming for this perfect thing and it never happens. From my point of view, it would always be better if she would just relax."

Vera saw their situation quite differently. From her perspective, the problem was more Neal's than hers. "I am always amazed at how our outlook on so many things is so similar," she said one morning over breakfast at a luncheonette a few blocks away from her apartment. "I think we're incredibly well suited to each other. Sex is just this one big bugaboo. There's something that prevents us from understanding each other in this one crucial area in our lives."

Recently, it had occurred to her that a sex therapist might be useful in her marriage. "In one way, I seem to have great faith in therapy," she said. "And yet, every time I think of saying something like 'Let's go to a sex therapist,' I immediately think of ten reasons we shouldn't. After I had a second affair with a woman, I thought, Well, perhaps I am just more homosexual than I would have believed. But I don't think that's the case—and the last person in my life was a man. Still, I sometimes feel that it takes me absurdly long to figure out the most basic things about my life. Why did Neal make such quick progress in his therapy? It was immediate. I don't feel that he says more to the therapist, but maybe he listens better. Sometimes I feel that I can say things easily in therapy, but I don't say things deeply. Quite a long time ago, my therapist suggested that I look at this neat little book. It took me over a year to get it and will probably take me another year to get to read it, though I'm truly eager to resolve this."

"What kind of book is it?" I asked.

"Its subject is, I think, basically how to live with the same person for forty years and enjoy sex all the time. I'm sure it's a fascinating book, but I don't dare open it, because I'm afraid it's going to tell me to do things I don't want to do."

"Like what?"

"I actually looked at two pages. It said modest things like 'Don't have sex for a week.' My kind of book! And it suggested that 'he' rub you with powder and perfume. Sounds terrific. But the problem, I believe, is more in the realm of Neal's needs being so great. If your needs are overwhelming, then you can't hear when someone else's needs are different. A certain gentleness is what I need. We've talked about all this, but we somehow always end up talking at cross-purposes. Sometimes, I think we don't have the *vocabulary* to talk about sex. I'd go to a sex therapist tomorrow if I thought I could get this across. But I'm so sure that it's Neal's problem—I'm sure that that in itself is part of the trouble. Do other people do better than we do? I know hardly anyone who actually talks about sex. It's the one taboo, despite the general impression you get that everyone speaks about it so easily. It's so taboo that it's not even the obvious taboo."

In the mid-eighties, Neal left his old sinecure at the human-rights agency to work as a counselor for high school dropouts at a local community center. He loved the new job, which he found through a newspaper ad, even though it left him less time than ever for his own work. The best thing about it from his point of view was that he had at last found work on his own and was out of the family orbit. Just about the time he began the new job, however, Mary began to weaken noticeably. Soon he and Vera found themselves spending much of their off-work time at her apartment. His diary reveals strong sympathy for Mary and equally strong bursts of guilty resentment. His sister rarely stops by Mary's apartment; both he and Vera consider her a hopeless case and have long since given up on expecting much cooperation from her—though after a big fight she agreed she would start to come by to spell them on a regular basis. Neal has agreed to make himself available for whatever Mary needs help with. He works on her taxes, and he and Vera cook many of her meals, hang around to keep her company, and help transport her to and from her doctors' offices. Vera has been going along as much to support Neal as to help Mary—for Mary, as she has weakened, has become increasingly irritable, and, Neal's sympathy for his mother tends to become overwhelmed by exasperation. But he accepts as a given his obligation to help her as often as he can.

In the diary he writes that one evening when his mother

seemed listless he wondered as she waved good-bye and managed a faint "Toodle-oo" from her bed, whether he might be seeing her for the last time, and tried to imagine how he would feel if this were the case. He knows he will regret that they were never able to have closer talks and that he hadn't pressed for her more about her own history. "At the same time, I can barely make it through our relationship as it is now—it is so draining," he writes. "Rallying around, being there, being the good, dutiful son. But still the missing, unspoken part—love."

As it happens, Mary has struggled on for several years now. Visiting nurses were found to help her, and Neal and Vera's life has settled into a routine of work, brief periods at home, and regular vigils at Mary's. Bill and Susanna are by now well established in their own lives. They are not anarchists, but, like their parents, they have a highly developed social consciousness. Bill works as a book designer and lives, with his wife, in another part of the city; Susanna works for a government-supported poverty agency in Chicago. Both of them keep in close contact with Neal and Vera, and if they are around, they always try to reconnect when Vera decides to run the New York City Marathon—something she has done three times. During each race, Neal and either one or both of the children take the subway out to Fourth Street in Brooklyn in the early morning to cheer her on in the first leg of the event; then they rush back to Manhattan to find a spot near the exit ramp of the Queensboro Bridge where she might glimpse them, then they walk over to Central Park and wait for her near the finish line. Neal is given to writing celebratory verses for birthdays and other noteworthy family events, and after the 1986 race he composed a poem for her, whose last lines went:

> So all hail, Vera, runner fair;
> At every step, why . . . I'll be there!

Neal wrote another poem when Vera turned fifty, and read it aloud at a packed party, attended by friends and family. The party and Neal's commiseration helped Vera recover from a bizarre four-page letter she had received that day from her mother, the gist of which was that Vera had not done *too* badly in life considering her (enumerated) inadequacies and the fact that "Mom was a hard act to follow." The letter is couched in weirdly cheerful, aggressive language and is nakedly revelatory of the letter-writer's competitive feelings toward her daughter and of her own unmotherly ill will. Vera was shocked by the letter, she told me later, but she hadn't felt nearly as furious as Neal, because, unlike him, she had by now become more or less reconciled to her mother's Wagnerian negativity and obliviousness.

That same year, Neal and Vera celebrated their twenty-fifth wedding anniversary. Vera had to work that day, but Neal took the day off. They had champagne, croissants, and hot chocolate for breakfast, and Neal played a record of "Undecided"—a song they had listened to a lot in Paris. They met for a meal when Vera took her lunch break, and during it they enjoyed reminiscing about their wedding day. Afterward, Neal walked Vera back to school, and Vera spoke of how happy she was. In the afternoon, Vera visited her therapist, and Neal went to an art show. Over another round of champagne that evening, according to Neal's diary, they counted their blessings and talked a little about the things they thought could be improved in their life—their sexual relationship, for one.

The sex book suggested to her by her therapist, Vera reported, had, upon closer examination, proved to be a dud. And she was not as sure that the era of sexual exploration had ended for her as Neal was that it had ended for him. Eventually, the words "sex therapist" had come up in a conversation, but Neal didn't think they needed one; he now felt that, though he knew sex was still an issue for Vera, their "problem" had become a negligible factor in their marriage. He would be surprised, he told me not long ago, if he ever had another outside sexual relationship; he couldn't remember the last time he'd thought about it. He and Vera had become so close as parents and as allies in a thousand and one crises that he could imagine no issue steering their marriage off course in any appreciable way.

For more than a year now, Mary's ongoing decline has absorbed nearly all of the Clarks' free time. In the fall of 1994 they began sleeping at Mary's apartment on weekends when they couldn't get anyone to care for her, and they rarely saw their friends or got out. When they were at home, they were usually in a state of nervous exhaustion, and, as a consequence, a number of their habits changed. They tended to eat in a more impromptu fashion, one or the other of them often shuffling over to the table at odd hours with a plate of spaghetti and some paperwork; they had wistful conversations about reconnecting with their friends and both of them began enthusiastically planning new work projects. According to Vera, Neal was about to start a new series of paintings. Nowadays, he seemed to be able to paint in a less trammeled way, she said, and no longer expected to bowl the world over. For all his soul-searching, she told me, she continued to be impressed by "the way, after all, he accepts himself, and by his basic self-confidence." She feels that "somewhere, underneath all those layers of introspection, he's terribly secure. Whereas I feel that if I don't strive all the time I'll be below the zero mark," she says.

Several years ago, Vera acquired a graduate degree in education, but she thinks she may return to school to study in a less organized way fairly soon. "All my studying has been to help me teach children. Now I'd like to learn just for the sake of learning. I feel terrific when I'm in school, and I don't think I'd ever have gotten any of my degrees if it weren't for Neal. He's wanted me to succeed because he knows how important it is to me. But now I'd like to just sort of allow myself to graze on information—to follow my nose. By the way, my mother seems to have undergone some kind of sea change recently. She's gone out of her way to be nice to me, and she's even mentioned that she feels bad about how hard she's been on me. Perhaps she's been confronting her own mortality."

Increasingly over the past few months, locked together as she and Neal were in their nurse-companion roles, Vera had noticed that they often seemed to be having the same thoughts at the same time. Neal had noticed that, too. Independently, they had both gone to a downtown art show, and on impulse, she had bought a painting that she planned to give Neal for his birthday. Meanwhile, he mentioned the painting one evening, saying that it had been the one he'd most admired at the show. "I feel really in tune with Neal, so in the one area where I don't I tend to bend, because it's so important to him. But the lack of unity in this one part of our lives continues to bother me. I don't know. I imagine everyone else has solved these problems by my age. Why is it I feel like such an oddball?"

Sometimes events occur in people's lives that make their ordinary worries or psychic itches seem as inconsequential as tumbleweed, and last fall, a gas explosion that blasted through one wall of the Clarks' building had that effect on Neal and Vera. Though they managed to salvage most of their things, the building was evacuated, and the rent-controlled apartment they'd lived in for most of their lives had to be abandoned. For the next six weeks, they camped out at Mary's and at a friend's place, searched in a state of shock for a new apartment that they could fit all their books and other belongings into and that they could afford, and, lacking a regular home base and familiar objects to reassure them, began to feel more than a little disoriented. Friends who observed them during this period, however, were struck by how unselfpitying and staunch they were about the whole business. It was almost as if, in lieu of a real home, they had wrapped a fence around themselves. Their friends noticed, too, how untrammeled they seemed as they began to throw away many of their belongings, having realized that not all their things would fit in the smaller place they would have to settle for, and how they gently endeavored to keep each other's spirits up.

Vera was more discouraged than Neal by the apartment-hunting process. If she'd had a choice, she would have preferred an apartment in Manhattan. She had recently switched jobs, and her new job was in a school in the Bronx, a long way from the Brooklyn neighborhoods they seemed to be able to afford.

The day after they signed a lease on a place that Vera was far from crazy about but that had a low rent and lots of space to recommend it, I met with them. Vera said that the street was OK and the landlord lived in the building and seemed to be nice, but that her heart did not rise when she thought of going home to the neighborhood each night. Neal pointed out that they had to be realistic—that the ideal apartment Vera presumably had in mind was surely out of their reach. To cheer her up after the lease signing, Neal had taken her to a Mexican restaurant. She has loved things Mexican ever since she took a trip to Mexico alone several years ago. "Everything looked better in the restaurant," Vera said. "Anyway, I believe that Neal and I could manage to make a good life together anywhere." Echoing the same optimistic assessment of the state of their marriage on another occasion not long before, Neal had remarked, "For five or ten years now, I've been certain that the marriage was going to last, but now we're on a different level. There are hardly any times now when we argue, few times when we even raise our voices with each other. You come to understand that faults are just part of the picture. I think we've finally come to accept each other as full people, but God, that doesn't really happen for a while. We're beyond just lasting. It's now kind of pure enjoyment."

EPILOGUE

LIKE A NOVELIST WHO LIVES WITH HIS OR HER characters over a long period, I have had the people in the pages of this book somewhat obsessively on my mind for a number of years now, and have thought long and hard about who they were or wanted to be. Unlike the characters in a novel, of course, it was not I, but they who determined the course of the plots of their lives. At the very least, their stories serve as a kind of social barometer, registering some of the pressing issues that absorb couples living in our time. But, more important, I hoped to convey my own appreciation of the reality that the small universe created by a marriage is infinitely complex and is always unique. The larger historical and sociological forces that affect people's lives seem to function like tectonic plates. Above them, in darkness or brilliant light, drifting and settling like delicate undersea creatures, couples send out exploratory tendrils toward each another, are swept up by powerful currents, encounter every sort of danger, and find places of repose and nourishment.

Whatever the strains on this, our smallest and most enduring of social institutions, its greatest virtue may be that it offers two people a chance to create a sustaining context, a world that is infinitely larger and richer than anything that either could invent alone—and one that draws on the deepest human capacities.

What, if anything, do the eight people who allowed me a privileged look at their lives have in common—apart from the age-old concerns about children and money and a more modern focus on their emotional and sexual well-being? The red thread that ran through all the couples' lives was something of a surprise to me. *Everyone* worked terribly hard all the time, and, with the exception of the McLanes, who could afford pleasant breaks from their labors, rarely got a chance to come up for air. This is undoubtedly more a reflection of the economic realities of our era than anything else, but, since the life of almost everyone else I know or meet is similar in this respect, it is nonetheless a sobering commentary on the times. Somehow, 350 years after the Pilgrims' experiment, we are still busily chopping down trees and clearing the land as if our lives depended on it. The postwar vision of a leisured, prosperous citizenry has faded from sight, as has the once much anticipated four-day workweek. Indeed, private life, like everything else in postindustrial America, has become more and more a rush job. In such a frenetic age, the institution of marriage recalls us to ourselves, and, if we are lucky, we are sustained and enlarged by it.

SELECT BIBLIOGRAPHY

Hundreds of books have been published over the past century, many of them in the last two decades, that explore themes touched on in this book. Some that I found particularly helpful were:

Anderson, Michael. *Approaches to the History of the Western Family 1500–1914*. London: The Economic History Society, Macmillan, 1980.

Bane, Mary Jo. *Here to Stay*. New York: Basic Books, 1976.

Barker-Benfield, G. J. *The Horrors of the Half-Known Life*. New York: Harper & Row, 1976.

Campbell, Angus. *The Sense of Well-Being in America: Recent Patterns and Trends*. New York: McGraw-Hill, 1981.

Campbell, William. *The Romantic Ethic and the Spirit of Modern Consumerism*. Oxford and New York: Basil Blackwell, 1987.

Cancian, Francesca. *Love in America*. Cambridge: Cambridge University Press, 1987.

Chafe, William H. *The American Woman*. New York: Oxford University Press, 1972.

Cherlin, Andrew J. *Marriage, Divorce, Remarriage*. Cambridge, Mass.: Harvard University Press, 1992.

Davidson, Cathy. *Revolution and the Word*. New York: Oxford University Press, 1986.

Degler, Carl D. *At Odds: Women and the Family in America from the Revolution to the Present*. Oxford and New York: Oxford University Press, 1980.

Ehrenreich, Barbara, and Deirdre English. *For Her Own Good: 150 Years of the Experts' Advice to Women*. Garden City, N.Y.: Anchor, 1978.

Evans, Sara. *Born for Liberty: A History of Women in America*. New York: The Free Press, 1989.

Fletcher, Ronald. *The Abolitionists*. London and New York: Routledge, 1988.

Fliegelman, Jay. *Prodigals and Pilgrims: The American Revolution Against Patriarchal Authority*. Cambridge and New York: Cambridge University Press, 1982.

Freidman, Jean E., and William G. Shade, eds. *Our American Sisters*. Lexington, Mass.: D. C. Heath, 1982.

Gans, Herbert J. *The Levittowners: Ways of Life and Politics in a New Suburban Community*. New York: Pantheon, 1967.

Gilman, Charlotte Perkins. *The Man-Made World, or, Our Androcentric Culture*. New York: Charlton, 1911.

Grossberg, Michael. *Governing the Hearth*. Chapel Hill: University of North Carolina, 1985.

Gutman, Herbert G. *The Black Family in Slavery and Freedom*. New York: Pantheon, 1976.

Hacker, Andrew. *U/S*. New York: Viking, 1983.

Harding, Vincent. *There Is a River: The Black Struggle for Freedom in America*. New York: Vintage, 1983.

Henslin, James M., ed. *Marriage and Family in a Changing Society*. New York: The Free Press, 1985.

Hochschild, Arlie. *The Managed Heart*. Berkeley: University of California, 1983.

———*The Second Shift*. New York: Viking, 1987.

James, Henry. *The Speech and Manners of American Women*. Lancaster House Press, 1973.

Karlson, Carol F. *The Devil in the Shape of a Woman: Witchcraft in Colonial New England*. New York: Norton, 1987.

Komarovsky, Mirra. *Blue-Collar Marriage*. New Haven: Yale University Press, 1962.

Leman, Nicholas. *The Promised Land*. New York: Knopf, 1991.

Lerner, Gerda, ed. *Black Women in White America* New York: Vintage, 1973.

Ostrader, Susan. *Women of the Upper Class*. Philadelphia: Temple University Press, 1984.

Outhwaite, R. B. *Studies in the Social History of Marriage*. New York: St. Martin's, 1981.

Phillips, Roderick. *Untying the Knot*. Cambridge and New York: Cambridge University Press, 1991.

Reiss, Ira L. *Premarital Sexual Standards in America*. New York: The Free Press, 1960.

Rothman, Ellen. *Hands and Hearts: A History of Courtship in America*. New York: Basic Books, 1984.

Rubin, Lillian Breslow. *Worlds of Pain: Life in a Working-Class Family.* New York: Basic Books, 1976.

Schwartz, Pepper, and Philip Blumstein. *American Couples.* New York: Morrow, 1983.

Skolnick, Arlene. *Embattled Paradise: The American Family in an Age of Uncertainty.* New York: Basic Books, 1991.

Stone, Lawrence. *The Family, Sex and Marriage in England, 1500–1800.* New York: Harper & Row, 1977.

Taylor, Charles. *Sources of the Self: The Making of the Modern Identity.* Cambridge: Harvard University Press, 1989.

Veroff, Joseph; Elizabeth Douvan; and Richard A. Kulka, eds. *The Inner American: A Self-Portrait from 1957–76.* New York: Basic Books, 1981.

Wall, Helena. *Fierce Communion: Family and Community in Early America.* Cambridge: Harvard University Press, 1990.

Weiner, Lynn Y. *From Working Girl to Working Mother: The Female Labor Force in the United States 1820–1980.* Chapel Hill: University of North Carolina, 1985.

Weitzman, Lenore. *The Divorce Revolution.* New York: The Free Press, 1985.

Wells, Robert V. *Revolutions in American Lives: A Demographic Perspective on the History of Americans, Their Families, Their Society.* Westport, Conn.: Greenwood, 1982.

Wharton, Edith. *A Backward Glance.* 1934. Reprint, Century, 1987.